RELIGIOUS PHILOSOPHY
A Group of Essays
By Harry Austryn Wolfson

As Mr. Wolfson deftly isolates and analyzes some of the most vital and often the most enigmatic ideas developed by the religious philosophers of the West, a cumulative and thoughtful continuity emerges from his interpretations. Philo, for example, appears as a dominant force throughout the sixteen centuries that preceded Spinoza's critique of his basic principles.

The ten essays which constitute the critical sequence of this penetrating book are derived from lectures, and from separate publications many of which are not readily available now. Among the pieces included are "Immortality and Resurrection in the Philosophy of the Church Fathers," "St. Augustine and the Pelagian Controversy," and "Causality and Freedom in Descartes, Leibniz, and Hume." Mr. Wolfson concludes with a perceptive distillation of his personal wisdom in an essay contrasting the professed atheist with the "verbal theist."

Harry Austryn Wolfson is Nathan Littauer Professor of Hebrew Literature and Philosophy, Emeritus, Harvard University, and author of *Crescas' Critique of Aristotle, Philo: Foundations of Religious Philosophy in Judaism, Christianity, and Islam,* and *The Philosophy of the Church Fathers, Volume 1: Faith, Trinity, Incarnation* (Harvard University Press, 1929, 1947, and 1956; see back of this jacket).

RELIGIOUS PHILOSOPHY
A GROUP OF ESSAYS

RELIGIOUS PHILOSOPHY

A Group of Essays

BY

HARRY AUSTRYN WOLFSON

THE BELKNAP PRESS OF
HARVARD UNIVERSITY PRESS
CAMBRIDGE, MASSACHUSETTS

1961

PREFACE

The papers collected in this volume are occasional pieces originally delivered as lectures or written for special or periodical publications. And yet a common theme runs through all of them. The common theme is the thesis which I have been trying to develop in a series of studies under the general title "Structure and Growth of Philosophic Systems from Plato to Spinoza."

Briefly stated the thesis is this.

If we are to follow the conventional method of dividing philosophy into ancient, medieval, and modern, then medieval philosophy is to be defined as that system of thought which flourished between pagan Greek philosophy, which knew not of Scripture, and that body of philosophic writings which ever since the seventeenth century has tried to free itself from the influence of Scripture. Medieval philosophy so defined was founded by Philo, who lived at the time of the rise of Christianity. Ostensibly Philo is only the interpreter of the Hebrew Scripture in terms of Greek philosophy. But actually he is more than that. He is the interpreter of Greek philosophy in terms of certain fundamental teachings of his Hebrew Scripture, whereby he revolutionized philosophy and remade it into what became the common philosophy of the three religions with cognate Scriptures, Judaism, Christianity, and Islam. This triple scriptural religious philosophy, which was built up by Philo, reigned supreme as a homogeneous, if not a thoroughly unified, system of thought until the seventeenth century, when it was pulled down by Spinoza.

The papers in this volume deal with some Philonic views as they were argued about and as they grew and developed in the triple scriptural religious philosophy during various stages in its history.

Harvard University   H. A. W.
July 18, 1961

CONTENTS

1

THE PHILONIC GOD OF REVELATION AND HIS LATTER-
DAY DENIERS   1

    Philo as founder of scriptural religious philosophy, 1.

    I. Philo's three ways of arriving at a knowledge of God, 2.
— His two meanings of revelation, 3. — Three characteristics
of the scriptural conception of an infinite God as contrasted
by Philo with the Greek philosophic conception of a finite
God: (1) God infinite in the sense of His unknowability,
5. — (2) God infinite in the sense of His infinite goodness, 7.
— (3) God infinite in the sense of His infinite power, 8.

    II. Denial of revelation by Spinoza, Hume, and John Stuart
Mill, and how a hypothetical spokesman of scriptural philosophers would comment upon it, 11. — How Spinoza and
Hume argue against the unknowability of God, and how the
hypothetical spokesman of scriptural philosophers would
answer their arguments, 12. — How Spinoza, Hume, and Mill
argue against the infinite goodness of God, and how the
hypothetical spokesman of scriptural philosophers would
comment upon their arguments, 16. — How Spinoza, Hume,
and Mill argue against the infinite power of God, and how
the hypothetical spokesman of scriptural philosophers would
answer their arguments, 17.

    The new climate with the same old storms and thunderings
and lightnings, 25. — Philosophies of labels, 26.

2

EXTRADEICAL AND INTRADEICAL INTERPRETATIONS OF
PLATONIC IDEAS   27

    Philosophical synthesizers and theological peacemakers, 27.

I. LOGOS   28

    How contradictory statements in Plato led to an extradeical
and intradeical interpretation of his view on the relation of
the ideas to God, 28. — How Philo integrated the Platonic
ideas in an intelligible world placed in a Logos and how he

harmonized Plato's contradictory statements by introducing
into the ideas and the Logos two successive stages of existence, an intradeical followed by an extradeical, 30.

II. TRINITY 38

The Logos in the Prologue of John, 38. — How the Johannine Logos came to be interpreted in terms of the Philonic
Logos as containing an intelligible world of ideas and as
having a twofold stage of existence, 39. — How the Logos
of John, unlike the Logos of Philo, came to be regarded
as God and thereby became both intradeical and extradeical,
not by succession but simultaneously, during both its first
and its second stage of existence, but how the ideas within the
Logos, during both these two stages of existence, were only
intradeical, 41. — How Origen introduced the conception
of eternal generation to take the place of the Philonic twofold stage theory, and how the Logos still continued to be
simultaneously both intradeical and extradeical and the ideas
still continued to be only intradeical, 44. — The Sabellian
conception of the Logos as only intradeical, 47. — Ammonius
Hermiae's intradeical interpretation of Platonic ideas, 48.

III. ATTRIBUTES 49

The rise of the problem of attributes in Islam, 49. — The
problem of attributes in Islam, like the problem of the persons
of the Trinity in Christianity, a problem of the extradeical
and the intradeical interpretation of Platonic ideas, 51. —
Why there was no problem of attributes in Christianity
during the Patristic period, 52. — Four events which led to
the appearance of a problem of attributes among the Schoolmen, 53. — How the problem of attributes was solved by the
Schoolmen, 60. — Attributes in Descartes, 65. — Attributes
in Spinoza, 66.
Now these are the generations of Platonic ideas, 67.

3

IMMORTALITY AND RESURRECTION IN THE PHILOSOPHY
OF THE CHURCH FATHERS 69

Did Jesus believe in the immortality of the soul? 69. — Immortality in the Church Fathers, as in Philo, by grace and
not by nature, 71. — Why Tertullian, Origen, and Augustine
are erroneously said to believe in immortality by nature,
72. — Two philosophic analogies of resurrection discussed
and rejected by the Fathers, 74. — Two characteristics of the

doctrine of resurrection as conceived of by the Fathers, and
the problems arising therefrom: (1) the problem of annihilation, 76. — (2) the problem of the identity of the body risen
with the body foregone, 77. — How the Fathers would answer three Epicurean arguments against immortality: (1)
the argument from the corporeality of the soul, 83. — (2)
the argument from the impossibility of a bodiless soul to have
any memory, 87. — (3) the argument from the impossibility
of a bodiless soul to experience any pleasure, 91. — Differences in the reward awaiting the immortal souls and the risen
bodies, 93. — Is there salvation for those who do not believe
in Christ? 96. — Difference between the meaning of "everything is possible to God" as used by the Fathers and the meaning of "nothing is impossible" as used by the Stoics, 98. —
The innate desire for immortality, 100. — The Fathers and a
certain bright young man, 101.

4

PHILOSOPHICAL IMPLICATIONS OF THE THEOLOGY OF
CYRIL OF JERUSALEM 104

Cyril speaking philosophy without being aware of it, 104.
— Philosophy behind his definition of faith, 106. — Problem
of the relation of faith to reason among the Fathers prior to
Cyril, 109. — Cyril's cryptic condemnation of philosophy in
his warning against the "enemy" and the "strange woman,"
112. — Cyril's two departures from the phrasing of the
Nicene Creed, 117. — How his omission of the expression
homoousion to patri cannot be explained on the ground of
the objection raised against the term *homoousios* because
it was used by Paul of Samosata or because it implied Sabellianism or because it does not occur in Scripture, 118. —
How it can be explained on the ground of a certain philosophic objection which, according to Athanasius and Basil,
was raised against that expression, 121. — A philosopher in
spite of himself, 125.

5

PHILOSOPHICAL IMPLICATIONS OF ARIANISM AND APOL-
LINARIANISM 126

Patristic statements about the Aristotelian background of the
Arian heresy, and the meaning of these statements, 126. —
What modern historians have made of these statements, and

the attempt of some historians to give a Platonic background to the Arian heresy, 131. — The Fathers not to be made to don the uniforms of Greek schools of philosophy, 136. — How the Fathers only partly followed the Philonic conception of the Logos in their interpretation of the Johannine Logos, and how Arius, by his complete acceptance of the Philonic conception of the Logos, was led to his denial of the divinity of the pre-existent Christ, 137. — The religious and philosophic motives of Arius for fully accepting the Philonic conception of the Logos, 144. — Arius' denial of a divine nature in the born Christ as a corollary of his denial of the divinity of the pre-existent Christ, 147. — The reasoning behind Apollinaris' denial of a human nature in the born Christ, 148. — Why both Arius and Apollinaris deny that Jesus had a rational soul, 149. — Why both Arius and Apollinaris at first also denied to Jesus an irrational soul and then changed their mind and endowed him with an irrational soul, 151. — How Apollinaris, by denying to Jesus a human nature, does not deny him a bodily quality or property, and the significance of this, 153. — Summary, 155. — Historical investigation and metahistorical speculation, 157.

6

St. Augustine and the Pelagian Controversy 158

The relative free will of Greek philosophy and the absolute free will of Philo, 158. — How the Philonic conception of free will was followed by the early Church Fathers, 160. — The innovation introduced by Augustine and the opposition of Pelagius, 161. — Origin of Augustine's identification of concupiscence with sexual desire and of his view that concupiscence is the source of all sin and is irresistible, 164. — His further view that concupiscence is resistible by divine grace, but that divine grace itself is irresistible, 168. — The debate between Augustine and Pelagius, 169. — How despite the irresistibility of both concupiscence and grace Augustine still maintains that man is free, 170. — Augustine's reinstatement of the relative freedom of Greek philosophy, and his new definition of man, 175. — Christianized Stoicism, 176.

7

Ibn Khaldūn on Attributes and Predestination .. 177

How by analyzing the proof of the existence of God, Ibn Khaldūn sets out to explain the reconcilability of attributes with the unity of God and of predestination with the justice of God, 177. — How the unity of God is derived from the proof of His existence, 180. — How at first Ibn Khaldūn suggests that one of the three theories of attributes enumerated by him would be reconcilable with the unity of God, 181. — How he then decides that the unknowability of God is the sovereign solution of the problem of attributes, 183. — How God's power over man's actions is derived from the proof of God's existence, 185. — How at first Ibn Khaldūn suggests that one of the three theories of the power of God over man's actions would be reconcilable with the justice of God, 188. — How he then decides that the unknowability of God is the sovereign solution of the problem of predestination, 190. — Choosing to suspend reason rather than to pervert it, 195.

8

CAUSALITY AND FREEDOM IN DESCARTES, LEIBNIZ, AND HUME 196

The Epicurean and the Philonic conception of absolute free will: the former a corollary of the denial of causality; the latter a corollary of the belief in miracles, 197.

I. How Descartes endows man with the Philonic miraculous kind of freedom, 198. — Still he denies miracles, 201.

II. How the pre-established harmony of Leibniz allows for the possibility of miracles, 203. — Still he denies freedom of the Philonic miraculous kind, 206.

III. How Hume's denial of causality is like that of the Epicureans, 207. — Still he does not allow man the Epicurean kind of freedom, 214.

The two roads to freedom, and those who travel without road maps, 215.

9

THE VERACITY OF SCRIPTURE FROM PHILO TO SPINOZA 217

I. THE PROBLEM AND ITS SOLUTIONS 217

How the narrative of events starting with the exodus was generally taken as authentic history, 217. — The arguments used in proving the divine origin of the scriptural teaching, 218. — The problem of proving the veracity of the events from the creation to the exodus, 222.

II. THE ORIGIN OF LANGUAGES, THE HEBDOM-
ADAL PERIOD, AND THE DENARY SYSTEM 223

Speculation about the origin of language in Greek philosophy,
Philo, the rabbis, the Church Fathers, and Islam, and how
it was used by Halevi and Maimonides to prove the Adamic
descent of mankind, 223. — How the hebdomadal week and
the denary system was used by Halevi to prove the Adamic
descent of mankind, 236.

III. THE SCRIPTURAL CHRONOLOGY 237

How Judaism and Christianity accepted the scriptural chronology, 237. — How Islam did not accept it, 238. — Treatment
of the subject by Halevi and Maimonides, 239.

IV. SPINOZA 241

Spinoza's critical attitude toward the historicity of the scriptural narrative; his denial of revelation, 241. — Scriptural
miracles and mythical tales, 243.

1 0

SPINOZA AND THE RELIGION OF THE PAST 246

Spinoza's "yes" and "but" to traditional religious philosophy,
246. — The stock philosophic terms God, substance, mode,
cause, attribute, extension, and thought as used by Spinoza,
247. — His so-called proofs for the existence of God, 254. —
A soul which was not breathed into Adam by God, 256. —
Freedom of the will not of the kind that is a divine gift,
259. — Virtues without the benefit of Scripture, 260. — Philosophy taking the place of religion as a consolation, 261. —
Immortality individual, but by nature, 263. — How for once
Spinoza plays the strange role of defending orthodoxy against
heresy by alluding to scriptural proof-texts, 267. — Daring
rather than novelty, 269.

1 1

SERMONETTE:

THE PROFESSED ATHEIST AND THE VERBAL THEIST 270

He who is called fool in Scripture and those who call themselves lovers of wisdom, 270.

INDEX OF NAMES, SUBJECTS, AND TERMS 273

RELIGIOUS PHILOSOPHY:
A GROUP OF ESSAYS

1

THE PHILONIC GOD OF REVELATION AND HIS LATTER-DAY DENIERS [*]

PHILO, professionally, was not a teacher of philosophy. He was a preacher, a preacher on biblical topics, who dispensed his philosophic thoughts in the form of sermons. And because he was not professionally a teacher of philosophy, some modern students of his works say that he was not a philosopher. For nowadays, as we all know, to be called philosopher one must be ordained and one must be hired to teach philosophy and one must also learn to discuss certain hoary problems as if they were plucked but yesterday out of the air. Some say that Philo was an eclectic. But there is one eminent scholar who would begrudge him even the title of eclectic without further qualification, for, after all, eclecticism is the name of a reputable system in ancient Greek philosophy. The eclecticism of Philo, he says, "is that of the jackdaw rather than the philosopher." [1] Still, while we may deny Philo the honorific title of philosopher, with the privilege of wearing ostentatiously a special garb like that affected by ancient Greek philosophers, we cannot deny him the humbler and more modest title of religious philosopher. As such, Philo was the first who tried to reduce the narratives and laws and exhortations of Scripture to a coherent and closely knit system of thought and thereby produced what may be called scriptural philosophy in contradistinction to pagan Greek philosophy.

Let us then analyze this scriptural philosophy of Philo into its essential elements, so that we may afterwards see how

---

[*] Based upon the Suarez Lecture delivered at Fordham University, 1952, and one of the three Walter Turner Candler Lectures delivered at Emory University, 1959. Published in the *Harvard Theological Review*, 53 (1960): 101–124.
[1] E. R. Dodds, "The Parmenides of Plato and the Origin of the Neoplatonic 'One,'" *Classical Quarterly*, 22 (1928): 132 n. 1.

these essential elements of the Philonic scriptural philosophy were treated in modern philosophy since the seventeenth century.

I

The starting point of Philo's philosophy is an enumeration and assessment of the various views with regard to the ways by which men have arrived, or may arrive, at a knowledge of God. He enumerates three views.

According to some, he says, the way by which men have arrived at a knowledge of God is the way of imagination. The belief in God, according to them, is a fictitious belief, the product of our imagination, like the belief in chimeras and centaurs and hydras. As restated by Philo, the belief in God, according to this view, was invented by some clever legislator in order to tame the rebellious spirit of the people and inspire them with awe and fear and reverence for the law. Philo does not give us the name of the author of this view. But he can be identified as Critias, the leader of the Thirty Tyrants in Athens at the beginning of the fifth century before the Christian era. His view, which may be summarized in the maxim that religion is the bugaboo of the people, has been revived in our own time in the maxim, so well familiar to all of us, that religion is the opiate of the people. In principle, if not in purpose, this view, insofar as it makes God a mere concept in our mind, may also be considered as the forerunner of the various forms of modern religious humanism, which identifies God with man's idealized consciousness or with human aspirations for ideal values or with the unity of all ideal ends.

Philo dismisses this view as atheism.[2]

According to others, says Philo, God is the discovery of human reason. God is not a figment of our imagination. He has real existence outside our mind, and we are able to dis-

[2] Cf. my *Philo*, rev. ed. (Cambridge, Mass., 1948), I, 165–167.

cover Him by the power of our mind. It is the God whom
Plato discovered when, starting with a world which he held
to have been framed out of an eternal formless matter, he was
compelled by reason to assume the existence of a Demiurge
or a God who has framed the world. It is also the God whom
Aristotle discovered when, starting with an eternal world
which is eternally in motion, he was compelled by reason to
arrive at the existence of a being who is an immovable mover.
It is also the God of the Stoics who, starting with a world in
which they saw order and beauty and purpose, found themselves compelled by reason to arrive at the existence of a God,
whom they call, among other things, the mind or the soul
of the world. In principle, if not in wording, this view is
the forerunner of all modern forms of religious rationalism,
whether its God is called substance, or central monad, or
spirit, or cosmic consciousness, or élan vital, or universal nisus,
or principle of concretion, or ground of being.

Philo does not deny that one may arrive by reason at some
knowledge of God. In his characterization of Greek philosophers, he distinguishes between those who were believers of
God and those who were deniers of God; and Plato, Aristotle,
and the Stoics are placed by him among the former. Still he
does not believe that reason is the only way of arriving at a
knowledge of God; nor does he believe that reason alone can
lead us to a true and full knowledge of God. There is to him
a third way of arriving at a knowledge of God, the way of
revelation.

As conceived by Philo, revelation meant two things.

First, it meant the historical revelation: an event which
took place in the past when at Mount Sinai God made himself known to men and gave them the Law. Indeed Philo refers to certain people in his own city who denied the divine
and revealed origin of Scripture. He describes them as a sort
of amateur students of comparative religions, whose only tool
of reasoning was that of analogy and, whenever they observed
among various peoples beliefs and customs which were alike

in some respects, they inferred that they must be alike in every respect. And so, because they found in Greek mythology stories about appearances of gods to men and the revelation of laws, stories which they themselves considered as false, they argued that the account of the appearance of God at Mount Sinai and the revelation of His Law there is similarly false. Philo does not argue against them; he simply dismisses them as "impious" [3] and asserts his faith in revelation. For revelation to him is a matter of faith and not of reason, though occasionally he tries to confirm his faith in revelation by such arguments as the intrinsic excellency of its teachings and the salutary effect of these teachings upon those who follow them.[4]

Scripture, despite its similarities to other books, is to him a unique book. All other books are man-made, and their stories and teachings may be either true or false. Scripture is of divine origin, and its stories and teachings are all true. As a philosopher who tried to introduce logical coherence in his religious beliefs, he tries to remove the apparent inconsistency between a God who was declared to be invisible and the story of His having made himself visible to men at Mount Sinai. In great detail he tells us how the revelation at Mount Sinai was not a physical appearance of God, how the "words" in which God "spoke" with His "voice" were not physical words, uttered, as he says, by means of "mouth and tongue and windpipe." [5] But still, while all this was a miraculous event and one unlike ordinary human communication, the event still had taken place actually as a historical fact, and is not to be explained away as a fancy or dismissed as a fiction.

Second, revelation meant to him progressive revelation, a continuous revealment of God to chosen individual human beings to make known to them the meaning of the revealed Law. For though he believed that the revelation was final and

[3] *Conf.* 2, 2.
[4] Cf. my *Philosophy of the Church Fathers*, I (Cambridge, Mass., 1956), 19.
[5] *Decal.* 9, 32f.

perfect, inasmuch as the Law was to be eternal, this belief did not mean to him that it was a closed revelation. Final and perfect indeed it was, but as a revelation to men, it had to be couched in ordinary language, in language intelligible to the ordinary run of man, and so the perfection of its teaching was often obscured by the imperfection of human language. Those to whom the Law was revealed, and who were to believe in it and to live by it were to search for those inner meanings hidden behind the uttered words. This search for the inner meaning of Scripture cannot be successfully pursued without the aid of God. It is this divine aid in the discovery of the inner meaning of Scripture, which is called by Philo the Unwritten Law and corresponds to what the rabbis call the Oral Law, that constitutes a new kind of revelation, a progressive revelation, and a revelation which comes in response to the search of human reason. For while Philo, like the rabbis of Palestinian Judaism, believed in the cessation of prophecy with the close of the Hebrew Scripture, it is only that special kind of prophecy which inspired the writings of the prophets of the Hebrew Scripture that ceased.[6] Divine inspiration and the work of the Holy Spirit continue to function as a supernatural source of human knowledge, by which man is to discover not new truths but the real meaning of the old truths which are embedded in the final historical revelation.

Revelation to Philo is not only a new way of coming to a knowledge of God, it also yields a truer conception of God; and hereupon in various places scattered throughout his homilies he explains what the conception of God is as taught by revelation and how that conception of God differs from that taught by reason in the works of the philosophers.

This scriptural conception of God as contrasted with that of Greek philosophers is presented by Philo under three headings, which may be subsumed as a contrast between the con-

[6] Cf. *Philo*, II, 52f.

ception of God as infinite and the conception of God as finite.

First, God is infinite in the sense that He is incomprehensible, for, that which is infinite, according to a current philosophic maxim, cannot be comprehended by the mind.[7] At the very beginning of his speculation about God Philo declares that in His essence God cannot be known. All that can be known of Him is the fact of His existence. This distinction between the knowability of God's existence and the unknowability of His essence was something new in Greek philosophy. It was introduced by Philo. Among the Church Fathers, about two centuries after Philo, and already under the influence of Philo's teaching of the incomprehensibility of God, the question arose as to whether Plato conceived of God as incomprehensible in His essence.[8] On independent grounds, however, it can be shown that the God of Plato, who was either one of the ideas or a being other than the ideas, could be known in His essence and could be described, though Plato was not unaware of certain logical difficulties arising from his view. Nor was the God of Aristotle unknowable in His essence.[9] The terms ineffable (ἄρρητος), unnamable (ἀκατονόμαστος), and incomprehensible (ἀκατάληπτος), by which the unknowability of God is expressed by Philo, do not occur as a description of God in extant Greek philosophic literature before Philo, but once these terms were used by Philo they begin to occur frequently in Greek philosophy. The chief source of Philo's view of the incomprehensibility of God was his rigid philosophical interpretation of the scriptural prohibition of the likening of God to anything that is in heaven above, or on earth beneath, or in the water under the earth. The unlikeness of God became with him the uniqueness of God. Uniqueness meant that God belonged to no

[7] Aristotle, *Physica* I, 4, 187b, 7; *Metaphysica* II, 2, 994b, 27–30.

[8] Cf. *Philo*, II, 112–113.

[9] Cf. my paper "The Knowability and Describability of God in Plato and Aristotle," *Harvard Studies in Classical Philology*, 56/57 (Cambridge, Mass., 1947): 233–249.

class. And since He belonged to no class, no concept of Him could be formed. He was thus incomprehensible.[10]

Second, God is infinite in the sense of infinite goodness.

As used by Philo, the infinite goodness of God means two things: (a) that God acts freely by will and design and purpose; (b) that God exercises His individual providence over human beings. This conception of the infinite goodness of God, with all its implications, is advanced by Philo as a view in opposition to the views held by various Greek philosophers. Indeed he knew that all Greek philosophers described God as good, and some of them, Plato and the Stoics, though not Aristotle, ascribe to God also providence. But the goodness which they apply to God is not used by them in its ordinary sense as a description of an act performed by will and design and for a purpose. It is applied by them to God in a figurative sense and only because the unwavering, uniform action flowing by necessity from the nature of God has the appearance of an action guided by some intelligent will toward a goal. This is the sense in which not only Aristotle and the Stoics apply goodness to God; it is the sense in which also Plato applies it to God. When Plato, in answer to the question "Why God made this world," says that it is because "He was good" and "desired that all things should be as like unto himself as possible," or that "He desired that all things should be good," [11] despite his use of the term desire there was no choice on the part of God in the creation of this form of the world. He could not create any other kind of world. There were "fated laws" (νόμοι εἱμαρμένοι), as he says later,[12] by which the Demiurge was guided in his act of creation.

Similarly the term providence used by them means inexorable, fated laws. As the Church Fathers, a century after Philo and speaking under the influence of Philo, try to show, the providence of the Greek philosophers means universal providence; not individual providence.[13] Against the Stoic

[10] Cf. *Philo*, II, 94ff.
[11] *Timaeus* 29 D–E.
[12] *Ibid.* 41 A.
[13] Cf. Justin Martyr, *Dial. cum Tryph.* 1.

saying, which in fact represents the view of the generality of Greek philosophers, that "the gods attend to great matters, but they neglect the small ones," [14] Philo says that God has "a providential regard not only for those which are of greater importance, but also for those which appear to be of less importance." [15]

Philo was not unaware of the many difficulties that may arise from applying to God the attribute of goodness. He was especially aware of the difficulty arising from the problem of evil, both physical and moral evil. He discusses this problem in great detail, both in terms of Scripture and in terms of philosophy.[16] Every answer given in native Jewish tradition and in philosophy is made use of by him. But despite all the answers, a residuum of the problem still remains, and this residuum of the problem is solved by him by the principle of the incomprehensibility of God. Not only do we not know the essence of God; we do not also know the ways of God and the purpose of God. "God," he says, "judges by standards more accurate than any which the human mind employs," [17] which is only a paraphrase of the words of Zophar the Naamathite in the Book of Job, with regard to the problem of evil, that one is not to try to find out the deep things of God or to try to attain unto the purpose of the Almighty (Job 11:7).

Third, God is infinite in the sense of infinite power or omnipotence.

By omnipotence Philo means four things: (a) God created the world out of nothing and implanted in it certain laws of nature by which it is governed.[18] (b) Before the creation of this world of ours, God, if He willed, could not have created it at all or could have created another kind of world governed by another kind of law.[19] (c) In this present world of ours,

---

[14] *Apud* Cicero, *De Natura Deorum* II, 66, 167; cf. III, 35, 86; Plutarch, *De Stoicorum Repugnantiis* 37, 2.

[15] *Migr.* 33, 186.

[16] Cf. *Philo*, II, 279–303.

[17] *Provid.* 2, 54; cf. *Philo*, II, 291 n. 49.

[18] Cf. *Philo*, I, 325–347.

[19] Cf. *ibid.*, I, 315–316.

God can override the laws which He Himself has implanted in the world and create what is called miracles.[20] (d) God, if He wills, can destroy this world and create in its stead a new heaven and a new earth, though Philo happens to be certain that God will not will to do so.[21]

This conception of the omnipotence of God, in all its four phases, is presented by Philo explicitly in opposition to every school of Greek philosophy. It is in accordance with this conception of the omnipotence of God that he rejects explicitly the Aristotelian conception of the eternity of the world, and this on the ground, as he says, that it "impiously" postulates in God "a vast inactivity." [22] By this he means that the assumption of a world existing eternally by the side of God would be a restriction on the power of God. By the same token, he makes the Platonic pre-existent matter out of which God created the world to have been itself created by God.[23] Here again the assumption of an eternal uncreated matter could be a restriction on the power of God. It is for this reason also that he rejects the Stoic conception of God as fate,[24] for fate means an internal limitation on the power of God to act according to the freedom of His will.

This conception of the omnipotence of God is most strikingly brought out by Philo in statements in which he tries to answer certain questions which must have arisen in his mind.[25] Why this order of nature? Why do stars sparkle in the sky? Why do birds fly in the air? Why do fish swim in water? Why do trees grow in the field? Pagan Greek philosophers had two answers. According to one answer, that order had been fixed, as if by fate, from eternity and it is unchangeable. According to another answer, that order is the result of chance and it may by chance break down. Against both these two views, Philo maintains that it is all the work of an omniptent Deity. Before the world came into being God, through

[20] Cf. *ibid.*, I, 347–356.
[21] Cf. *ibid.*, I, 316.
[22] Cf. *ibid.*, I, 295ff.

[23] Cf. *ibid.*, I, 300–316.
[24] Cf. *ibid.*, I, 328–330.
[25] Cf. *ibid.*, I, 315–316.

His omnipotence, could have created another kind of world, governed by another kind of law, a world in which there would have been no succession of day and night and of seasons, and one in which trees would grow in heaven and stars would sparkle on earth. And now that God created this world in its present order, God can upset that order, though He promised not to upset it unless He had to do it for some good purpose — a purpose, by the way, which more often than not He keeps hidden from us.

His opposition to the generally prevailing view among Greek philosophers as to the inevitability of the present order of nature is expressed by Philo in his oft-repeated statement that "all things are possible to God" (πάντα θεῷ δυνατά) [26] — a statement which reflects the Septuagint version of Job's address to God: "I know that Thou art able to do all things and that to Thee nothing is impossible" (Job 42:1).

These four principles of scriptural religion as laid down by Philo have been generally accepted in all the philosophies of the three revealed religions, Judaism, Christianity, and Islam. They all accept the fact of a historical and final revelation, though they may differ as to which historical revelation was final. They all accept the view that while there was one historical revelation that was final, that final revelation was not a closed revelation; there was progressive revelation supplementary to the final revelation. They all accept the principle of the incomprehensibility of God, though there may be some difference of opinion among them as to how to interpret the terms predicated of God in Scripture. Finally they all accept the principle of divine goodness and of divine omnipotence in the manner they are conceived by Philo, and, though they are conscious of the many difficulties arising therefrom, especially the difficulty of the problem of evil, they solve all these difficulties by the incomprehensibility of God's ways.

No wonder, then, that in modern philosophy, ever since

[26] *Opif.*, 14, 46; cf. *Jos.* 40, 244; *Mos.* I, 31, 174; *Qu. in Gen.* IV, 17.

the seventeenth century, those who undertook to depose scriptural philosophy concentrated their attack upon these four principles. Let us then examine some of the main arguments raised against the four points in scriptural philosophy as defined by Philo and let us also see how a hypothetical scriptural philosopher would try to refute these arguments.

II

As representative opponents of scriptural philosophy we shall take three philosophers, one from the seventeenth century — Spinoza; another from the eighteenth century — Hume; a third from the nineteenth century — John Stuart Mill; and let each one of us select a representative opponent of scriptural philosophy from the present century.

They all reject revelation. The arguments they use are all variations of the arguments used by those whom Philo described as "impious," arguments based upon analogy and upon the view that things alike in some respects must be alike in all other respects. Instead of the analogy with Greek myths used by the "impious" critic of Philo's time, Spinoza uses the analogy of "the Koran or the dramatic stories of the poets or ordinary chronicles." [27] Hume uses the analogy of "Arabians" in their records of the miracles of "Mahomet or his successors" and of "Grecian, Chinese, and Roman Catholic" authors.[28] John Stuart Mill endorses Hume [29] and adds a long ponderous argument to show how the alleged evidence for revelation will not pass muster in an English court of justice.

To this our hypothetical spokesman for scriptural philoso-

[27] *Tractatus Theologico-Politicus* 5 (*Opera,* ed. Gebhardt, Heidelberg, 1925, III, 79, ll. 19–20).

[28] *An Inquiry Concerning the Human Understanding* X, 2 (*Philosophical Works,* Boston, 1854, IV, 138).

[29] "Theism, Part IV: Revelation," in *Three Essays on Religion* (New York, 1878), p. 217.

phers would say: the same old argument for which we can only repeat Philo's answer.

Both Spinoza and Hume reject the principle of the infinity of God in the sense of the unknowability of God.

In Spinoza this rejection is expressed in the proposition that "the human mind possesses an adequate knowledge of the eternal and infinite essence of God." [30] The argument by which he has arrived at this conclusion is not directly and explicitly stated. It may, however, be unfolded as follows:

Spinoza begins by asking himself: What do scriptural philosophers mean when they speak of God as unknowable? They mean, of course, that He cannot be the subject of a definition. And what do they mean by definition? They mean, of course, the Aristotelian kind of definition, which consists of a genus and a specific difference and which is conceived of as prior to the *definiendum* and as its cause.[31] Spinoza refers to this kind of definition as that which must "include the proximate cause" [32] and describes it as applying only to created things.[33] Taken in this sense, Spinoza admits that God is indefinable and hence unknowable. It is in this sense that he says "every substance is absolutely infinite," [34] by which, in the context in which he uses this proposition, he means that God is indefinable and unknowable.[35] But God, according to Spinoza, is immediately known by his third kind of knowledge, the intuitive knowledge, for God being an uncreated thing, which is in itself or is the cause of itself, becomes known to us through himself. It is in this sense that he says that "the human mind possesses an adequate knowledge of the eternal and infinite essence of God." [36] Thereby Spinoza challenges scriptural philosophers: You say that the

[30] *Ethics* II, Prop. 47.
[31] Aristotle, *De Anima* II, 2, 413a, 15; *Anal. Post.* II, 10, 93b, 38ff.
[32] *Short Treatise* I, 7, § 9.
[33] *Tractatus de Intellectus Emendatione* § 96ff. (*Opera*, II, 35).
[34] *Ethics* I, Prop. 8.
[35] Cf. my *Philosophy of Spinoza* (Cambridge, Mass., 1934), I, 138.
[36] *Ethics* I, Prop. 47.

existence of God can be demonstrated only *a posteriori*, and hence you say that, while His existence can be known, His essence is unknown. I say that His existence can be known *a priori*, and so His essence is known no less than His existence.

To this, I imagine, our hypothetical refuter would answer that those for whom he speaks would deny that God is an object of immediate knowledge. He would remind Spinoza of his own reference to St. Thomas' denial that God could be proved *a priori*.[37] Indeed, some scriptural philosophers speak of direct vision of God, but this is not the same as the intuitive knowledge of Spinoza. None of the scriptural philosophers, their hypothetical spokesman would argue, would admit that the human mind can generate its own knowledge. All knowledge, he would say for them, must come from an external source, though not necessarily a sensible source. He would go further and maintain that no Greek philosopher ever believed that the mind generates its own knowledge. What is the so-called immediate knowledge of Plato if not the recollection of pre-existent ideas? And what are the indemonstrable immediately known premises of Aristotle if not something which have ultimately their source in sense perception? And the common notions of the Stoics, are they not based upon experience? Even the innate ideas of Descartes can be shown to have been considered by him as having an external source. Our hypothetical scriptural philosopher would admit, of course, that Spinoza has an explanation for his intuitive knowledge, which is consistent with his general system of philosophy, but he would challenge both the explanation and the system.

In Hume, the argument against the unknowability of God is more direct and more explicit. Referring to all the scriptural philosophers as mystics, he addresses them as follows: "How do you Mystics, who maintain the absolute incom-

---

[37] *Short Treatise* I, 1; cf. Thomas Aquinas, *Sum. Theol.* I, 2, 1c; *Cont. Gent.* I, 10–11.

prehensibility of the Deity, differ from Sceptics or Atheists, who assert that the first cause of all is unknown and unintelligible?"[38] He thus argues from a lack of knowledge of the essence of God to a lack of knowledge of His existence.

Let us see how our hypothetical scriptural philosopher would answer this argument.

First, he would say it is an old argument. It is to be found in Thomas Aquinas.[39] It occurs in St. Thomas' refutation of those anti-rationalist theologians who maintain that the existence of God is a matter of faith only and cannot be demonstrated by reason. For in God, they argue, existence is identical with essence and, inasmuch as God's essence cannot be known, His existence cannot be demonstrated. This argument of St. Thomas' antirationalist theologians is exactly the same as that of Hume, except that in St. Thomas the argument is put in the mouth of those who, denying that God can be demonstrated by reason, fall back upon faith, whereas in Hume it is quoted in the name of those who, denying that God can be demonstrated by reason, became sceptics or atheists.

The answer given by St. Thomas is that the existence of God which is said to be identical with His essence is not the same kind of existence of God which can be established by demonstration.[40] Our hypothetical scriptural philosopher, I think, could do better than that. He would go about answering Hume as follows. He would say that Hume's contention that a God who is not known is a God that does not exist has in it a touch of Berkleyan philosophy. It implies that to exist means to be perceived, or to be known, so that if a thing is not known it does not exist. Our hypothetical scriptural philosopher would admit that, if one really believed that only that exists which is known, one cannot consistently affirm both that God exists and that God cannot be known.

[38] *Dialogues Concerning Natural Religion* (*Philosophical Works*, II, 451).
[39] *Cont. Gent.* I, 12.
[40] *Ibid.*

But, scriptural philosophers, their hypothetical spokesman would continue, do not admit the main premise. They do not believe that to exist is to be known. They are old-fashioned philosophers, Aristotelians, if you please. With all their quarrels with Aristotle on matters divine, they are inclined to agree with him in matters mundane. And following the old custom of scriptural philosophers of documenting every statement they make, our hypothetical spokesman of scriptural philosophers would refer to Aristotle's discussion of the distinction between a relation in which the correlatives are simultaneous in nature and a relation in which the correlatives are not simultaneous in nature.[41] By a relation in which the correlatives are simultaneous in nature, Aristotle means a relation in which the existence of one of the correlatives necessarily implies the existence of the other, as, for instance, the correlatives "master" and "slave," in which the existence of "master" necessitates the existence of "slave" and *vice versa* the existence of "slave" necessitates the existence of "master." By a relation in which the correlatives are not simultaneous in nature, Aristotle means a relation in which one correlative may exist even when the other correlative does not exist. And he illustrates it by the example of the relation of "knowledge" to the "object of knowledge." This relation, he says, is one in which the correlatives are not simultaneous in nature, because the "object of knowledge" may have existence even when there is no "knowledge" of it, as, for instance, the squaring of a circle. And so, our hypothetical scriptural philosopher would conclude, there is a difference between the assertion that God's essence cannot be known and the assertion that God's existence, which is identical with His essence, can be demonstrated, for this is exactly a case of a relation between "knowledge" and the "object of knowledge," by which Aristotle illustrates the kind of relation in which the correlatives are not simultaneous in nature and of which he consequently says that one of

[41] *Categoriae* 7, 7b, 15–35.

the correlatives, "the object of knowledge," may exist, even though the other correlative, "knowledge," does not exist.

Then Spinoza, Hume, and Mill reject the infinity of God in the sense of infinite goodness by invoking the old problem of evil. Spinoza introduces the problem by the statement that "amidst so much in nature that is beneficial, not a few things must have been observed which are injurious" and he illustrates it by an old-fashioned list of evils: "storms, earthquakes, diseases." [42] Hume, with the scriptural expressions "cursed is the ground" (Gen. 3:17) and "the earth also was corrupted" (Gen. 6:11) and "the land was polluted" (Psalms 106:38) in the back of his mind, starts out with the general statement that "the whole earth . . . is cursed and polluted" and then proceeds to enumerate the various evils in the world in the form of an elaboration on an allusion to Hobbes' dictum about the war of every one against every one.[43] And John Stuart Mill, lugubriously pointing to history, shows how during all past ages in all countries mankind's lot was not a happy one.[44]

Logically, the problem presents itself to them in the form of a dilemma. Spinoza, dealing in general with the finitude of the world, which includes the evil therein, phrases the dilemma as follows: "If it is finite through its cause, this must be either because it *could* not give more, or because it *would* not give more. That He should not have been able to give more would contradict His omnipotence; that He should not have been willing to give more, when He could well do so, savors of *ill-will*, which is nowise in God, who is all *goodness* and perfection." [45] Hume, dealing directly with the problem of evil, phrases the dilemma in similar terms as follows: "Is He willing to prevent evil, but not able? Then He is impotent.

[42] *Ethics* I, Appendix (*Opera*, II, 79, ll. 18–20).
[43] *Dialogues Concerning Natural Religion*, part X (*Philosophical Works*, II, 496f).
[44] "Theism, Part II: Attributes," *Three Essays on Religion*, p. 192.
[45] *Short Treatise* I, 2, 5 (*Opera*, I, 20, ll. 18ff.).

Is He able but not willing? Then He is malevolent." [46] Both of them finally bring up the sovereign traditional solution, that of Zophar the Naamathite, to the effect that one cannot find out the deep things of God or attain unto the purpose of the Almighty. But Spinoza dismisses it contemptuously in his statement: "And so you fly to the will of God, the asylum of ignorance" [47] and Hume ironically remarks that he is willing to rest the argument with the statement "that these subjects exceed all human capacity, and that our common measures of truth and falsehood are not applicable to them." [48] John Stuart Mill somberly argues: "If the motive of the Deity for creating sentient beings was the happiness of the beings He created, his purpose . . . must be pronounced . . . to have been thus far an ignominious failure." [49]

To all this our hypothetical scriptural philosopher would say that all those for whom he speaks are willing to rest their case with a declaration of our ignorance of God's ways and would ask: Does anybody know of a better solution? and is not resignation out of faith better than resignation out of despair?

They all also reject the infinity of God in the sense of infinite power, which, of course, involves infinite goodness with its implication of will and design. They each have a different argument against it.

In Spinoza there is the implication of an argument that scriptural philosophers in their view on God's omnipotence contradict themselves. Evidently drawing upon statements of Maimonides and St. Thomas to the effect that God has no power over impossibilities, such, for instance, as making contraries to be in the same subject at the same time and in the

---

[46] *Dialogues Concerning Natural Religion* (*Philosophical Works*, II, 501; cf. p. 505).
[47] *Ethics* I, Appendix (*Opera*, II, 81, ll. 10–11).
[48] *Dialogues Concerning Natural Religion* (*Philosophical Works*, II, 505).
[49] *Three Essays on Religion*, p. 192.

same respect, or changing himself into a body, or producing a square the diagonal of which be equal to its side, or making the past not to have been,[50] he finds this to be contradictory with their expressed belief that "all things are possible with God." This is implied in his argument that to say that God, if He willed, could not have created the world, is like saying that "God could bring about that it should not follow from the nature of a triangle that its two angles should be equal to two right angles." [51] It is also implied in his argument that it is more in accord with the conception of the "omnipotence of God" to say that the world, and this world only, continuously flows from God by the same necessity and in the same way as it follows from the nature of a triangle that its three angles are equal to two right angles than to say that this world was created by a decision of God's absolute will out of many other possible worlds which He could have created.[52] Both these arguments mean that for scriptural philosophers to be consistent in their view of the infinite power of God they would also have to believe that God has power to change what is described by them as impossibilities.

Let us see how our hypothetical scriptural philosopher would deal with this argument.

To begin with, our hypothetical scriptural philosopher would say that not only Maimonides and St. Thomas, whom Spinoza undoubtedly had in mind in his criticism, but also all other scriptural philosophers would admit that God does not change impossibilities. In support of this he would refer offhand to Origen [53] and St. Augustine,[54] among Christian philosophers, to the Mutakallimūn, among Muslim philosophers,[55] to Saadia,[56] among Jewish philosophers. He would

---

[50] Maimonides, *Moreh Nebukim* II, 13 (3); *Cont. Gent.* II, 25.

[51] *Ethics* I, Prop. 17, Schol. (*Opera*, II, 61, ll. 27–32).

[52] *Ibid.* (p. 62, ll. 10–30).

[53] *Cont. Cels.* III, 70; V, 23.   [54] *Cont. Faust. Manich.* XXVI, 4–5.

[55] Ibn Hazm, *Fiṣal fī al-Milal* (Cairo, A.H. 1317–1327), IV, 192, ll. 13–14; Ghazālī, *Tahāfut al-Falāsifah*, XVII (ed. Bouyges), §24, p. 292, ll. 2ff.; *Moreh Nebukim* I, 73, Prop. 10.

[56] *Emunot ve-De'ot*, II, 13 (ed. Landauer), p. 110, ll. 4–7.

also add, in passing, that all these scriptural philosophers had been re-echoing a sentiment expressed in the same words and illustrated by the same examples by such pagan philosophers as Alexander Aphrodisiensis [57] and Plotinus [58] and others.[59]

Then he would try to show that scriptural philosophers themselves were aware of this apparent contradiction in their own belief. Such an awareness of it, he would show, is implied in a passage in Origen. In that passage Origen quotes Celsus as ascribing to Christians the statement "as if it were said by us, that 'God will be able to do all things' (δυνήσεται πάντα ὁ θεός)." [60] Origen does not disown the view expressed in this statement. His remark "as if it were said by us" merely means that it is not a verbatim quotation from the New Testament. On the contrary, Origen himself in another place in the same work reproduces with approval the same view in his statement that "all is possible to God (πᾶν δυνατὸν τῷ θεῷ)," [61] which is a paraphrase of the New Testament statement that "all things are possible with God" (πάντα δυνατὰ παρὰ τῷ θεῷ).[62] But while he agrees with this view, he admits that Celsus "might with a show of reason have opposed it." [63] How Celsus could have opposed it "with a show of reason" he does not explain here. But from Origen's statement elsewhere that Christians take the term "all" in the statement as not to include things that are "inconceivable" (τῶν ἀδιανοήτων) [64] it may be inferred that Celsus could have opposed the statement on the ground that it is contradictory to the Christians' own belief that God has no power over things that are "inconceivable." By things "inconceivable," incidentally, he means things which are in violation of such logical rules as the Law of Contradiction or the rules of mathe-

---

[57] *De Fato* 30. [58] *Enneades* VI, 8, 21.

[59] Cf. chapter on "Omnipotence" in R. M. Grant, *Miracles and Natural Law in Graeco-Roman and Early Christian Thought* (Amsterdam, 1952), pp. 127–134. [61] *Ibid.*, V, 23.

[60] *Cont. Cels.* III, 70. [62] Mark 10:27; cf. Matt. 19:26.

[63] *Cont. Cels.* III, 70. Incidentally, Celsus' statement would seem to be a paraphrase of the Septuagint version of Job's address to God (Job 42:1): I know that Thou art able to do all things (πάντα δύνασαι)."

[64] *Ibid.* V, 23.

matics and geometry. Our hypothetical scriptural philosopher would also show that this objection is explicitly quoted by pseudo-Dionysius in the name of a fictitious "Elymas the Magician" (cf. Acts 13:8), who found a contradiction between the Christian belief that "God is omnipotent" and Paul's statement that God "cannot deny himself" (2 Tim. 2:13).[65]

Finally he would try to answer this objection. It is not for lack of power, he would argue, that God does not change impossibilities; it is rather out of wisdom and justice. God could have created another world in which these impossibilities would have been possibilities. He can also destroy this world and create a new world in which the impossibilities would become possibilities. But having by His wisdom created this world and implanted in it these laws, He would not change these laws except when it served a certain purpose. For God does not change the laws of nature in vain, nor does He, like a stage magician, perform miracles to amuse or to impress the spectators. Miracles are performed and laws of nature changed by God only in His exercise of individual providence, for the purpose of preserving those who deserve to be preserved or for the purpose of instructing those who deserve to be instructed. Now, in the wisdom of God, the world is so ordered that to attain that purpose of miracles there is only a need for a change of the physical laws of nature; there is no need for a change of the laws of thought or of the laws of mathematics. All miracles recorded in the scriptures, from the creation of the world to the resurrection of Jesus, are miracles which involved only a transgression of the physical laws of nature, for these miracles had purpose. No conceivable purpose could be served in the world as it is presently constituted for a miraculous change in the laws of thought or in the laws of mathematics. When scriptural philosophers, therefore, say that God does not change, in this world as it is presently constituted, the Law of Contradiction or the geo-

[65] *De Divinis Nominibus* VIII, 6.

metrical proposition about the three angles of a triangle, it is not an indication of a lack of power; it is an indication of the fact that God uses His power in accordance with His wisdom and His goodness.

This answer is implied in Origen's explanation of the statement that with God all things are possible by saying that "in our judgment God can do everything which it is possible for Him to do without ceasing to be God, and good, and wise" [66] or that "we maintain that God cannot do what is disgraceful, since then He would be capable of ceasing to be God, for if He do anything that is disgraceful ($ai\sigma\chi\rho\acute{o}v$), He is not God." [67] In the same way, some Muslim Mu'tazilites explain that the impossibility for God to do evil is not because God has no power to do evil, but rather because He does not want to exercise that power, and this because of "His wisdom and mercy" [68] or because of "its being disgraceful (*qabīḥah*)." [69] So also Isaac Israeli (or Judaeus) says that "the fact that it was impossible for Moses to appear at the time of Adam is not due to the powerlessness of God, but to the fact that such a thing would not belong to wisdom but to absurdity." [70] Similarly Maimonides, speaking of the impossibility on the part of God to change human nature with regard to its freedom of action, says that this is not because God has not the power to do it but rather because, in His wisdom, "it has never been His will to do it, and it never will be." [71] It is also implied in St. Thomas' explanation of why God cannot do that which implies a contradiction by saying that a contradiction implies the notion of non-being and is therefore not "the proper effect" (*proprius effectus*) of God's power.[72]

---

[66] *Cont. Cels.* III, 70.

[67] *Ibid.* V, 23. Cf. H. Chadwick's notes in his translation of *Contra Celsum, ad loc.*

[68] Al-Ash'arī, *Maqālāt al-Islāmīyīn* (ed. Ritter), p. 555, ll. 6–8.

[69] Al-Shahrastānī, *Al-Milal wa'l-Niḥal* (ed. Cureton), p. 37, ll. 8–9.

[70] The Book of Substances, Fragment II, in A. Altmann and S. M. Stern's *Isaac Israeli* (London, 1958), p. 82.

[71] *Moreh Nebukim* III, 32; cf. II, 29.

[72] *Cont. Gent.* II, 22, *Item.*

In Hume the argument against the infinite power of God begins with the general proposition that "like effects prove like causes" [73] and then proceeds as follows: "For as the cause ought only to be proportioned to the effect; and the effect, so far as it falls under our cognizance, is not infinite; what pretensions have we, upon our suppositions, to ascribe that attribute to the divine Being?" [74]

Here, again, our hypothetical spokesman of scriptural philosophers would begin by pointing out that this is an old argument. And he would go on to sketch briefly the history of that argument. He would show how it appears in Plotinus in the form of the following questions: "How from the One, as we conceive it to be, can any multiplicity or duality or number come into existence?" [75] or, "How could all things come from the One which is simple and which shows in its identity no diversity and no duality?" [76] Substitute Hume's terms "infinite" and "finite" for Plotinus' terms "one" and "multiplicity" and you get exactly the same argument, based upon the same principle that "the cause ought only to be proportioned to the effect."

Then our hypothetical scriptural philosophers would show how Plotinus tried to solve this difficulty by making Nous, the first emanation from the One, a being who was one numerically but in whose nature there was an inner duality.

He would then go on to show how scriptural philosophers, such, for instance, as Maimonides [77] among the Jews and Thomas Aquinas among the Christians,[78] have discussed the problem raised by Plotinus as well as his solution, how they refuted his solution of the problem, and how, while agreeing with the principle that "the cause ought only to be proportioned to the effect," they argued that this principle applies only to a cause which produces an effect by necessity, but does not apply to an agent who acts by intelligence and will

---

[73] *Dialogues Concerning Natural Religion*, Part V (*Philosophical Works*, p. 459).
[74] *Ibid.* (p. 461).
[75] *Enneades* V, 1, 6.
[76] *Ibid.* V, 2, 1.
[77] *Moreh Nebukim* II, 22.
[78] *Cont. Gent.* II, 21–24.

and design, such as God's is conceived by all of them. Being an intelligent agent acting by will and design, their God, they all argued, could produce a plurality of things, though He is himself one, and could produce a finite world, though He is himself infinite.

What Hume really did here, our hypothetical scriptural philosopher would conclude, was to rake up an old difficulty raised against the non-scriptural conception of God, to overlook the arguments of scriptural philosophers that this difficulty cannot be raised against their scriptural conception of God, and to flaunt it before an innocent world as a new argument against the scriptural conception of God.

An argument against the infinite power of God is also advanced by John Stuart Mill.[79] But as the argument has not been summarized by him in one quotable passage, we shall try to summarize it ourselves in some brief intelligible form; and, despite Mill's disparagement of the syllogism, we can find no better method of making his argument intelligible than by reducing it to a syllogism. Thus syllogistically stated, his argument runs as follows:

Everyone who employs means in carrying out his purpose is finite;

God employs means in carrying out His purpose;

Therefore, God is finite.

Here, too, the scriptural philosopher would begin his refutation of this argument by pointing out that the implication of powerlessness in the attribution to God of action for a purpose and by the use of means was a difficulty not unknown to scriptural philosophers of the past. It is this very difficulty that had moved a certain class of Muslim theologians to deny that God acts by the use of means. As represented by Averroes, they believed "that the One, that is, God, acts upon all beings without any intermediary" [80] and, as represented

---

[79] "Theism, Part II: Attributes," *Three Essays on Religion*, pp. 126–167.
[80] *In IX Metaph.*, Comm. 7 (Venice, 1574), fol. 231H; XII, Comm. 18, fol. 305F.

by Maimonides, they believed "that God does not do one
thing for the sake of another and that there are no causes
and effects, but that His actions are all the direct result of
His will," [81] and, as represented by Thomas Aquinas, they
believed "that God alone is the immediate cause of everything wrought." [82] This view of Muslim orthodoxy, which
was repudiated alike by Averroes and Maimonides and St.
Thomas, was later accepted, for the very same reason of safe-
guarding the infinite power of God, by the Christian philosopher Nicolaus of Autrecourt.[83]

Then our hypothetical scriptural philosopher would try
to show how this argument could be answered. He would
try to show how God's employment of means differs from
the employment of means by other beings. All other beings
employ those means because, without them, they are powerless to do the things they are resolved to do. Not so is God.
He has the power to do everything directly himself without
any means. In fact, whenever He wishes, He does things directly himself without any means. And even when, for certain
reasons, known or unknown to us, He employs means, those
means act in complete obedience to His will and nowise do
they limit His power. Supporting this assertion of his, our
hypothetical scriptural philosopher would quote such statements of Thomas Aquinas as that "it is erroneous to say that
God cannot himself produce all the determinate effects which
are produced by any created cause" [84] and that "it is clear
that . . . nothing is a cause of being except in so far as it
acts by God's power." [85] He would also quote the view of
Maimonides, according to whom the creation of the world
was a direct act of the divine will without any intermediate
causes [86] and that if in the created world God in His wisdom
acts through intermediate causes, these intermediate causes
are said by him to act as if commanded by God, with the

[81] *Moreh Nebukim* III, 25.   [82] *Sum. Theol.* I, 105, 5c.
[83] Cf. J. R. Weinberg, *Nicolaus of Autrecourt* (Princeton, 1948), pp.
84ff.   [85] *Cont. Gent.* III, 67.
[84] *Sum. Theol.* I, 105, 2c.   [86] *Moreh Nebukim* II, 18 (2).

result that "of everything which is produced by any of these causes it can be said that God commanded that it shall be made or said that it shall be so." [87] And all this, he could conclude, ultimately goes back to Philo who divided God's actions into those which were performed by Him directly and into those performed by Him by means of intermediary causes,[88] and those intermediary causes have no power of their own but act only at the bidding of God.[89]

What Mill really did here, our hypothetical scriptural philosopher would conclude, was to rake up an old difficulty, to overlook the answer given to it, and garnish it up as a new argument.

*   *   *

In my brief survey of some of the reactions to the Philonic conception of God in modern philosophy I have tried to deal with the subject as a historian and not as a theologian. Knowing that scriptural philosophers in the past have raised difficulties against their own belief in revelation and in the various meanings of the infinity of God, I wanted to find out how the difficulties raised by themselves compared with the arguments raised against them by their opponents ever since the seventeenth century. We are often told that the intellectual climate in modern philosophy ever since Spinoza is different and therefore the arguments raised against such beliefs as revelation and the incomprehensibility, goodness, and omnipotence of God are also different. But while indeed it is to be granted that the climate is different, the storms and thunderings and lightnings, as we have seen, are the same. They are not the clash of newly discovered facts with old beliefs. They are still the clash of one kind of interpretation of facts with another kind of interpretation of the same facts.

When philosophers since the seventeenth century deny revelation it is not because new facts have been discovered

---

[87] *Ibid.*, II, 48.
[88] Cf. *Philo*, I, 223, 269–270, 282.   [89] Cf. *ibid.*, I, 332–347.

to discredit it, but rather because, as in the time of Philo, the belief in revelation is held to have no greater historical validity than the myths of the Greeks, though in modern times a greater verisimilitude is lent to this argument by the greater knowledge we now possess of similar myths among other peoples. Logically the argument is still, as Philo characterized it, the refusal to distinguish between Scripture and myth, except that nowadays more people are apt to refuse to distinguish between them.

When they deny the belief that God is infinite in the three senses in which He has been described as infinite it is again not because new facts have been discovered to discredit this belief but rather because, like Job of old, they refuse to acknowledge that one cannot find out the deep things of God and to attain unto the purpose of the Almighty. Logically it is still the same old question whether God is like the world or unlike the world, whether He is part of nature or is above nature, leading on the one hand to the assertion that our knowledge of nature is now greater than in the past and on the other hand to the contention that with all our increased knowledge of nature the facts thereof, not only in their raw state but even in their scientific correlations, are still susceptible of the age-old interpretation of rationalized scriptural theology.

The Philonic type of religious philosophy may be described after Matthew 9:17 as a process whereby old wine is put into new bottles. The speculation about God in modern philosophy, ever since the seventeenth century, is still a process of putting old wine into new bottles. There is only the following difference: the wine is no longer of the old vintage of the revelational theology of Scripture; it is of the old vintage of the natural or verbal theology of Greek philosophy. Sometimes, however, even the bottles are not new; it is only the labels that are new — and one begins to wonder how many of the latter-day philosophies of religion would not prove to be only philosophies of labels.

2

EXTRADEICAL AND INTRADEICAL INTERPRETATIONS OF PLATONIC IDEAS *

THE history of philosophy, especially that philosophy which hired itself out as a handmaiden to theology, is a succession of conflicting views and of attempts to reconcile them. Philosophy, which affects a language of its own, would describe it as a dialectical process of thesis, antithesis, and synthesis. Theology, which occasionally stoops to speak the language of ordinary men, would describe it as a process of peacemaking between mutually misunderstood friendly opinions. But, while in theology peacemakers are pronounced blessed and are they who inherit the kingdom of dogma, in philosophy synthesizers are often blasted and castigated as infringers upon the Law of Contradiction.

In my talk tonight I shall deal with two opposite interpretations of Platonic ideas and the attempts to reconcile them, tracing their history through successive generations of descendants of these Platonic ideas down to the philosophies of Descartes and Spinoza. I shall try to tell the story briefly, simply, sketchily, confining myself to highlights and to the main plot of the story, without going into the intricacies of the topics that come into play. My purpose in selecting this topic for a lecture dedicated to the memory of Whitehead is to illustrate to some extent the truth of his saying that "the safest general characterization of the European philosophical tradition is that it consists of a series of footnotes to Plato." [1]

* Delivered as the Alfred North Whitehead Lecture at Harvard University, 1960. Published in the *Journal of the History of Ideas*, 22 (1961): 3–32. Parts of Sections I and II, in expanded form, were delivered as the Grace A. and Theodore de Laguna Lecture at Bryn Mawr College, 1957, and as one of the three Walter Turner Candler Lectures at Emory University, 1959.

[1] A. N. Whitehead, *Process and Reality* (New York, 1929), p. 53.

I. LOGOS

Among the things which Plato somehow left unexplained about his theory of ideas is the question of how these ideas are related to God. His statements on this point create conflicting impressions. Sometimes he uses language which lends itself to the interpretation that the ideas have an existence external to God, either ungenerated and coeternal with God [2] or produced and made by God.[3] They are thus extradeical. Sometimes, however, he uses language which lends itself to the interpretation that the ideas are the thoughts of God.[4] They are thus intradeical. Modern students of Plato, from Karl Friedrich Hermann to our own Raphael Demos, try to solve these as well as all other real or seeming contradictions by a method which may be called the method of periodization. They assume that these different views about ideas in their relation to God were held by Plato at different periods of his life, and so they classify his dialogues according to certain chronological schemes and speak of early dialogues, middle dialogues, and later dialogues.

In antiquity, however, students of Plato did not know of this convenient method of exegesis. They followed another method, equally convenient. It may be described as the method of selection and rejection. What the followers of this method did was simply to select one set of statements in Plato and accept them as representative of his true philosophy and to reject all the other statements as of no account. And so among the early students of Plato, there were two opposing interpretations of his ideas in their relation to God. According to one interpretation, the ideas have a real existence outside of God: they are extradeical. According to another interpretation, which identifies Plato's God with mind, they are

---

[2] *Timaeus* 28 A, 29 A, 52 B; *Philebus* 15 B.

[3] *Republic* X, 597 B–D.

[4] Early modern students of Plato who found such a view in Plato are listed by Zeller, *Philosophie der Griechen* II, 1, 4th ed. (Leipzig, 1921), 664 n. 5 (*Plato and the Older Academy*, London, 1876, 243 n. 53).

thoughts of God: they are intradeical.[5] The problem concerning Platonic Ideas in their relation to God is brought out most poignantly in a statement which comes from the third century, but may reflect earlier traditions. "Plato," it says, "asserted that there are three first principles of the universe, God and matter and idea," and then, referring to the passages which gave rise to the two opposite interpretations of Plato, it goes on to say that, with respect to the idea, Plato at one time says that "it subsists by itself" and at another time says that "it is in thoughts [of God]." [6]

It is to be noted, however, that in the various passages restating the intradeical interpretation, two modes of expression are used. In the passage quoted, the expression used is that the idea is in thoughts ($\dot{\epsilon}\nu$ $\nu o\acute{\eta}\mu a\sigma\iota$). Similarly in two other passages, the expression used is that "the idea is an incorporeal substance in the thoughts ($\dot{\epsilon}\nu$ $\tau o\hat{\iota}s$ $\nu o\acute{\eta}\mu a\sigma\iota$) and fancies of God" [7] or that "the ideas are substances separate from matter, subsisting in the thoughts and fancies of God, that is, of mind." [8] But in a fourth passage, the expression used is that "the idea, in relation to God, is His act of thinking ($\nu\acute{o}\eta\sigma\iota s$)" and that "whether God be mind ($\nu o\hat{\upsilon}s$) or something mental, He has thoughts ($\nu o\acute{\eta}\mu a\tau a$), and these thoughts are eternal and immutable, and, if this be so, there are ideas," and the author then goes on to explain that by saying that there are ideas he means that God acts by certain rules and plans and that the order observed in nature is not the result of mere chance.[9] Similarly in a fifth passage, the expression used is that the idea is "the thought ($\delta\iota\acute{a}\nu o\iota a$) of God." [10] The difference between these two modes of expression on the face of them would seem to be quite striking. But still, taken in their textual and historical setting, the two mean the same, the difference

[5] On this interpretation, see M. Jones, "The Ideas as Thoughts of God," *Classical Philology*, 21 (1926): 317-326.

[6] Pseudo-Justin Martyr, *Cohortatio ad Graecos* 7 (PG 6, 256A).

[7] Pseudo-Plutarch, *De Placitis Philosophorum* I, 3, 21.

[8] *Ibid.* I, 10, 3 (309).

[9] Albinus, *Didaskalos* (ed. P. Louis) IX, 1 and 3.

[10] Hippolytus, *Refut. Omn. Haer.* (ed. P. Wendland) I, 19, 2.

between them being only verbal. When in the third passage, for instance, ideas are spoken of as substances separated from matter and as subsisting in the thoughts of God, it means the same as when in the fourth passage ideas are spoken of as the well regulated and planned process of God's thinking and thoughts. The different form of expression used in the third passage, as well as in the first and second passages, is only to show pointedly how, on the one hand, Plato differed from Aristotle who "admitted the existence of forms or ideas, but not as separated from matter or as patterns of what God has made" [11] and how, on the other hand, he differed from Zenonian Stoics, who "profess that the ideas are nothing but the conception of our mind." [12] In fact, all those who interpreted the Platonic ideas intradeically were already under the influence of the Aristotelian teaching that in God, because He is immaterial and a mind ($\nu o\hat{v}s$) which is always actual, the process of thinking ($\nu\acute{o}\eta\sigma\iota s$) and the object of thinking ($\nu oo\acute{v}\mu\epsilon\nu o\nu$) are identical with His own self.[13] Even Plotinus, who in his interpretation of Plato, as we shall see later, does not identify God with mind, but still believes that according to Plato the ideas are intramental, argues, quite evidently on the basis of that Aristotelian teaching, that though in our thought we distinguish between Nous, which is that which thinks, and the ideas, which are the object of its thinking, still they are both one and even identical, seeing that Nous is always in a state of "repose and unity and calm," [14] that is, in a state of actuality, for in Nous, as he says elsewhere, there is no transition "from the potentiality of thinking to the actuality of thinking." [15]

While these two contrasting methods of interpreting the Platonic ideas were followed by pagan philosophers, a new method — one less convenient but more subtle — was intro-

[11] Pseudo-Plutarch, op. cit. I, 10, 4.
[12] Ibid. I, 10, 5.
[13] Aristotle, Metaphysica XII, 9, 1074b, 34; 1075a, 3–5.
[14] Plotinus, Enneades III, 9, 1.
[15] Ibid. II, 5, 3.

duced by the Jewish philosopher Philo of Alexandria. His method may be described as that of harmonization. According to this method, all the statements in Plato, however contradictory they may appear to be, are assumed to be true, and out of all of them a harmonious composite view is molded, in which all the apparently contradictory statements are made to live in peace with each other. Such a method of interpretation was used by Jewish rabbis in their effort to harmonize contradictory statements in the Hebrew Scripture and by Augustine, in his *De Consensu Evangelistarum*, as a way of harmonizing the contradictory statements in the Gospels.

Philo's interpretation of Platonic ideas occurs in his various comments on the story of creation in the Book of Genesis. A composite summary of these comments may be stated as follows: When God by His own good will decided to create this world of ours, He first, out of the ideas which had been in His thought from eternity, constructed an "intelligible world," and this intelligible world He placed in the Logos, which had likewise existed previously from eternity in His thought. Then in the likeness of this intelligible world of ideas, He created this "visible world" of ours.[16]

Students of Plato cannot fail seeing a resemblance between this version of the story of creation of the Book of Genesis with the story of creation in Plato's *Timaeus*. As told by Plato in the *Timaeus*, there is a God, who is called the Demiurge, the Creator. Then, besides the Demiurge, there is a model (παράδειγμα),[17] which is coeternal with the Demiurge. This model is called the "intelligible animal" [18] and contains in itself "intelligible animals." [19] The Demiurge is said to have looked at the intelligible animal and in its likeness he created this world of ours, which is called "the visible animal." [20]

Comparing these two accounts of the creation of the world, one can readily see that what Philo was trying to do was to

---

[16] *Opif.* 5, 20ff. Cf. chapter on "God, the World of Ideas, and the Logos," in my *Philo*, rev. ed. (Cambridge, Mass., 1948), I, 200–294.
[17] *Timaeus* 29 B.
[18] *Ibid.* 39 E.
[19] *Ibid.* 30 C.
[20] *Ibid.* 29 D.

interpret the story of creation of the Book of Genesis in terms of the story of creation in the *Timaeus*. In fact, we know that this was his purpose.

But, though there is a resemblance between these two accounts of creation, there are also some differences. I shall mention here three such differences.

The *first* difference between them is that in the *Timaeus* the contrast between the pre-existent ideas and the created world is described as a contrast between the "intelligible animal" (ζῷον νοητόν) and the "visible animal" (ζῷον ὁρατόν), whereas in Philo the contrast is described as one between the "intelligible world" (κόσμος νοητός) and the "visible world" (κόσμος ὁρατός). At first sight the change would seem to be only verbal and of no significance. But upon further study of Plato's and Philo's philosophies we may discover that it involves two problems upon which Philo differed from Plato. To begin with, it involves the problem of the existence of a world-soul. To Plato, there is a world-soul, a soul which exists in the body of the world, just as there is a soul which exists in the body of any living being. The world is therefore to him a visible animal, and the ideas are therefore described by him as an intelligible animal. To Philo, however, there is no world-soul. Though occasionally he uses the expression "soul of the world," he never uses it in the sense of a soul immanent in the world. The function of the Platonic, as well as the Stoic, world-soul, which is a soul immanent in the world, is performed in Philo's philosophy partly by the Logos, which with the creation of the world becomes immanent in it, and partly by what he calls the Divine Spirit, which is an incorporeal being not immanent in the world. Without a soul, the world to Philo was not an animal being. Then, it involves the problem of the existence of ideas as segregate beings. To Plato in the *Timaeus*, the intelligible animal contains only the ideas of the four kinds of living creatures in the universe, namely, the celestial bodies, birds, fishes, and land-animals.[21] There is no

[21] *Ibid.* 39 E.

evidence that it contains even the ideas of the four elements, though such ideas are mentioned or alluded to in the *Timaeus*.[22] All the ideas, therefore, with the exception of those of living creatures, exist in segregation from each other. To Philo, however, all the ideas are integrated into a whole, namely, the intelligible world; and their relation to the intelligible world is conceived by him as that of parts of an indivisible whole, which as such have no real existence of their own apart from that of the whole.

The *second* difference between them is that in the *Timaeus* there is no mention of a place where the ideas exist, whereas in Philo the ideas are said to have their place in the Logos. Now, while the term Logos occurs in Greek philosophy, having been used ever since Heraclitus in various senses, it was never used in the sense of the place of the Platonic ideas. We must therefore try to find out how Philo happened to come to this concept of a Logos as the place of the Platonic ideas.

In trying to find an answer to this question, let us start by examining carefully the passage in which Philo introduces the Logos as the place of ideas. In that passage, he begins by saying that, just as the plan conceived by the mind of an architect, prior to its execution, exists in no other place but the soul of the architect, so the intelligible world of ideas, prior to creation of the visible world, existed in no other place but "the divine Logos." He then adds the following rhetorical question: "For what other place could there be . . . sufficiently able to receive and contain, I say not all, but any one" of the ideas of this intelligible world? [23] This rhetorical question quite evidently contains a challenge. It implies that somebody did suggest some other place for the ideas and Philo, convinced that that other place, or any other place that might be suggested, could not properly be the place of the ideas,

[22] *Ibid.* 51 Bf. Cf. R. D. Archer-Hind in his introduction to his edition of the *Timaeus* (London, 1888), 34–35; F. M. Cornford, *Plato's Cosmology* (London, 1937), 188–191.
[23] *Opif.* 5, 20.

challenges that somebody as well as anybody else to show whether any other place could properly be the place of the ideas. Fortunately we are able to identify that somebody who suggested another place for the ideas. It is Plato. In several passages Plato touches upon the question of the place of the ideas. In one of these passages, he states that the idea of beauty, and quite evidently any of the other ideas, is "never any-where in anything else," [24] a statement on the basis of which Aristotle generalizes that Plato's ideas are "nowhere" [25] or "not in place." [26] In other passages he speaks of the ideas as existing in a "supercelestial place" [27] or in an "intelligible place." [28] Combining these passages, we may conclude that what Plato means to say is this: the ideas do not exist in any place in the visible world, but they exist in the "supercelestial place" or "intelligible place," which is outside the visible world. But what is that supercelestial or intelligible place out-side the world? It can be shown, I believe, that Philo took this supercelestial or intelligible place of Plato to mean an infinite void outside the world, for, though Plato explicitly denied the existence of a void within the world,[29] there are statements in his writings which could have been interpreted by Philo to refer to the existence of a void outside the world. It happens, however, that Philo, under the influence of Aris-totle, denied the existence of a void even outside the world.[30] And so, with the elimination of what Plato designated as the place of the ideas, he locates the ideas in "the divine Logos" and, challenging one and all, he asks rhetorically, "for what other place could there be" for the ideas?

But how did Philo come to substitute the Logos as the place of ideas for Plato's infinite vacuum outside the world? The answer is that he came to it by a process of reasoning arising from a passage in Plato's own works. He started, we may imagine, with a passage in *Parmenides* (132 BC), in which

---

[24] *Symposium* 211 A.
[25] *Physica* III, 4, 203a, 9.
[26] *Ibid*. IV, 2, 209b, 34.
[27] *Phaedrus* 247 C.

[28] *Republic* VI, 509 D; VII, 517 B.
[29] *Timaeus* 80 C.
[30] Cf. *Philo*, I, 241–242.

Socrates, who poses as one not altogether convinced of the existence of ideas as real beings, raises the question whether an idea may not be only a "thought (νόημα), which cannot properly exist anywhere except in souls (ἐν ψυχαῖς)." Souls here means human souls, for it is in this sense that the term was understood by Aristotle in a passage where, with evident reference to this passage in the *Parmenides*, he says that "it has been well said that the soul is a place of forms or ideas," adding, however, "that this does not apply to the soul as a whole but only to thinking soul (ψυχὴ νοητική)." [31]

Now it can be shown that Philo made use of this statement of Aristotle,[32] and we may be justified in assuming that he also knew the original statement in *Parmenides*. Let us then imagine that, on reading these two statements, Philo asked himself: if ideas, according to those who question or deny their real existence, exist in a human thinking soul, which exists in a body, why should not those who believe in the existence of real ideas say that they exist in a thinking soul which does not exist in a body? Does not Plato himself believe in a bodiless pre-existent soul as well as in a bodiless immortal soul? And so Philo has arrived at the conclusion that the ideas exist in a bodiless thinking soul. It is perhaps on the basis of these passages, too, and by the same kind of reasoning that those who interpreted the Platonic ideas intradeically came to identify the God of Plato's philosophy with its Nous.

Then, let us further imagine that, on having arrived at this conclusion. Philo began to look for a single Greek word for the expression "thinking soul" used by Aristotle. It happens that the Greeks, by the time of Philo, had two words for it, *nous*, "mind," and *logos*, "reason." Philo, therefore, had before him the choice of one of these two words, and he decided in favor of Logos. What made him decide in favor of Logos may be assumed to be a threefold consideration. First, that which was to contain the intelligible world of ideas as the model for the visible world that was to be created, was,

---

[31] *De Anima* III, 4, 429a, 27–28.   [32] Cf. *Philo*, I, 233, 247.

according to Philo, to serve as a sort of instrument by which the visible world was to be created by God.[33] Second, the Greek term "Logos," which besides "reason" means also "word," is used in the Greek version of Scripture as a translation of the Hebrew term *dabar*, "word," so that in the verse "by the word of the Lord the heavens were established" (Ps. 33/32:6) the Logos is represented as a sort of instrument by which the world was created. Third, a parallel to this use of the term Logos in the scriptural verse quoted may have been seen by Philo in Plato's statement that all animals and plants and inanimate substances "are created by *logos* [that is, reason] and by divine knowledge that comes from God." [34]

It is this threefold consideration, we may assume, that has led Philo to decide in favor of the use of the term Logos to that of Nous. An indication that the term Logos is used by him as the equivalent of Nous, as well as a substitute for it, in the sense of a bodiless Nous, in contrast to the embodied Nous implied in Aristotle's statement that the "thinking soul" is the place of ideas, is his statement that the Logos is "the Nous above us" in contrast to the human thinking soul which is "the Nous within us." [35] And as an indication that it is the scriptural verse that caused him to decide in favor of the Logos is his use of the term Wisdom (σοφία) as the equivalent of Logos and his description of Wisdom also as that "through which the world came into existence," [36] for in Scripture, corresponding to the verse "by the word (*logos*) of the Lord the heavens were established" (Ps. 33/32:6) there is the verse "by wisdom (*sophia*) God founded the earth" (Prov. 3:19).

Since by Logos is meant Nous, when Philo speaks of the Logos as the place of the intelligible world, he means thereby that the relation of the Logos to the intelligible world, and hence also to the ideas which constitute the intelligible world, is after the analogy of the relation of the thinking mind to

---

[33] Cf. *ibid.*, I, 261–282.
[34] *Sophist* 265 C.

[35] *Heres* 48, 236.
[36] *Fug.* 20, 109; cf. *Deter.* 16, 54.

its object of thought. Now, according to Aristotle, in the case of immaterial things, the thinking mind is identical with its object of thought.[37] The Logos is, therefore, conceived by Philo as being identical with the intelligible world and hence also with the ideas which constitute the intelligible world.[38]

The *third* difference between Philo and the *Timaeus* is his departure from the representation of the ideas in that dialogue as ungenerated [39] and as being outside the Demiurge, so that they were looked at by the Demiurge and were used by him as a model in the creation of the visible world.[40] Philo undoubtedly knew of the other kind of statements about the ideas in the other dialogues of Plato and presumably he would also know of the two contrasting interpretations current in his time. Neither of these interpretations, however, was acceptable to him. The extradeical interpretation was unacceptable, because it implied the existence of eternal beings besides God, but to Philo, besides God, there could be no other eternal being.[41] Nor could the intradeical interpretation be acceptable to him. For, if it meant that the ideas were in thoughts of God as real beings really distinct from Him, then it implied that in God there existed something other than himself. But this was contrary to Philo's interpretation of the scriptural doctrine of the unity of God as meaning absolute simplicity.[42] And if it meant that the ideas were thoughts of God and hence identical with Him, then it meant a denial of the existence of ideas as such, but, according to Philo, those who denied the existence of incorporeal ideas are condemned in Scripture as "impious" and "unholy," [43] for, on the basis of certain scriptural verses and a Jewish tradition, he held that the belief in the existence of ideas as real beings was one of the fundamental teachings of Moses.[44] And so, what did he do? He introduced a new interpretation of the Platonic ideas in their relation to God. According to this new interpreta-

---

[37] *Metaphysica* XII, 9, 1075a, 3–4.
[38] Cf. *Philo*, I, 248–252.
[39] *Timaeus* 52 A.
[40] *Ibid*. 28 A.

[41] Cf. *Philo*, I, 322.
[42] *Ibid*., 172–173; II, 94ff.
[43] *Ibid*., 164.
[44] *Ibid*., 181–186.

tion, the Logos, together with the intelligible world of ideas within it, at first, from eternity, existed as a thought of God; then, prior to the creation of the world, it was created as a real incorporeal being distinct from God.

In Philo, then, Platonic ideas were integrated into an intelligible world of ideas contained in a Nous called Logos, so that the original problem of the relation of Platonic ideas to God became with him a problem of the relation of the Nous or the Logos to God, and the problem was solved by him by the assumption of two successive stages of existence in the Logos, an intradeical one followed by an extradeical.

From now on, in the history of philosophy, ideas will be treated either, after the manner of Plato himself, as segregated beings, or, after the manner of his interpreter Philo, as integrated into an intelligible world placed in a Logos or a Nous, and the original problem of extradeical and intradeical, or the solutions thereof, will be applied either to the ideas themselves or to the Logos or Nous.

II. TRINITY [45]

Philo preached his philosophical sermons in the synagogues of Alexandria at the time when Jesus, known as Christ, preached his hortatory and admonitory sermons in the synagogues of Galilee. About half a century later there appeared one of the four standard biographies of Christ, the Fourth Gospel, the Gospel according to St. John. This biography of Christ is based upon the theory, introduced by Paul, that before Christ was born there was a pre-existent Christ, an ideal Christ, an idea of Christ. This pre-existent idea of Christ, which in the epistles of Paul is called Wisdom or perhaps also Spirit is described in this biography of Jesus by the term Logos, which is conventionally rendered into English by the

[45] This section is based upon the chapters dealing with the Trinity in my *Philosophy of the Church Fathers*, I (Cambridge, Mass., 1956), 141–364. (Henceforth *Church Fathers*.)

term Word. And we are all acquainted with the opening verse in the Gospel according to St. John: "In the beginning was the Word, and the Word was with God, and the Word was God" (1:1). Then, like the Logos of Philo, which became immanent in the created world, the Logos of John, which is the pre-existent Christ, became immanent, or, as it is commonly said, incarnate, in the born Christ. And we are all, again, acquainted with the verse toward the close of the Prologue of the Gospel according to St. John: "And the Word was made flesh" (1:14).

In this Prologue of the Fourth Gospel, there are similarities between the Logos of Philo and the Logos of John. But two main characteristics of the Philonic Logos are missing in the Johannine Logos, or, with regard to one of them, it is not clearly stated. There is no hint at all that the Logos of John, which is the idea of Christ, contains in itself the intelligible world of ideas and there is no clear statement that before its incarnation it had two stages of existence, one from eternity as the thought of God, and then, with the creation of the world, as a real being distinct from God.

These two missing characteristics were supplied in the second century by those Church Fathers known as Apologists, who, having been born pagans, were before their conversion to Christianity students of philosophy. As they themselves tell us, what has led them to their conversion was the reading of Scripture, the Hebrew Scripture, naturally in the Greek translation. From internal evidence of their writings, we may gather that they used the works of Philo as a sort of commentary upon Scripture. From these works of Philo they became acquainted with Philo's interpretation of Platonic ideas, at the center of which was the term Logos. When, therefore, in the Fourth Gospel they read the opening sentence, "In the beginning was the Logos," they identified this Logos with the Philonic Logos and thus, without the Johannine Logos ceasing to mean the pre-existent Christ, it acquired the two main characteristics of the Philonic Logos.

To begin with, like the Philonic Logos, the Johannine Logos began to contain the intelligible world of ideas, so that it was no longer a single idea, the idea of Christ, but it became the place of the intelligible world consisting of all ideas. Then, again, like the Philonic Logos, it was made to have two stages of existence prior to its incarnation: first, from eternity it was within God and identical with Him; second, from about the time of the creation of the world it was a generated real being distinct from God. Once these two innovations were introduced, Fathers of the Church began to look in the New Testament for proof-texts in support of them. For the first of these two innovations, two Fathers of the Church, Origen and Augustine, at one time thought that they had found a supporting proof-text in Jesus' saying, "I am not of this world" (John 8:23), from which they tried to infer that there was another world, and that that other world was the intelligible world of ideas.[46] Ultimately, however, this inference was rejected, for different reasons, by both of them.[47] A satisfactory proof-text for this first innovation was, however, discovered by them in the verse stating that through the Logos were all things made by God (John 1:3). Following Philo in his description of the Logos, they interpreted this verse to imply that the Logos was used by God as a sort of architect's blueprint, which contained the plan for the structure of the world and thus it contained the intelligible world of ideas.[48] As for the second innovation, again, two of the Fathers of the Church, Tertullian and Clement of Alexandria,[49] took the verse "In the beginning was the Logos" to mean that "in the beginning of the creation of the world the Logos came into being." Now the Greek ἦν which is used in this verse for the English "was," in classical Greek means "was" and not "came into being," for the latter of

---

[46] Origen, De Princ. II, 3, 6; Augustine, De Ordine I, 11, 32 (PL 32, 993).
[47] Origen, loc. cit.; Augustine, Retractiones I, 3, 2.
[48] Origen, In Joannem XIX, 5 (PG 14, 568BC); Augustine, In Joannem I, 9; cf. Church Fathers, pp. 277–278, 283–284.
[49] Cf. Church Fathers, pp. 198, 213–214.

which the Greek would be ἐγένετο. But their interpretation of ἦν as meaning "came to be" may be justified on the ground that in the Greek translation of the Hebrew Scripture, the Septuagint, the Greek ἦν, through its use as a translation of the Hebrew *hayah*, which means both "was" and "came to be," acquired the additional meaning of "came to be." [50]

Following Philo, too, these early Fathers of the Church added to the Logos another pre-existent incorporeal being, the Holy Spirit, thus together with God and the Logos making three pre-existent real beings, subsequently to become known as hypostases or persons. Now the Holy Spirit is mentioned in the New Testament, but it is not clear whether it is meant to be the same as the pre-existent Christ, and hence the same as the Wisdom of Paul and the Logos of John, or whether it is meant to be a pre-existent being different from the pre-existent Christ. The Apostolic Fathers, who flourished before and up to the middle of the second century, were still uncertain about it. But the Apologists, under the influence of Philo, definitely declared the Holy Spirit to be distinct from the Logos. Like the Logos, the Holy Spirit was held by them to have been at first intradeical and then became extradeical.

But on one point did the Apologists differ radically from Philo.[51] To Philo, who followed the traditional Jewish conception of God as the maker of things after the analogy of an artisan, the Logos entered its second stage of existence by an act of making or creating, except that the making was out of nothing, since God is an omnipotent artisan and is in no need of material for any of his acts of making. Consequently, like any product of an artisan's making, which is not the same as its maker, the Logos is not the same as God. Though Philo applies to the Logos several terms meaning divine, he never applies to it the term God in the real sense of the term. The Apologists, however, who followed the Christianized mytho-

[50] Cf. below, "Philosophical Implications of Arianism and Apollinarianism," p. 139.

[51] On what follows, see the chapter on "The Mystery of Generation," in *Church Fathers*, p. 287–304.

logical conception of God as the begetter of things, after the
analogy of natural procreation, conceived of the entrance of
the Logos into its second stage of existence as having been
effected by an act of begetting or generating and consequently, as in any act of natural generation, where that which
is generated is like that which generated it, the Logos to them
is God like the God who generated it. Later Christian theologians, Augustine, followed by Thomas Aquinas, tried to
explain the Godship of the Logos by referring to the philosophic principle that all living beings reproduce their kind.
They illustrated it by quoting the Aristotelian statement that
"man begets man," [52] to which St. Augustine added "and dog
dog" [53] and which St. Thomas paraphrased by saying "as a
man proceeds from a man and a horse from a horse." [54] Subsequently the term God was extended to the Holy Spirit, so
that each of the persons, the Father, the Son or Logos, and
the Holy Spirit, was God.

These three persons of the Trinity, however, though each
of them a real being and each of them God and each of them
really distinct from the others, constituted one God, who was
most simple and indivisible. Consequently, the Logos, in so
far as it was really distinct from God the Father and God the
Holy Spirit, was extradeical: but, in so far as it was an indivisible part of an indivisible triune God, it was intradeical.
This was a new kind of harmonization of extradeical and
intradeical. It may be described as harmonization by unification, which was added by the Apologists to the Philonic harmonization by succession. How three distinct real beings,
each of them God, could be harmonized and unified into one
God, without infringing upon the Law of Contradiction, the
Fathers of the Church tried to explain by various analogies
up to a certain point, but beyond that point they admitted
that the Trinity was a mystery.

[52] *Metaphysica* VII, 7, 1032a, 23–24; cf. IX, 8, 1049b, 27–29.
[53] *Cont. Maximin.* II, 6.
[54] *Sum. Theol.* I, 27, 2c.

As part of the mystery of the Trinity is the conception of the relation of the ideas within the Logos to the triune God. According to Philo, so also according to the Church Fathers, the ideas within the Logos were identical with the Logos. But, whereas to Philo, by reason of their being identical with the Logos, they were, like the Logos during its second stage of existence, extradeical, to the Apologists, despite their being identical with the Logos, they were not, like the Logos during its second stage of existence, both extradeical and intradeical by unification: they were only intradeical. The reason for this is as follows: It happens that among the Church Fathers from the earliest times there existed the view that the distinction between the persons of the Trinity is only with respect to some causal relationship existing between them, which later came to be described by the terms paternity, filiation, and procession. In every other respect they are one, their unity consisting in the indivisible unity of the one God which they all constitute. Since they all constitute one God, whatever is said of any of the persons of the Trinity, with the exception of the terms which describe the one single distinction between them, applies to the one indivisible God which they all constitute. Accordingly, when the intelligible world of ideas is said to exist in the Logos and to be identical with the Logos, it really means that it exists in the one indivisible God, which the three persons constitute, and it is with that one indivisible God that it is identical.

This, then, was the philosophic situation during the second century after the Christian era. Three interpretations of Platonic ideas existed side by side. Among pagan philosophers, the Platonic ideas were treated as segregated beings, and were interpreted either (1) extradeically or (2) intradeically. In Philo and the Church Fathers they were treated as integrated into an intelligible world placed in a Logos, but, whereas to Philo the Logos together with the ideas within it (3) was both intradeical and extradeical by succession, to the Apologists (4) the Logos was extradeical and intradeical both by succession and by unification, but the ideas were only intra-deical.

Then, in the third century, something new happened both in Christian philosophy and in pagan philosophy. Christian philosophy had its center in Alexandria under Origen and pagan philosophy had its center in Rome under Plotinus.

Both Origen and Plotinus start their philosophy with three principles, which are coeternal. Both of them call these principles hypostases.[55] Both of them describe the first hypostasis, who is God, as Father.[56] Both of them describe the second hypostasis as being eternally generated from the first[57] and call him son[58] and image.[59] Both of them make their second hypostasis contain the intelligible world of ideas.[60] So far forth they are in agreement. But then they begin to differ. Origen, as in Christianity, calls his second hypostasis Logos. Plotinus calls it Nous. In direct opposition to those who called it Logos, he explicitly denies that the second hypostasis is the Logos of the first[61] and, especially aiming at the Christian use of Logos as a technical term designating the second hypostasis only, he says: "The Soul is a *logos* and a certain *energeia* of the Nous, just as the Nous is of the One."[62] Again, the third hypostasis is called by Origen, as in Christianity, Holy Spirit; Plotinus calls it Soul[63] and, again, in direct opposition to those who called it Spirit, he uses the term spirit in a material sense and therefore argues that it cannot be Soul.[64] Then, also, following Christian tradition, Origen calls his Logos God; and, while a real being distinct

[55] Origen, *De Princ.* I, 2, 2; *In Joan.* X, 21 (PG 14, 376B); *Cont. Cels.* VIII, 12 (PG 11, 1533C); Plotinus, *Enneades* II, 9, 2; V, 1, 7; V, 8, 12; VI, 7, 29.
[56] Origen, *De Princ.* I, 2, 6; Plotinus, *Enneades* III, 8, 11.
[57] Origen, *De Princ.* I, 2, 4; *In Jeremiam*, Hom. IX, 4 (PG 13, 357A); Plotinus, *Enneades* V, 1, 6; VI, 8, 20.
[58] Origen, *De Princ.* I, 2, 4; Plotinus, *Enneades* III, 8, 11.
[59] Origen, *De Princ.* I, 2, 6; Plotinus, *Enneades* V, 1, 7; V, 4, 2; V, 6, 4; V, 9, 2; VI, 2, 9.
[60] Origen, cf. above at n. 48; Plotinus, *Enneades* V, 9, 9.
[61] *Enneades* VI, 7, 17.
[62] *Ibid.* V, 1, 6.
[63] *Ibid.* V, 1, 10.
[64] *Ibid.* IV, 7, 3-4.

from his first hypostasis, it constitutes with it one God. Plotinus, however, is reminiscent of Philo. Like Philo, who calls his Logos simply "God," without the definite article "the," in contrast to the true God, who is called "the God," with the definite article "the," [65] Plotinus calls his Nous God in the sense of πᾶς, "all," that is, in an indefinite sense, in contrast to God in the sense of τίς, that is, a certain particular God.[66] Again, like Philo, who describes his Logos as "the second God" [67] in contrast to the true God who is "the first God," [68] Plotinus describes his Nous as "the second God" [69] in contrast to the God, whom he usually refers to as "the First" [70] or whom he may have even described as "the first God." [71] Accordingly, to Origen, the Logos is eternally both extra-deical and intradeical by unification, but the ideas within it are intradeical, whereas, according to Plotinus, the Nous, together with the intelligible world of ideas within it, are extradeical.

How did these two systems at once alike and different originate?

Here I am going to suggest an answer for which there is no direct documentary evidence. There is only circumstantial evidence, the kind of evidence on which a defendant standing trial for murder may be acquitted by a jury of his peers, and on which, I believe, a student of the history of philosophy may venture to build a theory even at the risk of being condemned by fellow historians as indulging in flights of fancy.

My explanation is this: Both Plotinus and Origen were students at one time, though not at the same time, of Ammonius Saccas in Alexandria. "Ammonius," according to Porphyry as quoted by Eusebius, "was a Christian, brought up in Chris-

---

[65] *Somn.* I, 39, 239–240.
[66] *Enneades* V, 5, 3.
[67] *Qu. in Gen.* II, 62; cf. *Leg. All.* II, 21, 86.
[68] *Migr.* 32, 181; 35, 194; *Mos.* II, 26, 205.
[69] *Enneades* V, 5, 3.
[70] *Ibid.* V, 5, 11.
[71] *Ibid.* III, 9, 9, according to some readings of the text. See ed. Bréhier (Paris, 1925) and ed. Henry and Schwyzer (Paris, 1951) *ad loc.*

tian doctrines by his parents, yet, when he began to think and study philosophy, he immediately changed his way of life to conform to that required by the laws." [72] We may assume, I believe, that during his Christian period, like Clement of Alexandria,[73] he interpreted Plato in terms of the Philonic twofold stage theory and applied the same interpretation to the Johannine Logos and, by reason of the mystery of the Trinity, while the Logos during its second stage of existence was both extradeical and intradeical by unification, the ideas within it were only intradeical. Then, when Ammonius gave up Christianity, we may further assume, he gave up the interpretation of Plato in terms of the Philonic twofold stage theory and substituted for it the theory of eternal generation; he also gave up the primarily Biblical term Logos and the strictly Biblical term Holy Spirit and substituted for them the purely philosophical terms Nous and Soul; finally, discarding the Christian mystery of the Trinity, his Nous, the substitute for the Christian Logos as the place of the intelligible world of ideas, was no longer equal with God, no longer the same as God, and no longer forming together with God and the Soul one God, and hence no longer intradeical and extradeical by unification. Plotinus, a pagan, adopted this new philosophy of Ammonius in its entirety. Origen, a Christian, adopted from it only the concept of eternal generation, which he applied to the Christian Logos, but this he did only on purely Christian religious grounds, considering the principle of eternal generation less open to misunderstanding and misinterpretation than the twofold stage theory.

Truly speaking, then, the philosophy of Plotinus, known as Neoplatonism, in so far as its theory of ideas is concerned,

---

[72] Eusebius, *Hist. Eccl.* VI, 19, 7. It must be noted that Eusebius denies the apostasy of Ammonius (VI, 19, 9–10). Among modern scholars, some say that Eusebius was mistaken in denying the apostasy of Ammonius Saccas (cf. Lawlor and Oulton's note on VI, 19, 10 of their English translation of Eusebius), while others say that Porphyry was mistaken in making Ammonius Saccas born a Christian (cf. Bardy's note on VI, 19, 7 of his French translation of Eusebius).

[73] *Church Fathers*, p. 266–270.

is a paganized version of the Christian version, which in turn is a Christianized version of the Philonic Jewish version of Plato's theory of ideas. Thus the theory of ideas of both Origen and Plotinus are a third generation of the Platonic ideas.

In Christianity, the Origenian harmonization of extradeical and intradeical by the method of unification prevailed and it became the orthodox creed of the Church. But it met with opposition. It was felt by many Christians, described by Origen as those "who sincerely profess to be lovers of God," [74] that the conception of a God, in whom there was a distinction of three real beings each of whom was God, was incompatible with the conception of the unity of God, which was the common profession of all Christians. The various attempts at explaining the unity of God ultimately meant the reduction of the conception of unity to a relative kind of unity,[75] which to them was unacceptable. They had before them, therefore, two choices, either to deny that the Logos was God or to deny the reality of its existence.[76] Some followed the first alternative. They are the Arians. Others followed the second alternative. This had many exponents. But we shall refer to them, after one of its exponents, as Sabellians. Denying the reality of the Logos, in a passage in which they refer to the Logos as the Son, they declared that "the Father is Son and again the Son Father, in hypostasis one, in name two." [77] And when the Holy Spirit was proclaimed by orthodoxy to be also God, they declared that "the term Father and Son and Holy Spirit are but actions and names." [78] In other words, they rejected the orthodox conceptions of the Logos as being simultaneously both extradeical and intradeical by unification and made it only intradeical, in the sense of identical, and, of course, with it also the ideas within it were intradeical.

---

[74] *In Joan.* II, 2 (PG 14, 108C); cf. *Church Fathers*, pp. 580ff.
[75] *Church Fathers*, p. 312ff.
[76] Cf. *ibid.*, chapter on "Heresies," p. 575ff.
[77] Athanasius, *Orat. cont. Arian.* IV, 25 (PG 26, 505C).
[78] Epiphanius, *Adv. Haer. Panar.* LXII, 1 (PG 41, 1052B).

In pagan philosophy, similarly, the Plotinian conception of a Nous, in which the ideas integrated into an intelligible world was located, prevailed until the pagan schools of philosophy were closed by the order of Emperor Justinian in 529. But one notable exception is to be mentioned, and that is the theory of Ammonius Hermiae, who was at the head of the pagan school of philosophy in Alexandria at about the middle of the fifth century. In his commentary on the *Isagoge*, a work by Porphyry, who was a student of Plotinus, this Ammonius tries to answer questions raised by Porphyry with regard to the ideas of Plato — questions not with regard to the relation of the ideas to God but rather with regard to their relation to individual things in the world. After solving in his own way the phase of the problem with regard to ideas which was raised by Porphyry, Ammonius, of his own accord, tries to solve the problem of the relation of the ideas to God. His answer is contained in the following statements. First, he says, "He who fabricates all things contains in himself the paradigms of all things" [79] and "if He knows that which He makes, it is at once evident that the forms exist in the Fabricator." [80] Then, trying to prove that this is also the view of Plato, he says [81] that Plato, who, in contradistinction to Aristotle, describes the ideas as being "intelligible, subsisting in themselves" (νοηταὶ, αὐταὶ καθ' ἑαυτὰς ὑφεστῶσαι),[82] as being "really substances" (ὄντως οὐσίας),[83] and as "first substances" (πρώτας οὐσίας),[84] means thereby that "God contains in himself the models of the genera and species." Here then we have in pagan philosophy a continuation or revival of the old pre-Plotinian, or rather pre-Philonic, treatment of

---

[79] *Ammonius in Porphyrii Isagoge sive V Voces* (ed. A. Busse), p. 41, ll. 20–21.

[80] *Ibid.*, p. 42, ll. 5–6.   [81] *Ibid.*, p. 44, ll. 1–4.

[82] Reflecting Plato's description of ideas as νοητά (*Timaeus* 30 C) and as things which are αὐτὰ καθ' αὐτὰ ὄντα (*Timaeus* 51 B).

[83] Reflecting Plato's description of ideas as οὐσία ὄντως οὖσα (*Phaedrus* 247 C).

[84] Not found in Plato as a description of ideas, but it probably reflects Plato's description of ideas as ἀΐδιος οὐσία (*Timaeus* 37 E).

ideas as beings segregated from each other and as the thoughts of God.

Thus beginning with the third century both in pagan philosophy, as represented by the Neoplatonism of Plotinus, and in Christian philosophy, as represented by orthodoxy and Sabellianism, the Platonic ideas were integrated into an intelligible world. In pagan philosophy it existed in a Nous which was extradeical; in Christian philosophy it existed in a Logos which was either, as in orthodoxy, both extradeical and intradeical by unification or, as in Sabellianism, only intradeical. As for the ideas within the Logos or Nous, in Christianity they were purely intradeical; in Neoplatonism they were extradeical along with the Nous with which they were identical.

III. ATTRIBUTES

Six hundred and twenty-two years roll by since the rise of Christianity and a new religion appears — Islam. In the Scripture of this new religion, the Koran, God is described by what the followers of this religion like to refer to as "the ninety-nine most beautiful names of God," such, for instance, as "the living," "the powerful," "the wise," and so forth up to ninety-nine. Early in the history of this religion there arose a view, first with regard to only two of that list of ninety-nine names and then also with regard to other names of that list, that each name by which God is designated reflects some real being existing in God as something distinct from His essence, but inseparable from it and coeternal with it. Thus, for instance, when God is described as living or wise or powerful, it means that life or wisdom or power exist in Him as real, eternal beings, distinct from His essence. These real beings in God corresponding to the names by which God is designated are known in Arabic by two terms, one of which, as we shall see, came to be known to philosophers of the West as "attributes."

This view, it can be shown, could not have originated in Islam spontaneously but it could have originated under Christian influence in the course of debates between Muslims and Christians shortly after the Muslim conquest of Syria in the VIIth century.[85] In these debates, we may assume, Christians tried to convince the Muslims that the second and third persons of the Trinity are nothing but the terms "wisdom" and "life" or "wisdom" and "power," which in the Koran are predicated of God, and that there is nothing in the Koran against the Christian belief that the predication of God of either pair of these terms reflects the existence in God of real beings, or persons or hypostases, as they called them. The Muslims could find no flaw in the reasoning and no objection to the conclusion. They therefore accepted the view that in God there were real beings to correspond to certain terms predicated of Him in the Koran. But then, when the Christian debaters continued to argue that these two persons of the Trinity, the second and third, are each God like the first person, the Muslims balked and quoted against them the Koranic verses, "say not three . . . God is only one God" (4:169) and "they surely are infidels who say, God is the third of three, for there is no God but one God" (5:77). Thus there had arisen in Islam the belief, which became the orthodox belief, that certain terms predicated of God have, corresponding to them, real existent beings in God, called attributes, which are coeternal with God, but eternally inseparable from Him, and because they were eternally inseparable from God and because also they were not called God, the unity of God, so vehemently insisted upon in the Koran, is preserved.

That this is how the problem of attributes had originated in Islam can be shown by arguments evidential, terminological, and contextual. To begin with, among Muslims themselves

[85] See my papers "The Muslim Attributes and the Christian Trinity," *Harvard Theological Review*, 49 (1956): 1–18, and "The Philosophical Implications of the Problem of Divine Attributes in the Kalam," *Journal of the American Oriental Society*, 79 (1959): 73–80.

there were those who in this doctrine of attributes saw an analogy to the Christian doctrine of the Trinity. Then, the two Arabic terms for what we call "attributes," namely ṣifāt and maʿāniyy, are translations of two Greek terms, χαρακτηριστικά and πράγματα, which were part of the technical vocabulary of the Trinity. Finally, the two "most beautiful names of God," which originally were taken by Muslims to reflect real attributes in God, correspond exactly to the names by which the second and third persons of the Trinity came to be known to Muslims through Christians writing in Arabic.

This, we imagine, is how the theory of attributes was introduced in Islam.

No sooner, however, had the belief in real attributes been introduced than there arose opposition to it. This opposition was like the Sabellian opposition in Christianity to the reality of the second and third persons of the Trinity. It saw in the assumption of real attributes, even though not called Gods, a violation of the true unity of God. Like Sabellianism in Christianity, therefore, which declared the second and third persons of the Trinity to be mere names of God designating His actions, this opposition declared the terms predicated of God in the Koran to be only names of God, designating His actions, and hence the so-called attributes are not real beings and other than the essence of God: they are identical with His essence.

And so the controversy in Christianity over the persons of the Logos and the Holy Spirit in their relation to God the Father, became in Islam a controversy over the relation of the attributes to God. The orthodox Muslim position was like, though not exactly the same as, orthodox Christian position. The attributes, like the second and third persons of the Trinity, were both extradeical and intradeical, except that, unlike the second and third persons of the Trinity, which were intradeical and extradeical by unification, that is, they were at once the same as God and other than He, these orthodox Muslim attributes were intradeical and extradeical by location, that is, they were in God but other than He. The unorthodox position of the Antiattributists in Islam corresponds to Sabellianism in Christianity.

The Muslim attributes are not ideas. They lack the essential characteristic of the Platonic ideas, that of being pre-existent patterns of things that come into existence. But they may be considered as the fourth generation of Platonic ideas through two generations of Logos, being as they were direct descendants of Logos and the Holy Spirit of the Christian Trinity. It can be further shown that with the gradual introduction of Greek philosophy into Islam, the problem of attributes became identified with the problem of Platonic ideas, or rather with the problem of universals, as the problem of Platonic ideas was known by that time, and with that the controversy between Attributists and Antiattributists in Islam became a controversy over universals as to whether they were extradeical or intradeical.[86] It was during this new phase of the problem that a new conception of the relation of attributes to God, or perhaps only a new way of expressing their relation to God, made its appearance. It is known as the theory of modes (aḥwāl). Dissatisfied with the orthodox view that attributes are really "existent" in God and with the unorthodox view that attributes, being mere names, are "nonexistent," the exponents of this new theory declared that attributes, now surnamed modes, are "neither existent nor nonexistent." [87] Of course, they were charged with infringing upon the Law of Excluded Middle, but theologians and philosophers that they were they were not fazed by this difficulty: they found a way of getting around it.

While in Islam the problem of attributes was raging, there was no such a problem in Christianity, that is to say, there was no controversy over the question as to what was the meaning of terms, outside the terms Father, Logos or Son,

[86] To be fully discussed in my work "The Philosophy of the Kalam," in preparation.

[87] Baghdādī, Al-Farq bayn al-Firaq (Cairo, A.H. 1328), p. 182, l. 5; Shahrastānī, Nihāyat al-Iqdām (ed. Guillaume), p. 133, l. 4.

and Holy Spirit, in their relation to God, when predicated of Him. The implied distinction between the Logos, which was both extradeical and intradeical by unification, and the ideas within the Logos, which were only intradeical, was formally made explicit by the last of the Church Fathers, John of Damascus, in the distinction drawn by him between "persons" and "names." [88] The Logos, as one of the three persons of the Trinity is a real being, but the ideas within the Logos, such as the ideas of goodness, greatness, powerfulness, and the like, are not real beings; they are only "names," so that their distinction from the Logos as well as from one another is only nominal, derived from the various ways in which the Logos appears to the mind of man through its various operations in the world. Since they are only various names of the Logos, by the principle that whatever is predicated of one of the persons of the Trinity is predicated of the triune God as a whole, they are various names of the triune God as a whole. Accordingly, when you say God is Father and Logos the Holy Spirit, the relation between the three predicates and the subject as well as the relation between the three predicates themselves is a real relation and they are all one by the mystery of the Trinity. But when you say that God is good or great or powerful you merely predicate of God different "names." Thus, without using the term "attribute" and without raising a problem of attributes, the Fathers of the Church arrived at a position like that of the Antiattributists in Islam. In fact, it can be shown, that the Antiattributists in Islam were influenced by this view of the Church Fathers.

This distinction between "persons" and "names," or between the Logos as the place of ideas and the ideas within it, in their relation to God, was generally accepted in Christianity. The ideas within the Logos continued to be called "names" and there was no problem of "attributes" corresponding to such a problem in Islam. But then four events happened which resulted in the introduction of the problem

[88] Cf. *De Fide Orthodoxa*, I, 6–8, 9.

of divine attributes into mediaeval Christian philosophy. Let us study these four events.

The first event was the publication and subsequently the condemnation of the *De Divisione Naturae* by John Scotus Erigena. In that work, published in 867, Erigena deals with what he calls "the primordial causes of things," which he says the Greeks call "ideas" and "prototypes." [89] Following the Church Fathers, these ideas are placed by him in the Logos, but, departing from the Church Fathers, who considered the ideas within the Logos as identical with the Logos, Erigena distinguished them from the Logos. This may be gathered from his statements that "before the ages, God the Father begot (*genuit*) His Word, in whom and through whom He created (*creavit*) the most perfect primordial causes of all natures" [90] and also that while "we believe that the Son is wholly coeternal with the Father, with regard to the things which the Father makes (*facit*) in the Son, I say they are coeternal with the Son, but not wholly coeternal." [91] Note the two distinctions drawn between the Logos and the ideas within it: the former is begotten, the latter are created or made; the former is wholly coeternal with God, the latter are not wholly coeternal with the Logos. Being thus not identical with the Logos, they are not identical with God, and therefore they are not mere "names" of God. Accordingly, while God is described by him as "that which creates and is not created," the ideas in their totality are described as "that which is created and creates." [92] Here then we have, in deviation from the traditional Christian view, a view approaching the orthodox Muslim view on attributes.

Erigena's deviation from the traditional Christian view on the relation of the ideas to God passed unnoticed by his contemporaries. While his *De Praedestinatione* was condemned

---

[89] *De Divisione Naturae* II, 2 (PL 122, 529B); II, 36 (615D–616A). Cf. E. Gilson, *History of Christian Philosophy in the Middle Ages* (London and New York, 1955), pp. 117–119.
[90] *Ibid*. II, 21 (560B).
[91] *Ibid*. (561C).　　　　　　　　　　　　[92] *Ibid*. I, 1 (441B).

twice during his lifetime, his *De Divisione Naturae* was not molested during his lifetime, nor was it molested for a long time after that. The Schoolmen during the four centuries following Erigena were engaged in the problem of universals, which is concerned primarily with the problem of the relation of ideas to sensible objects, and paid little attention to the problem of the relation of the ideas to God. It was not until the beginning of the XIIIth century, at the Council of Paris (1209) that his *De Divisione Naturae* was condemned; and one of the reasons for its condemnation was its theory of ideas. The writ of condemnation on this point reads as follows: "The second error is his view that the primordial causes, which are called ideas, that is forms or exemplars, create and are created, whereas, according to the holy Fathers, in so far as the ideas are in God, they are the same as God, and therefore they cannot be created." [93]

This is event number one.

Then, prior to the condemnation in 1209 of Erigena's work, Gilbert of la Porrée was accused at the Council of Rheims, in 1148, of believing that, when such terms as goodness, wisdom, greatness and the like are predicated of God, they are not designations of perfections which are identical with God, but rather a "form" which is placed in God and by which He is God, analogous to the universal term "humanity," which, when predicated of the subject "man" does not designate that which is identical with the subject but rather a "form" in the subject by which the subject is man.[94] This prompted the Council to draw up a profession of faith, which, directly in opposition to the alleged view of Gilbert, maintained that "God is wise only by a wisdom which is God himself; eternal by an eternity which is God himself; one only by a unity

[93] "secundus est, quod primordiales causae, quae vocantur ideae i. e. forma seu exemplar [*sic*], creant et creantur: cum tamen secundum sanctos idem sint quod Deus: in quantum sunt in Deo: et ideo creari non possunt" (quoted in Johannes Huber, *Johannes Scotus Erigena*, Munich, 1861, p. 436).

[94] Cf. Geoffrey d'Auxerre, *Libellus contra Capitula Gilbert Pictavensis Episcopi* (PL 185, 597CD; 617A).

which is God himself; [God] only by a divinity which is He himself; in short, He is by His own self wise, great, eternal, one, God." [95] The difference between Gilbert and the Council is strikingly like the difference between the Muslim Attributists and Antiattributists. The formula used by the Council is exactly the same as that reported in the name of the Anti-attributist, or perhaps Modalist, Abū al-Hudhayl, which reads as follows: "God is knowing by a knowledge which is himself, and He is powerful by a power which is himself, and He is living by a life which is himself." [96]

This is event number two.

Then something else happened. Early in the XIIIth century, certainly before 1235, there appeared a Latin translation of Maimonides' work *The Guide of the Perplexed*, which contained an account of the Muslim controversies over the problem of divine attributes and a presentation of his own elaborate theory in opposition to the reality of attributes. This Latin translation was made not from the original Arabic, in which the book was written, but from one of its two Hebrew versions. In that Hebrew version, the Arabic term *ṣifah*, which, as said above, reflects the Greek term χαρακτηριστικόν used in connection with the Trinity, was translated by two Hebrew terms, *middah* and *to'ar*. These two terms, in turn, are translated by three Latin terms: *dispositio*, *attributio*, and *nominatio*.[97] Of these three terms, each of which reflects one of the senses of the two Hebrew terms as well as of their underlying Arabic term, the term *attributio*, used in this translation in the sense of a divine predicate, is of special interest. By the time this translation was made, the Latin term *attributio* or *attributum* in the technical sense of "predicate" was not altogether unknown. According to the *Thesaurus Linguae Latinae* it was used in that technical sense by Cicero. But it was

[95] *Ibid.* (618A).

[96] Al-Ashʿarī, *Maqālāt al-Islāmiyīn* (ed. Ritter), p. 165, ll. 5–7; *Al-Shahrastānī, al-Milal waʾl-Niḥal* (ed. Cureton), p. 34, ll. 17–20.

[97] Rabi Mossei Aegyptii, *Dux seu Director dubitantium aut perplexorum*, lib. I, cap. XLIX, fol. XVIIIa, l. 28; cap. LI, fol. XVIIIb, l. 41 (Paris, 1520).

never used, as far as I know, as a designation of terms predicated of God, either in a work originally written in Latin or in a work translated from the Arabic into Latin. In the Latin translation of Ghazālī's *Maqāsid al-Falāsifah*, which was made in the XIIth century by John Hispalensis, the Arabic *sifah* is translated, not by *attributio* or *attributum*, but by *assignatio*.[98] The verb *attribuere* [99] and the noun *attributio* [100] do indeed occur in the Latin translation of Avicebrol's *Fons Vitae*, also made in the XIIth century by John Hispalensis, but from the context it may be gathered that in both its forms the term is used not in the sense of "predicate" and still less in the sense of "divine predicate" but rather in the sense of "gift," "addition," "cause."

This is event number three.

The fourth event is a double header.

Between the years 1245–1250 and between the years 1254–1256 Albertus Magnus and Thomas Aquinas respectively published their commentaries on the *Sentences* of Peter Lombard. In these commentaries, both of them for the first time use the term "attributes" instead of the traditional term "names" as a description of the ideas within the Logos predicated of God. Moreover, both of them, as soon as they introduced the term "attributes," raised the question, which, as phrased by Albert, reads: "Whether attributes in God are one or many?" [101] and, as phrased by Thomas, reads: "Whether in God are many attributes?" [102] The meaning of the question is whether the attributes are really distinct from God and from each other or not. Once this question was raised with regard to attributes, St. Thomas raised it also with regard to "names," phrasing his question to read: "Whether names predicated of God are synonymous?" [103] meaning, again, whether the ideas

[98] *Algazel's Metaphysics*, ed. J. T. Muckle (1933), p. 62, l. 2; cf. Arabic text: *Maqāsid al-Falāsifah*, p. 149, l. 12.

[99] Avencebrolis (Ibn Gebirol), *Fons Vitae*, ed. Baeumker (1895), p. 92, l. 27.   [101] Albertus Magnus, *In I Sent.* III, 4.

[100] *Ibid.*, p. 182, l. 9.   [102] Thomas Aquinas, *In I Sent.* II, 1, 2.

[103] *Sum. Theol.* I, 13, 4; cf. *Cont. Gent.* I, 35; *De Potentia* 7, 6; *Compend. Theol.* 25.

contained in the Logos and traditionally designated by the term name are really distinct from God and from each other or not. Moreover, once St. Thomas raised the question of the relation of the ideas to God under the guise of the question with regard to attributes and names, he raised the question directly with regard to ideas. Thus in the very same work, the commentary on the *Sentences*, in which he for the first time introduced the term attribute and the problem of attributes, he raised the question "Whether the ideas are many?" [104] and the same question appears also in some of his later works.[105] Here again the question is whether the ideas are really distinct from God and from each other or not. In other words, he raised the question whether the Fathers of the Church were right in their assumption that the ideas within the Logos were only names and intradeical or whether they were wrong in that assumption of theirs.

This is the succession of events in the history of post-Patristic Christian philosophy relating the problem as to whether the ideas within the Logos are intradeical or not: (1) the condemnation of the alleged Gilbert's view on the reality of the distinction between the perfections of God; (2) the condemnation of Erigena's theory of ideas; (3) the introduction into Christian Latin philosophy of the term "attributes" in the sense of divine predicates and withal a knowledge of the Muslim controversies about it; (4) the use of the term "attribute" and the raising of the problem of attributes by Albertus Magnus and Thomas Aquinas. The question naturally arises in our mind whether there is any causal connection between the first three events and the fourth event. In answer to this question, it may be said that with regard to the first two events there is an argument from silence showing that there is no connection between these two events and the fourth event. Neither Albert nor Thomas, throughout their discussions of the problem of attributes, makes any reference

[104] *In I Sent.* XXXVI, 2, 2.
[105] *Sum. Theol.* I, 15, 2; *De Veritate* 3, 2; *Cont. Gent.* I, 54; *Quodl.* IV, 1.

or allusion to Erigena or to Gilbert. Besides, while Gilbert was accused of believing in a real distinction between the perfection predicated of God and God, he was not accused of believing in a real distinction between the perfections themselves; quite the contrary, he is said to have believed that all the perfections predicated of God constitute one form in God.[106] There is, however, evidence of a connection between the new problem raised about attributes and the Latin translation of the work of Maimonides. First, there is St. Thomas himself, who in his commentary on the *Sentences*, after introducing the term attribute and raising the problem of attributes, quotes Maimonides and takes issue with him.[107] Second, there is Occam, who says: "The holy men of old did not use that word attributes (*attributa*) but in its stead they used the word names (*nomina*), whence, in contrast to certain moderns who say that divine attributes are distinct and diverse, the ancients and those who were at the time of the ancient masters said that divine names are distinct and diverse, wherefrom it follows that they laid down a distinction only with reference to names and a diversity only with reference to signs, but with reference to the thing signified they assumed identity and unity";[108] and in support of this Occam goes on to quote Augustine and Peter Lombard. The term "attributes" was thus regarded by Occam as a new-fangled term, of recent origin, which had come to replace the old traditional term "names," and he makes it unmistakably clear that there was no problem of the relation of attributes to God as long as "names" was used instead of "attributes," and that the problem arose only with the introduction of the term "at-

---

[106] *Op. cit.* above, n. 94 (597 C–D).   [107] *In I Sent.* II, 1, 3c.

[108] *Quodlibet* III, 2 (Strasburg, 1491): "Sancti antiqui non utebantur isto vocabulo attributa, sed pro isto utebantur hoc vocabulo nomina. Unde sicut quidam moderni dicunt quod attributa divina sunt distincta et diversa, ita dicebant antiqui et qui erant tempore antiquorum doctorum quod nomina divina sunt distincta et diversa, ita quod non posuerunt distinctionem nisi in nominibus et unitatem in re significata et diversitatem in signis" (quoted with omissions by P. Vignaux in *Dictionnaire de Théologie Catholique*, vol. 11, col. 757).

tributes." With all this, are we not justified in assuming that the use of the term attribute and the rise of the problem of attributes in medieval Christian philosophy had its origin in the Latin translation of Maimonides' *Guide of the Perplexed?*

In their attempt to solve the problem, the Schoolmen were all unanimous in rejecting the reality of attributes predicated of God. So far forth, they were all aligned against the Muslim Attributists. But there were differences of opinion among them as to how to express this opposition to the reality of attributes. Three different ways of expressing it developed in the course of the discussion.

First, Thomas Aquinas, having introduced the term attribute and having raised the problem of attributes, laid down certain fundamental views which were shared by all other Schoolmen.

The starting point in St. Thomas' discussion of the problem raised by him is that ideas and attributes are in God. With regard to ideas, having in mind his own statement elsewhere that "the Word of God is rightly called conceived or begotten Wisdom, as being the wise conception of the divine mind," [109] he says that the "ideas" are "in the divine Wisdom" or "in the divine mind," and this divine wisdom or "divine mind" is subsequently spoken of by him as the "divine essence" and "God himself." [110] Elsewhere he explicitly says that "we cannot suppose the ideas to exist outside of God; they exist in the mind of God only." [111] With regard to attributes, in answer to the question "Whether in God are many attributes," he starts by saying that "in God there is wisdom, goodness, and the like." [112]

Then, as an explanation of the statement which was his starting point, St. Thomas tries to show that, while ideas and attributes are in God, they are not in God as real beings. With regard to the ideas which are in God, he argues against their reality on the ground that there is no "real plurality in God

[109] *Cont. Gent.* IV, 12.
[110] *Sum. Theol.* I, 44, 3c.
[111] *De Veritate* 3, 1c.
[112] *In I Sent.* II, 1, 2c.

other than the plurality of persons," [113] maintaining, therefore, that the relations between the ideas in God "are not real relations, such as those whereby the persons are distinguished, but relations understood (*intellecti*) by God," [114] so that ideas are many only in the sense that "God understands many models proper to many things," [115] or "that many ideas are in His intellect as understood by Him," [116] or that "although these ideas are multiplied in their relations to things, they are not really distinct from the divine essence." [117] Combining these statements, we gather that in reality all the ideas in God are one and, of course, identical with God, but God in His wisdom causes them to be multiplied in things. Similarly with regard to attributes, he says that, unlike the persons of the Trinity, each of which signifies "a real thing" (*res*) [118] and which are "really (*realiter*) distinct from each other," [119] so that "there are many real things (*res*) subsistent in the divine nature," [120] the plurality of attributes which are affirmed of God are "in God wholly one in reality (*re*) but they differ in reason (*ratione*)"; [121] or, as he also phrases it, "the names attributed to God signify one thing" but "they signify that thing under many and diverse distinctions of reason (*sub rationibus multis et diversis*)," [122] so that God "is one in reality (*re*), and yet multiple according to reason (*secundum rationem*), because our intellect apprehends Him in a manifold manner, just as things represent Him in a manifold manner." [123]

Thus St. Thomas' way of expressing his denial of any distinction between the attributes and the essence of God, as well as between the attributes themselves, is to say that the attributes of God are "multiple only according to reason."

Another expression, however, for the same purpose of de-

[113] *Ibid*. I, 15, 2, obj. 4.
[114] *Ibid*., ad. 4.
[115] *Ibid*., c.
[116] *Ibid*., ad. 2.
[117] *Sum. Theol*. I, 44, 3c.
[118] *Ibid*. I, 29, 2c; I, 30, 4c.

[119] *Ibid*. I, 30, 2c.
[120] *Ibid*. I, 30, 1c.
[121] *In I Sent*. II, 1, 3c.
[122] *Sum. Theol*. I, 13, 4c.
[123] *Ibid*., ad. 3.

nying any real distinction between the attributes and God and between the attributes themselves, is used by Duns Scotus. The expression used by him is "formal distinction" (*distinctio formalis*).[124] Whether this "formal distinction" is something different from St. Thomas' "distinction of reason" is a moot point.[125] But if it is assumed to be different, the difference has been stated as follows: "The attributes are distinguished from the essence not indeed actually in reality (*realiter*) or by reason only (*ratione tantum*) but formally (*formaliter*) or by a distinction which is midway between real and of reason."[126] If this is what the expression "formal distinction" means, then it reminds one of the expression "neither existent nor nonexistent" used by the Muslim Modalists;[127] and, like the Modalists' expression it could be objected to on the ground of its being an infringement on the Law of Excluded Middle; but, if such an objection were raised, it could be answered in the same way as the Modalists answered the objection raised against their expression.

Opposed to the description of the anti-realistic conception of attributes by either the expression "distinction of reason" or the expression "formal distinction" is Occam. As we have seen, he prefers the good old term "names" to the new-fangled term "attributes." He therefore maintains that the terms predicated of God are distinguished from God and from each other only "with reference to names" (*in nominibus*) or "with reference to signs" (*in signis*).[128] As the equivalent of "names" and "signs," he uses also the term "concepts" (*conceptus*),[129]

---

[124] *Opera Oxoniensis, I Sent.* II, 7 (Op. VIII, 602–605). See Gilson, *History of Christian Philosophy in the Middle Ages*, pp. 461–462, 765, n. 63.
[125] Cf. Bernard Jansen, "Beiträge zur geschichtlichen Entwicklung der Distinctio formalis," *Zeitschrift für Katholische Theologie*, 53 (1929): 318.
[126] Francis Noel, *Theologiae R. P. Fr. Suarez, Summa, seu Compendium,* I: *De Deo Uno et Trino*, I, i, 10, 2 (I, 24).
[127] Cf. above at n. 87.
[128] Cf. above n. 108.
[129] *In I Sent.* Dist. II, Qu. II F (Lugdunum, 1495), where with reference to divine attributes, he says: "non sunt nisi conceptus quidam vel signa quae possunt praedicari vere de Deo" (quoted with an omission by P. Vignaux in *D. T. C.*, vol. 11, col. 756).

though in St. Thomas *conceptio*, which he uses as the equivalent of *conceptus*, means the same as *ratio*, and hence *distinctio conceptus* would mean the same as *distinctio rationis*.

These three expressions are all meant to be a denial of the reality of attributes. The difference in phrasing, to my mind, does not mean a difference in the degree of reality which they each deny. St. Thomas in his detailed explanation of what he means by his "distinction of reason" makes it clear that, even with the qualification that the "reason" is not "from the side of the reasoner only" (*tantum ex parte ipsius ratiocinantis*) but also "from the peculiarity of the very thing" (*ex proprietate ipsius rei*),[130] he does not mean by it any diminution in the degree of his denial of the reality of attributes; he only means by it to emphasize that the attributes, which are in no sense real, are not definable, that is to say, they are not univocal terms, and also that they are not generic or fictitious or equivocal or synonymous terms.[131] And to my mind, again, just as the phrases used by St. Thomas as qualifications of his "distinction of reason" do not mean a diminution in the degree of his denial of the reality of divine attributes, so does not also the expression "formal distinction" used by Duns Scotus. If there is at all any difference in meaning between the different expressions used by them, it is to be found with reference to something in which they openly and outspokenly disagree with each other. Now they happen to be openly and outspokenly in disagreement as to whether attributes are predicated of God univocally or not. St. Thomas takes the negative;[132] Duns Scotus takes the affirmative.[133] But, as we have seen, St. Thomas explains his "distinction of reason" plus its qualification to mean the negation, among others, also of the univocal interpretation of divine attributes. We may therefore conclude that, if Duns Scotus had chosen the expression

[130] *In I Sent.* II, 1, 3c.
[131] *Ibid.*; cf. *Sum. Theol.* I, 13, 4–5; *Cont. Gent.* I, 32–35.
[132] *Ibid.*
[133] Hieronymus de Montefortino, *Ven. Johannis Duns Scoti Suma Theologica* (Rome, 1900), XIII, 5 (Vol. I, pp. 318–322).

"formal distinction" with a view to emphasizing some difference between himself and St. Thomas on the question of divine attributes, the difference which he wanted to emphasize was the difference between them on the univocal interpretation of attributes, a difference which can be shown to be only semantic. Similarly the different formula used by Occam, to my mind, once more, does not mean an increase in the degree of his denial of the reality of attributes; it only means that he felt that the denial of the reality of attributes should be expressed more strongly and more clearly and in a form, such as suggested by him, which would be less likely to be misunderstood by the unwary and to mislead them into endowing attributes with some measure of reality. In the history of religions, many a hotly debated problem was not so much over actual beliefs as over the manner in which to formulate actual beliefs, behind which there was always the fear that a wrong formulation might lead the unwary astray.

Thus at about the middle of the XIVth century there were in medieval Christian philosophy two types of descendants of Platonic ideas, the Logos and Attributes. The Logos was the place of the ideas and, through the Logos of Philo, was the third generation of Platonic ideas; attributes were the terms by which the ideas within the Logos were designated and, through the Muslim attributes, were the fifth generation of Platonic ideas. It is to these two types of Platonic ideas that the original question as to whether the Platonic ideas were extradeical or intradeical was transferred. The answer given to this question differed in each of these two types of descendants. The Logos was both extradeical and intradeical by unification; attributes were only intradeical.

Centuries roll by and the scene is shifted from the Schoolmen, who were professional teachers of philosophy, to Descartes and Spinoza, who were free-lance philosophers, Descartes a free-lance roving philosopher, Spinoza a free-lance non-roving philosopher.

Descartes, heir to medieval Christian philosophy, followed faithfully the traditions of that philosophy. God to him was still immaterial and hence he insists upon the simplicity and indivisibility of God.[134] Following Christian tradition, he declares that the Logos, as one of the persons of the Trinity is both extradeical and intradeical by unification and that hence the Trinity is a mystery. Thus bearing in mind the traditional view that the distinction between the persons is only with respect to some causal relation between them, he says with regard to the persons of the Trinity that he denies that "there can be discerned between them a real distinction in respect of the divine essence, whatever be admitted to prevail in respect to their relation to one another"; [135] and, with regard to the Trinity itself, he says that it is a doctrine "which can be perceived only by a mind illumined by faith." [136] Following the vocabulary of the Schoolmen, he refers to such terms predicated of God as "eternal, infinite, omniscient, and the creator of all things which are outside of himself" [137] as "attributes." [138] From his classification of attributes into those which are "in things themselves" (*in rebus ipsis*) and those which are "only in our thought" (*in nostra tantum cogitatione*) [139] it may be inferred that divine attributes belong to to the latter and that the distinction between these attributes and God and between these attributes themselves is what he describes, after St. Thomas, as being a "distinction of reason (*distinctio rationis*)," [140] and, like St. Thomas, he explains that by that "distinction of reason" he does not mean a "reason" which is only of the "reasoner" (*ratiocinantis*) but one which has a "foundation in things" (*fundamentum in rebus*).[141] In

---

[134] *Meditatio* III (*Oeuvres*, ed. Adam et Tannery, Paris, 1897–1910, VII, 50, ll. 16–19).
[135] *Sextae Responsiones* 10 (*Oeuvres*, VII, 433, l. 27 to 444, l. 2).
[136] *Ibid.* (443, ll. 23–27).
[137] *Meditatio* III (*Oeuvres*, VII, 40, ll. 16–18).
[138] *Correspondance* 299 (*Oeuvres*, III, 297, ll. 15–17).
[139] *Principia Philosophiae* I, 57.
[140] *Ibid.* I, 62.
[141] *Correspondance* 418 (*Oeuvres*, IV, 349, ll. 26–30); cf. above at n. 130.

fact, Descartes himself confesses that in his conception of God and His attributes he follows tradition, for in his letter to Mersenne (July 1641) he writes: "by the idea of God I understand no other thing than that which all other people are accustomed to understand when they speak of Him." [142]

Spinoza, heir to medieval Jewish philosophy supplemented and panoplied by medieval Christian philosophy, parted from the fundamental conception of God as an immaterial being common to both these philosophic traditions. He boldly asserts that God is not pure thought; He is both thought and extension. How he came to this view he explains in geometrical language in Propositions II–VI of *Ethics* I and in plain language in Chapter II of *Short Treatise* I.[143] But, while his God is extension as well as thought, He is simple and indivisible. How extension can be simple and indivisible is explained by him in a Scholium to Proposition XV of *Ethics* I and in Epistola XII addressed to Ludovicus Meyer.[144] But still, while thought and extension are each simple and indivisible, they are different from each other. How then could he say of God that He is both thought and extension, without making Him composite and divisible? His answer is that thought and extension are related to God after the analogy of goodness and greatness and the like in their relation to God as conceived by philosophers before him, including Descartes. They are attributes of God, which are distinguished from God only in thought or by a distinction of reason. And so he formally defines attribute as "that which the intellect perceives of substance, as if constituting its essence," [145] or, as he informally describes it, as that which is the same as substance but is called attribute with respect to the intellect (*respectu intellectus*).[146] And the same holds true of the distinction between the at-

---

[142] *Ibid.* 245 (*Oeuvres*, III, 393, ll. 25–27).
[143] Cf. chapter on "The Unity of Substance" in my *Philosophy of Spinoza* (Cambridge, Mass., 1934), I, 79–111.
[144] Cf. chapter on "Infinity of Extension," *ibid.*, 262–295.
[145] *Ethics* I, Def. 4.
[146] *Epistolae* 9 (*Opera*, ed. Gebhardt, Heidelberg, 1925, IV, 46, l. 4).

tributes themselves: it is a distinction only in thought. Knowing also that, in the history of the problem of attributes, those who denied their reality, spoke of them as names, Spinoza refers to the attributes of extension and thought as two names of God and explains the unity of God, despite His having two attributes, by the example of the third patriarch, who is one, despite his having two names, Jacob and Israel.[147]

And yet, with all this background, reaching far and wide into history, students of Spinoza treat the attributes in his philosophy as if they were inventions of his own mind. With their bare wit they try to extract some rootless meaning out of his mnemonic phrases and, if sometimes they happen to summon aid from without, they make him split hairs with Descartes or share honors with Berkeley.

At the beginning of my talk I said that I would trace the history of the two interpretations of Platonic ideas through the successive generations of descendants of these ideas. Let me now, by way of summary, list the generations through which I have tried to trace the continuity of these two interpretations. As there is no better method of showing the continuity of a historical process than that used by the Biblical historiographers in those genealogies which begin with the words "Now these are the generations," I shall adopt this literary device and begin:

Now these are the generations of Platonic ideas.

And Plato lived forty years and begat the ideas.

And the ideas of Plato lived three hundred years and begat the Logos of Philo.

And the Logos of Philo lived seventy years and begat the Logos of John.

And the Logos of John lived six hundred years and begat the attributes of Islam.

And the attributes of Islam lived five hundred and fifty years and begat the attributes of the Schoolmen.

[147] *Ibid.* (ll. 9–11).

And the attributes of the Schoolmen lived four hundred years and begat the attributes of Descartes and Spinoza.

And the attributes of Spinoza lived two hundred years and begat among their interpreters sons and daughters who knew not their father.

IMMORTALITY AND RESURRECTION
IN THE PHILOSOPHY
OF THE CHURCH FATHERS *

LAST year, on this platform, under the auspices of this lecture-
ship, an eminent New Testament scholar, Professor Oscar
Cullmann, depicted for us two scenes. One scene was laid in
Athens, in a prison, where Socrates awaited death cheerfully,
courageously, and without complaint. This cheerful, coura-
geous, and uncomplaining attitude of Socrates toward death,
said Professor Cullmann, was due to his belief in the immortality of the soul. The other scene was laid in Jerusalem, at Geth-
semane and Golgotha, where Jesus awaited death amazedly,[1]
sorrowfully,[2] and "with strong crying and tears." [3] From this
Professor Cullmann inferred that Jesus did not believe in the
immortality of the soul; that to him death meant the death
of both body and soul; and hence that resurrection, in which
he explicitly expresses a belief, meant to him a new creation
of soul as well as of body.[4]

Let us depict for you another scene, one laid not in far-off
Athens about 492 years before the crucifixion but in a village
about thirty miles from the place of the crucifixion and only
about half a century after its occurrence.

We are told [5] that when Rabban Johanan, the son of Zakkai, fell ill and was about to die, his disciples came to visit him.
Upon seeing them, he began to weep. His disciples said to him:
"Light of Israel, right pillar, mighty hammer, wherefore
weepest thou?" In his answer he explained that he wept because his soul, which would survive his body, would have to

---

* Delivered as the Ingersoll Lecture on the Immortality of Man at the
Harvard Divinity School, 1956, and published in the *Harvard Divinity
School Bulletin*, 22 (1956–57): 7–40.
[1] Mark 14:33.   [2] Matt. 26:37, 38.   [3] Heb. 5:7.
[4] Cf. *Harvard Divinity School Bulletin*, 21 (1955–1956): 5–36.
[5] *Berakot* 28b.

face the inscrutable judgment of the supreme King of Kings, the Holy One, blessed be He.

This, ladies and gentlemen, is exactly the reason why Jesus awaited death amazedly, sorrowfully, and "with strong crying and tears." It is because he believed his soul was immortal and would have to face the inscrutable judgment of the Lord his God, the Most High; for, even though, as we are told, "in him is no sin," [6] certainly there was not in him the sin of being righteous in his own eyes.

But whatever one may be pleased to prove with regard to what Jesus thought of immortality and resurrection, to the Fathers of the Church these two beliefs were inseparably connected with each other. To them, the belief that Jesus rose on the third day after the crucifixion meant that his soul survived the death of the body and was reinvested with his risen body. Similarly the belief that in the end of days there will be a general resurrection of the dead meant the reinvestment of surviving souls with risen bodies. To all of them, in the interval between death and resurrection, the soul had a life of its own without a body, though there was some difference of opinion as to what was the state of the soul's life during that interval. And this conception of resurrection as implying immortality was attributed by the Fathers also to Jesus. Accordingly the verse, "I am the God of Abraham and the God of Isaac and the God of Jacob," [7] which Jesus, in his answer to the challenge of the Sadducees, used as a proof-text for the belief in resurrection,[8] was used by Church Fathers like Justin Martyr [9] and Irenaeus [10] as proof-text for both resurrection and immortality. And in their effort to strengthen the belief in immortality and the belief in resurrection as Christian doctrines, the Fathers not only followed the example of their Master in trying to prove, by quoting additional verses, that these beliefs have their roots in the Old Testament, but they also

[6] 1 John 3:5.
[7] Exod. 3:6.
[8] Matt. 22:23–32; Mark 12:27; Luke 20:37.
[9] *Apologia* I, 63.
[10] *Adv. Haer.* IV, 5, 2.

went beyond their Master's example and undertook to show that these beliefs were not contrary to reason. With this in view, they set out in search of philosophic testimonials for immortality and resurrection.[11]

With regard to immortality, the Fathers did not have to go far afield in their search. This belief is writ large upon the pages of Plato's *Phaedo* and it peers out from between the lines of other philosophic writings. But already forewarned by Philo, or reasoning like Philo from the same scriptural principles, the Fathers knew that the Platonic philosophic conception of immortality is not exactly the same as the scriptural conception of it. To Plato, immortality belonged to the soul by nature, for by its very nature the soul could not be mortal. In scripture, immortality was a gift of grace of God to the soul, for by its own nature the soul was mortal.[12] This distinction between the Platonic and the scriptural conception of immortality is constantly stressed by the Fathers. One of the first of the Fathers to discuss this problem, Justin Martyr, commenting upon the statement that "according to some who are termed Platonists," the soul is immortal,[13] says "I pay no regard to Plato" and then, proceeding to expound what he considers "the truth" of the matter, argues, evidently against Plato's conception of immortality, that, if the soul lives, "it lives not as being itself life, but as the partaking of life," and this because "God wills it to live, and hence it will cease to live whenever he may please that it shall live no longer, for it is not the property of the soul to have life in itself as it is the property of God." [14] The same view is expressed also by Irenaeus,[15] Tatian,[16] Theophilus,[17] Arnobius,[18] Lactantius,[19] and others.

---

[11] Certain parts of the discussion which follows deal with topics which I have treated more fully in the as yet unpublished Volume II of *The Philosophy of the Church Fathers*.

[12] Cf. my *Philo*, rev. ed. (Cambridge, Mass., 1948).

[13] *Dial. cum Tryph.* 5.

[14] *Ibid.* 6.

[15] *Adv. Haer.* II 34, 4.

[16] *Orat. ad Graec.* 13.

[17] *Ad Autol.* II, 27; cf II, 24.

[18] *Adv. Gent.* II, 14, 32.

[19] *Div. Inst.* VII, 5.

Occasionally, indeed, some of the Fathers use language loosely, so that what they say, when taken out of its context, may lead to a misunderstanding of their view. Thus three Fathers, at least, have been misunderstood and taken to believe that the soul is immortal by its own nature.[20]

The first of these Fathers who gave rise to a misunderstanding is Tertullian, and this because he speaks of the soul as being "immortal by nature" (*immortalis natura*) [21] and of immortality as being one of the things that are "known by nature" (*natura nota*).[22] But the context of the passages in which these expressions occur makes it clear that by the first expression Tertullian means that the soul "cannot be killed by men" [23] and by the second expression he means that the belief in the immortality of the soul can be attained by natural reason "from common notions" (*de communibus sensibus*).[24] When, therefore, in explanation of his use of his second expression, he says, "I may use, therefore, the opinion of Plato, when he declares, 'Every soul is immortal,'" [25] he does not mean that he agrees with the Platonic conception of the immortality of the soul; it only means that Plato has arrived at his conception of immortality, imperfect though it be, by natural reason. In still another place, Tertullian explains that the expression "that which was lost" (*quod periit*, τὸ ἀπολω-λός) in the verse that the "Son of man is come to seek and to save that which was lost," [26] if referred to the soul, means not "destruction" but "punishment," and this on the ground that the soul "is safe already in its own nature by reason of its immortality." [27] Here, it is only the "safety" of the soul and not its "immortality" that is described by him as being "in its own nature;" the immortality itself is conceived by him, as by all other Fathers, as being a gift of God, a gift which, while

[20] Cf. A. Stockl, *Geschichte der Philosophie der patristischen Zeit* (1859), pp. 197, 235, 393; W. Capitaine, *Die Moral des Clemens von Alexandria* (1903), pp. 119–120.

[21] *De Resur. Carn.* 35.

[22] *Ibid.* 3.

[23] *Ibid.* 35.

[24] *Ibid.* 3.

[25] *Ibid.*

[26] Luke 19:10.

[27] *De Resur. Carn.* 34.

God could take away, He will not take away. This, as we shall see, is the view also of some other Fathers, and among those them who explicitly deny that the soul is immortal by nature.[28] Nor, finally, does his statement that the soul is indivisible because it is immortal [29] mean that its immortality, which is the cause of its indivisibility, is itself by nature and not by the will of God. It only means that inasmuch as the soul is endowed by God with immortality, by virtue of its immortality it is also indivisible.

Origen is another who is alleged to have believed that the soul is immortal by its own nature, and this because of his speaking of "the essence" (*substantia*) of the human soul as being immortal and of his explaining its immortality as being due to the fact that it "partakes" of the divine nature [30] and because also of his repudiating anyone who ventures to ascribe to it "essential (*substantialis*) corruption." [31] But all this only means, as may be gathered from his reply to Celsus,[32] that the soul, having been created by God as partaking of His own nature, will not be destroyed by God; it does not mean that God could not destroy it, if He so willed.

The third Father who is supposed to have believed that the soul is immortal by nature is Augustine, and this evidently because, in his *De Immortalitate Animae* and *Soliloquia*, he attempts to prove the immortality of the soul by arguments which are reminiscent of those used by Plato and Plotinus in proving that the soul is immortal by nature. But the use of philosophic arguments by any Father in support of a religious doctrine does not necessarily mean that his conception of that religious doctrine is the same as the conclusion which philosophers sought to establish by those arguments. What Augustine's own conception of immortality was may be gathered from his statement that though "the soul of man is, according to a peculiar sense of its own (*secundum quemdam modum*

---

[28] Cf., for instance, Lactantius in the passages referred to above n. 19 and below n. 54.
[29] *De Anima* 14 and 51.
[30] *De Princip.* IV, 9 (36).
[31] *Ibid.* IV, 10 (37).
[32] Cf. *Cont. Cels.* V, 22, and below at n. 168.

suum), immortal, it is not absolutely immortal as God is, of whom it is written that He 'alone hath immortality' " [33] and as he proceeds he explains that the soul is described as being, "according to a peculiar sense of its own, immortal" and as "not wholly ceasing to live by its own nature" [34] only in the sense that it is not annihilated, that is to say, it is not annihilated by God, who by His will had brought it into existence and who could, therefore, annihilate it, if He so willed.

While the Fathers found direct philosophic support for immortality, no such support could they find for resurrection. Pseudo-Justin Martyr declares that "the Greeks refuse to believe" in resurrection and, when he thought that in the myth of the punishment of Aridaeus, as retold by Plato, he had discovered traces of a belief in resurrection, he said, "Here Plato seems to me to have learned from the prophets not only the doctrine of the judgment but also that of resurrection." [35] Cyril of Jerusalem, speaking of resurrection, proclaims that "Greeks contradict it," [36] and Augustine complains that, while "on the immortality of the soul many gentile philosophers have disputed at great length and in many books they have left it written that the soul is immortal, when they came to the resurrection of the flesh, they doubt not indeed, but they most openly deny it, describing it to be absolutely impossible that this earthly flesh can ascend to heaven." [37] Still, while they could find no direct support for resurrection, they found in the teachings of philosophers two doctrines which were cited by some of the Fathers as two analogies of the Christian doctrine of resurrection.

The first analogy is the Stoic doctrine of palingenesis or regeneration, according to which in the infinite succession of destroyed and created worlds each newly arising world is an

[33] 1 Tim. 6:16.
[34] *Epistolae* 166, 2, 3. Cf. *De Natura Boni* 39; *De Genesi ad Litteram* VII, 28, 43.
[35] *Cohortatio ad Graecos* 27; c. Plato, *Republic* X, 615C–616A.
[36] *Catecheses* XVIII, 1.   [37] *Enarr. in Psalm.* 88, 5 (PL 37, 1134).

exact duplicate of the past destroyed world, so that every individual who died in one world will be regenerated exactly in the same way in every other world. Socrates and Xanthippe, Plato and his successor, Speusippus, Aristotle and Alexander, all of whom were born and lived and died in this world of ours, had already repeatedly been born and lived and died in the infinite succession of worlds before this world of ours and will repeatedly be born and live and die in the infinite successive worlds after this of ours. An analogy between these two beliefs is sometimes suggested by the Fathers themselves. Thus Tatian [38] and Clement of Alexandria [39] and Origen [40] hint at such an analogy, and Lactantius [41] and Augustine [42] explicitly advance it as proof for the possibility of resurrection, and Nemesius quotes it as something said by "some people." [43] But having hinted at or mentioned this analogy, the Fathers who happened to discuss it further tried to show that these two beliefs are not exactly the same. The essential difference between these two beliefs, mentioned explicitly in Tatian, Augustine, and Nemesius and implied in Origen and Lactantius, is that the Stoic palingenesis means an infinite succession of resurrections to a temporary life, whereas the Christian resurrection means one resurrection to an eternal life. The philosophic basis of this essential difference, as stated by Tatian, is that the Stoic palingenesis is an endless repetition of the same thing "for no useful purpose," whereas the Christian resurrection is "for the purpose of passing judgment." The same view is also more or less clearly expressed by Augustine, Nemesius, Origen, and Lactantius. In other words, to the Stoics, it is an act of fate or necessity or what they would also call an act of nature; to the Christians, it is an act of divine will and design.

The second philosophic analogy is the theory of the transmigration of souls, which the Fathers usually attribute to

[38] *Orat. ad Graec.* 6.
[39] *Stromata* V, 1. 9 (PG 9, 21A). Section reference here and in nn. below is to ed. Stählin. [40] *Cont. Cels.* V, 20. [41] *Div. Inst.* VII, 23.
[42] *De Civ. Dei* XXII, 28. [43] *De Natura Hominis* 38 (PG 40, 761A).

such philosophers as Pythagoras, Empedocles, and Plato. Tertullian describes it as a belief which "most nearly approaches" the Christian doctrine of resurrection.[44] Origen quotes Celsus as having taunted the Christians that their doctrine of resurrection has its origin in a misunderstanding of "the doctrine of the transmigration of souls." [45] Gregory of Nyssa says that the philosophic theory of transmigration of souls is "not absolutely out of harmony with the resurrection which we hope for." [46] Similar assumptions as to the analogy between these two beliefs are to be found also in Irenaeus,[47] Lactantius,[48] and Augustine.[49] Here, again, having become conscious of the analogy between these two beliefs, the Fathers undertake to show that the two beliefs are not exactly the same. The difference found by them between these two beliefs is that in transmigration the soul enters another human body or even the body of an animal or a plant, whereas resurrection means the return of souls to their own restored bodies.[50]

From these discussions by the Fathers, as well as from their discussions in other places of their writings, we may gather that, according to them, two principles are to be regarded as distinctive characteristics of the Christian conception of immortality and resurrection. First, both immortality and resurrection are volitional acts of God and not necessary acts of nature. Second, in resurrection the body risen to life must be identical with the body that had existed before.

Each of these principles gave rise to a question, and each question gave rise to various answers.

The first principle, that of volition, implying as it does that if God willed He could bring annihilation to the soul as well as withhold resurrection from the body, gave rise to the ques-

---

[44] *De Resur. Carn.* 1.
[45] *Cont. Cels.* VII, 32.
[46] *De An. et Resur.* (PG 46, 108D).
[47] *Adv. Haer.* II, 33, 1; Cf. II, 34, 1.
[48] *Div. Inst.* VII, 23.
[49] *De Civ. Dei* XXII, 27.
[50] Cf. Irenaeus, *loc. cit.;* Tertullian, *Apologeticus* 48; Origen, *loc. cit.;* Lactantius, *loc. cit.;* Augustine, *loc. cit.*

tion whether God will ever will to annihilate a soul. Now to
ascertain the will of God on any of such matters one must
go first to consult the oracles of Scripture. But the oracles of
Scripture on this question are as vague as the oracle of Delphi
on any question and, if not vague, then they are downright
contradictory. According to one set of scriptural utterances,
the wicked will suffer "everlasting punishment" (κόλασις
αἰώνιος); [51] according to another set of utterances they are
destined to everlasting "destruction" (ὄλεθρος) [52] or "perdition" (ἀπώλεια). [53] And so the Fathers had their choice, either
to follow the verses which threaten the wicked with "destruction" and make those which threaten them with "punishment"
yield to some kind of interpretation, or the other way around.
No unanimity of opinion was arrived at by the Fathers. The
generality of them felt that eternal punishment is that which
the wicked deserve and tried to show that the "destruction"
and "perdition" could not have meant annihilation. [54] Arnobius, on the other hand, felt that the punishment which the
wicked deserve is annihilation. [55] Origen, however, is opposed
not only to annihilation [56] but also to a punishment which is
eternal, contending that there will be a final restoration of all
the wicked who are dead, [57] and, as for the term "everlasting"
(αἰώνιος), by which the term "punishment" is described in
the New Testament, he tried to show that that Greek term in
the New Testament, like its corresponding Hebrew term
'olam in the Old Testament, is to be taken to mean not everlasting but a very long time. [58]

The other principle, that of identity, gave rise to the question of how to reconcile it with certain verses in the New Testament which would seem to teach that the resurrected bodies
would not be identical with their respective counterparts be-

[51] Matt. 25:46; John 5:29; Rom. 2:8, 9.
[52] 2 Thes. 1:9; cf. Matt. 7:13; Heb. 10:39; 2 Pet. 3:7.
[53] Rom. 9:22; Phil. 3:19; 2 Thes. 2:3.
[54] Cf. Tertullian, De Resur. Carn. 35; Lactantius, Div. Inst. VII, 11;
Augustine, Epist. 166, 2, 3.
[55] Adv. Gent. II, 14.
[56] De Princip. IV, 4, 9 (36).
[57] Ibid. I, 6.
[58] In Exod., Hom. 6, 13.

fore death. The verses which are usually brought into play in this connection are two: (1) Jesus' statement concerning those who will rise that "in the resurrection they . . . are as the angels of God in heaven" [59] or "equal unto angels;" [60] (2) Paul's statement concerning the body as buried and the body as risen that "it is sown a natural (ψυχικόν) body; it is raised a spiritual (πνευματικόν) body." [61] Of the various views found among the Fathers on the principle of identity, we shall deal here only with two.

The first view is that of Origen. As his starting point, he takes the words of Jesus and Paul we have just quoted. Drawing upon Paul's description of that body as "spiritual" and upon Jesus' description of it as being "as the angels of God" or "equal unto angels," he says that the "sons of resurrection," even as the "angels of God," will be adorned "with the clothing of a spiritual body," [62] and as such it will differ from the "animal body" of man during his first lifetime on earth.[63] Wishing, however, to preserve the principle of identity, he says that the resurrected body, with all its being spiritual, is not a new and different body. It is still essentially the same as the original animal body. We are to believe, Origen maintains, that the body "which we now make use of in a state of meanness and corruption and weakness, is not a different body from that which we shall possess in incorruption and in power and in glory," [64] for "we are to hold that this very body which now, on account of its service to the soul, is styled an animal body, will — by means of a certain progress, when the soul has been united to God and made one spirit with Him so that the body is then rendering service as it were to the spirit — attain a spiritual condition and quality." [65]

But what is that which remains undestroyed throughout the change of the body from its being animal to its being spiritual, so as to serve as a common element in the two successive states

[59] Matt. 22:30; Mark 12:25.
[60] Luke 20:36.
[61] 1 Cor. 15:44.
[62] De Princip. II, 2, 2; Cf. I, 8, 4.
[63] Ibid. II, 10, 1; II, 10, 3.
[64] Ibid. III, 6, 6.
[65] Ibid.

of the body and thus to constitute its identity? Origen gives two answers to this question, which two answers, however, may be considered as complementing one another and as constituting two steps in one single argument.

The first step in the argument is to establish that there is an element which is common to sublunar bodies, celestial bodies, and the so-called spiritual bodies, such as angels and resurrected bodies. Whatever differences there are between them are not differences in kind but only differences in degree, described by him as differences in the degree of purity (*puritas*) or of subtileness (*subtilitas*) or of glory (*gloria*).[66] This common element is called by him "ether" — a term which is used by Plato in the sense of one of the four elements, air,[67] and by Aristotle in the sense of a fifth element.[68] Origen, preferring to follow Plato, uses it in the sense of one of the four elements, air,[69] and, referring to the Aristotelian conception of ether as fifth element constituting the celestial bodies, he says that "the faith of the Church" is against "certain Grecian philosophers" who believe that "there is besides the body composed of four elements another fifth element, which is different in all its parts and diverse from this one present body."[70] Accordingly, the celestial bodies, angels, and the resurrected bodies are all described by him as ethereal, with the understanding, of course, that they are of different grades of purity or subtileness of glory. Even among the various celestial bodies, he remarks, do such differences exist.[71] There is thus an element which is common to our present animal body and our future spiritual body.

But this element, Origen must have felt, is common to all bodies and consequently, while the assumption of the existence of such an element establishes negatively the fact that resurrected spiritual bodies are not generically different from animal bodies before their death, it does not establish an iden-

[66] *Ibid*. III, 6, 4.
[67] *Timaeus* 58 D; *Phaedo* 111 A.
[68] *De Caelo* I, 3, 270b, 22.

[69] *De Princip*. II, 1, 1.
[70] *Ibid*. III, 6, 6.
[71] *Ibid*. II, 10, 2.

tity between any individual resurrected spiritual body and its corresponding animal body before its death. In the second step of his argument, Origen, therefore, undertakes to analyze the concept of identity with a view to showing that such an identity exists between the animal and the spiritual body.

When identity is asserted of any given body, he seems to argue, it does not mean that that body remains the same in every respect. No human being, even during man's lifetime, retains a body which remains the same in every detail: it undergoes changes in size, in color, in weight, and in many other similar respects. What is it then that constitutes the identity of any individual body? Plunging himself into the problem of the principle of individuation, on which there is to be found in Aristotle a variety of statements, Origen maintains, not in opposition to Aristotle, I think, but rather as an interpretation of him, that the principle of individuation is not the underlying proximate matter (πρῶτον ὑποκείμενον) but rather the form (τὸ εἶδος). But that form is taken by him not as something common to all members of the species, as the Greek term for form, εἶδος, would imply, but as something peculiar to a single member of a species as its individual property, a sort of individual form added to a specific form. Origen thus describes that form as "the characteristic form" (τὸ εἶδος τὸ χαρακτηρί-ζον), that is to say, the form which stamps individual bodies with distinctive characteristics, inhering in them as one of their peculiar properties (ἰδιώματα) and molding them into permanent impressions (τύποι), that is to say, into permanent individualized impressions. It is this individual form of the animal body that is reunited with the soul at the time of the resurrection.[72] This individual form is described by Origen as a "reason" (ratio) which, like "the power (virtus) which is in the grain of wheat," is implanted in our bodies and contains a "bodily substance" (substantia corporalis) out of which a body will arise on the day of resurrection.[73] This individual

[72] In Psalm. I, 5 (PG 12, 1093B–C).
[73] De Princip. II, 10, 3.

form or "reason" (*ratio*) is also described by him more fully by the Stoic expression "seminal reason" (λόγος σπέρματος = σπερματικός).[74] Thus the resurrected spiritual body has, according to him, the same individuality as the animal body of its former existence. But the sameness of individuality does not mean that it has the same figure and shape and limbs and organs and those other appurtenances of the animal body.[75]

The extreme opposite of this is the view of the generality of the Fathers. All of them stress identity in its literal sense as the main principle in the Christian conception of the resurrected body. While Tatian merely says that God, "when He pleases, will restore the substance that is visible to Him alone to its pristine condition," [76] Irenaeus expresses himself more clearly in his description of those rising at the general resurrection that they will rise "with their very own bodies." [77] Still more explicit is Tertullian when he maintains that "the flesh shall rise again, wholly, in every man, in its identity, in its absolute integrity," [78] retaining all the parts of our body, the various limbs, such as mouth, teeth, throat, stomach, belly, bowels, hands, feet, and also the differences of sex, with the various organs of generation in the two sexes.[79] Cyril of Jerusalem insists that the body that will be raised will be the very same body (αὐτὸ τοῦτο).[80] Gregory of Nyssa, speaking through St. Macrina, defines resurrection as "the restitution of our nature to its original form," [81] which means, as may be gathered from its context, that the body will arise fully equipped with all its organs. Augustine similarly insists that those who will rise "will be bodies and not spirits" and that "as far as regards substance, even then it shall be flesh," [82] maintain-

---

[74] *Cont. Cels.* VII, 32 (PG 11, 1465 A).
[75] *Ibid.* V, 19; VII, 32; *In Psalm.* I, 5.
[76] *Orat. ad Graec.* 6.
[77] *Adv. Haer.* II, 33, 5; cf. II, 34, 1.
[78] *De Resur. Carn.* 63.
[79] *Ibid.* 60.
[80] *Catecheses* XVIII. 18.
[81] *De An. et Resur.* (PG 46, 148A, 155C).
[82] *Enchiridion* 91.

ing, furthermore, like Tertullian, that there will be a distinction of sex among those who will rise.[83]

But, if the resurrected body will be exactly the same as it was before death, what then is the meaning of Jesus' statement that those who will rise will be "as the angels of God" or "equal unto angels" and of Paul's statement that they will have a "spiritual body"?

The question is discussed by many Fathers.

As for the description of the resurrected body as angels, Tertullian points out that Jesus did not say that they shall be "angels"; he only said "equal unto angels," [84] which, he argues, merely means that, while possessing the same body as that before they died, they shall "no more be exposed to the usual solicitations of the flesh in their angelic garb," especially mentioning the fact that, like angels, they shall be "not marrying, because of not dying." [85] Augustine toward the end of his life declared that his earlier statement that "we ought to believe that the angelic bodies which we hope to inhabit are most luminous and ethereal " [86] should not be taken to mean that "we shall not have the same members of the body or the same substance of our flesh." [87] And as for the use of the term "spiritual," Augustine explains that it is not because the resurrected body "is converted into spirit, as some fancy," but "because it is subject to the spirit with a perfect and marvellous readiness of obedience," for, "as when the spirit serves the flesh, it is fitly called carnal, so, when the flesh serves the spirit, it will justly be called spiritual." [88] Gregory of Nyssa, with reference to the description of the resurrected as both angelic and spiritual explains that "all that blessed state which arises for us by means of the Resurrection is only a return to our pristine state of grace," [89] that is, to the state of Adam before his fall.

This conception of a body fully equipped with all its mem-

---

[83] *De Civ. Dei* XXII, 17.
[84] *De Resur. Carn.* 62.
[85] *Ibid.*
[86] *De Diversis Quaestionibus LXXXVIII*, 47.
[87] *Retractiones* I, 26.
[88] *De Civ. Dei* XIII, 20.
[89] *De An. et Resur.* (PG 46, 156D).

bers but resurrected to a life in which none of these members will be needed for the preservation of that life, gave rise to a question which is expressed by Tertullian as follows: "What will be the use of the entire body, when the entire body shall become useless?" [90] Back of this question is Plato's explanation [91] of how every bodily organ has a certain utility for the preservation and perpetuation of life as well as Aristotle's statement that "God and nature do nothing in vain." [92] After trying at various answers, Tertullian finally concludes with this general statement: "If, indeed, it has existence, it will be quite possible for it not to be useless; it may possibly have something to do; for in the presence of God there will be no idleness." [93] In other words, it must be assumed that the organs in the resurrected body will serve some purpose, though what that purpose will be is known only to God and it is past our understanding. Similarly Gregory of Nyssa, after describing, in the manner not only of Plato but also of Galen,[94] how the various members of the body have their special useful operations, raises, with regard to the resurrected, the following question: "When, therefore, all these operations will be no more, how and wherefore will their instruments exist?" [95] His answer is like that of Tertullian. "The true explanation of all these questions," he says, "is still stored up in the hidden treasure-rooms of Wisdom, and will not come to light until that moment when we shall be taught the mystery of the Resurrection by the reality of it; and then there will be no more need of phrases to explain the things which we now hope for." [96]

This then is what the Fathers believed about immortality and resurrection and this is how, whenever necessary, they explained themselves philosophically.

But the Fathers, learned in philosophy as many of them

[90] De Resur. Carn. 60.
[91] Cf. Timaeus 70–76.
[92] De Caelo I, 4, 271a, 33.
[93] De Resur. Carn. 60.
[94] Cf. De Usu Partium Corporis Humani.
[95] De An. et Resur. (PG 46, 144 D-145A).
[96] Ibid. (PG 46, 145B).

were, knew that besides those philosophers who believed in immortality, there were others, chief among them the Epicureans, who were outspoken opponents of immortality and argued against it. While no formal and direct refutation of the Epicurean arguments is to be found, as far as I could ascertain, in the Fathers of the Church, answers in anticipation of those arguments are provided by them in their discussions of the nature, origin, and functions of the soul as well as in their positive arguments for immortality. Let us then see how the Fathers would answer the Epicurean arguments against immortality.

One of the Epicurean arguments against immortality is that the soul is corporeal, composed as it is, according to the Epicurean view, of atoms, and that it is born, grows, and ages with the body, and therefore it is dissolved with the body.[97]

An indirect answer to this argument, or an answer in anticipation of this argument, may be found in the Fathers' discussion of the nature and the origin of the soul.

Superficially, on the basis of the language in which the Fathers express themselves, it would seem that they are divided into two camps on the question of the nature of the soul. In one camp are the majority of the Fathers who argue that the soul is incorporeal. In the other camp is Tertullian, who, in splendid isolation, or perhaps with a few insignificant camp followers, maintains that the soul is corporeal, and, quoting the Stoics, he rejects altogether the use of the term incorporeal. The contrast between these two camps emerges all the bolder when both these camps are found to bolster up their respective views by the same scriptural proof-text. The proof-text is the verse, "And the Lord God . . . breathed into his nostrils the breath (*nishmat, πνοήν, spiraculum*) of life." [98] The question arose: What does the term "breath" or *neshamah* or πνοή or *spiraculum* mean? Most Fathers, following Philo, say it means something which is not body, some-

[97] Lucretius, *De Rerum Natura* III, 418–458.
[98] Gen. 2: 7.

thing incorporeal. Tertullian says that it means a material breath, which filled the body of Adam, became condensed, and assumed the shape of the body.[99]

But when we begin to scrutinize these statements of the Fathers, we find that the battle between the two camps is a sham battle, only a battle of words. On the one hand, we find that those Fathers who say the soul is incorporeal qualify the term incorporeal. They say that this term should not be taken in an absolute sense. God alone is incorporeal in the absolute sense of the term. The soul is incorporeal only in a relative sense: in relation to the body; it is not a body like the body with which it united.[100] On the other hand, we also find that Tertullian, who maintains that the soul is corporeal, qualifies the term corporeal. He says that the soul is corporeal in the sense that it is a "body of a quality and kind peculiar to itself (*propriae qualitatis et sui generis*),"[101] and not in the sense in which bodies are corporeal.

Since therefore the incorporeality of those who say that the soul is incorporeal only means that it is not corporeal like the body and since also the corporeality of Tertullian who says that the soul is corporeal does not mean that the soul is corporeal like the body, the difference between them is only verbal.

But how did they happen to come to such a verbal difference? Here is the answer, in short. In Scripture, whether the Old or the New Testament, the term incorporeal does not occur — a fact already pointed out by Origen.[102] The scriptural equivalent for the philosophic "incorporeality" is "unlikeness." It was Philo who introduced into religious philosophy the term "incorporeal" as the equivalent of the term "unlike."[103] Now, if all the Fathers and also Tertullian were to describe the soul in scriptural terms, they would all de-

[99] *De Anima* 9.
[100] Cf., for instance. Irenaeus, *Adv. Haer.* V, 7, 1.
[101] *De Anima* 9.
[102] *De Princip.* I, Praef. 8.
[103] Cf. *Philo*, II, 94–100.

scribe it as being unlike the body. But since, as philosophers, they chose to use philosophic terms, most Fathers preferred the term incorporeal to express that unlikeness, whereas Tertullian preferred the term corporeal qualified by the expression *sui generis*.

Similarly with regard to the problem of the origin of the soul, we find that the Fathers are divided into different camps. In this case, there are three camps. In technical language, the views of these three camps are known as those of creation, prexistence, and traducianism. In plain English, they may be described, respectively, as the theory of custom-made souls, the theory of ready-made souls, and the theory of second-hand souls.

According to the custom-made theory, at the birth of each child God creates a soul especially for that child. According to the ready-made theory, at the time of the creation of the world, God in his foresight created individual souls which in number and variety were sufficient to supply the need of all the future generations of men. These souls are kept in a place the exact name of which is variously given by various authorities who are expert in the knowledge of these matters. At each child's birth a soul suitable to his body is placed within him — though, judging by the great number of misfit souls in the world, one may infer that mistakes frequently occur. According to second-hand theory of the soul, God, at the time of the creation of the world, created only one soul, and that is the soul of Adam. All our souls are only slices of the worn-out soul of our first ancestor, which, without being thoroughly cleansed and destained, are cut down and made to fit our own peculiar bodies.

Here, we must confess, the difference is more than verbal. Still, in so far as the problem of the relation of soul to body is concerned, there is no difference between them. All these three views agree that the soul, whatever its origin, may be described in the language of Philo and Scripture as being in the body as in a "garment," as in a "house," as in a "temple," as in a "tabernacle." [104] In short, it has an existence apart from the body.

And so, when the Epicureans argued that the soul cannot be immortal because it is "corporeal" and because it is "born" with the body, the Fathers would answer as follows: However the nature of the soul is described by us, whether as corporeal or as incorporeal, and however the origin of the soul conceived of by us, whether as created with the body or as pre-existent or as inherited, the soul is unlike the body and is not an inseparable part of the body. It can therefore survive the body.

Another Epicurean argument against immortality is that a soul without a body can have no consciousness, no knowledge, and no memory, for all consciousness and knowledge and memory are the result of sensation and sensation has its seat in body.[105] In raising this objection, Lucretius adds, evidently referring to the Stoic theory of regeneration, that even if our body should be regenerated, "it would not concern us at all, when once the remembrance of our former selves were snapped in twain." [106] This thus becomes an argument not only against immortality but also against resurrection. What good is resurrection without consciousness and knowledge and remembrance of our former selves! What is such a resurrection but a disinterment like that of the body of an Egyptian Pharaoh dug out of his tomb in a pyramid! And what are the glories promised to the risen saints but useless trinkets surrounding the mummified corpse of a Tutankhamen!

It is in anticipation of such an argument that the Fathers in their discussion of resurrection maintain that the resurrected body remembers its former life. Thus Fathers of different conceptions of resurrection, such as Irenaeus,[107] Ori-

---

[104] Cf. my *Philosophy of the Church Fathers*, I (Cambridge, Mass., 1956), 366–369.

[105] Lucretius, III, 624ff.; 830–842.

[106] *Ibid*. 846–851.

[107] *Adv. Haer.* II, 34, 1.

gen,[108] Lactantius,[109] and Augustine [110] say explicitly that the resurrected dead will remember their former lives.

When we read these statements about the existence of memory in the resurrected bodies, it would seem that this assertion of memory is taken by the Fathers as a part of the mystery of resurrection. In Irenaeus there is no attempt at an explanation. But, when immediately before his statement that the souls of the resurrected bodies "remember the deeds which they have done here" [111] he says of bodily resurrection in general that "God is not so poor or resourceless" [112] as not to be able to bring this about, it would seem that the existence of memory in the resurrected bodies, like resurrection itself, is due to the plenitude and resourcefulness of God. Moreover, when he indicates that sometimes the resurrected bodies not only remember the past but also possess the prophetic gift of knowing the future,[113] it may be inferred that memory in the resurrected bodies is a divine gift like that of prophecy. Origen, speaking of the punishment of the wicked in the hereafter and trying to explain how they could remember the evil doings of their past life, says that "the mind itself or conscience," which "by divine power" (*per divinam virtutem*) had received them "into memory" (*in memoriam*), "will see a kind of history, as it were, of all the foul and shameful and unholy deeds, which it has done, exposed before its eyes." [114] By the same token, we may reason, when Origen, speaking of the reward awaiting the saints in the hereafter, says that "they are to be instructed regarding all the things which they had seen on earth," [115] so that "they may enjoy an unspeakable joy" by their acquisition "of full knowledge" [116] of those things which they had seen on earth, he means thereby that "the mind itself or conscience" had "by divine power"

[108] *De Princip.* II, 10, 4.
[109] *Div. Inst.* VII, 23.
[110] *De Civ. Dei* XX, 22.
[111] *Adv. Haer.* II, 34, 1.
[115] *Ibid.* II, 11, 6 (ed. Koetschau, p. 190, 11, 4–5).
[116] *Ibid.* II, 11, 6 [5] (p. 189, 11, 9–13).

[112] *Ibid.* II, 33, 5.
[113] *Ibid.* II, 34, 1.
[114] *De Princip.* II, 10, 4.

received those things "into memory." Lactantius, like Irenaeus, attempts at no explanation. But in that very same passage, where he says of the resurrected bodies that "they will
remember their former life and all its actions," he makes the
following statement about resurrection in general: "Let no
one ask of us how this is possible, for no reason can be assigned for divine works (*divinorum operum*)." [117] To him,
therefore, memory in the resurrected bodies would be one of
the "divine works" for which "no reason can be assigned."
Augustine explains it as having been brought about "by means
of that indwelling of God in their . . . minds" (*per hoc
quod erat Deus . . . in eorum . . . mentibus*), by which
prophets were able to know things that had not yet happened.[118] To him, therefore, the resurrected saints will remember the past by an "indwelling of God" like that by
which prophets know the future — an explanation which, as
we have seen, is hinted at by Irenaeus.

But this plenitude and resourcefulness of God or this work
of God or this divine power or this indwelling of God by
which the resurrected bodies are said by the Fathers to possess memory of the past, we shall try to show, is not part of
what the Fathers consider the mystery of resurrection but is
rather a logical corollary of their conception of the soul.

The conception of the soul common to all the Fathers is
essentially Platonic. The main characteristic of that Platonic
conception of the soul is its separability from the body. But,
as to how that Platonic conception of the separability of the
soul is to be understood, there are two interpretations. According to one interpretation, in every human being, from
his very birth, there are two souls, one separable and one
inseparable, and it is the inseparable soul in which memory,
that is, memory of past sensations, originates. According to
another interpretation, in every human being, at his birth,
there is only one soul, a separable soul, and it is from this
one separable soul, as a result of its contact with the body,

[117] *Div. Inst.* VII, 23.   [118] *De Civ. Dei* XX, 22.

that another soul is exuviated, which other soul becomes inseparably entangled with the body. Still it is in that original separable soul that the power of memory resides, even the power of memorizing the impressions and images of past sensations and, because memory originates and resides in that separable soul, it can be preserved in that soul even after it has become separated from the body.

This is a statement of the two contrasting interpretations of the Platonic conception of the separability of the soul presented simply without the obfuscation of technical terminology and without the incrustation of historical data as to origin and exponents. Suffice it to say that Philo represents the two-soul theory, and some Fathers, mainly unorthodox, follow him. Orthodox Fathers who are conscious of the implications of the problem follow, as a rule, the one-soul theory. It is also to be noted that both those who follow the two-soul theory and those who follow the one-soul theory support their view by the verse, "And the Lord God . . . breathed into his nostrils the breath of life," [119] each side interpreting that verse in accordance with its own view. It is in this philosophic conception of one-soul, that the Fathers find a philosophic rationalization for the attribution of memory to the resurrected dead. The plenitude and resourcefulness of God or the divine work or the divine power or the indwelling of God by which the Fathers mentioned above try to explain the possibility of memory in the resurrected bodies refers to that power of memory with which God has endowed the human soul and which that soul can retain even after its separation from the body. Thus also Plotinus, starting with a Platonic conception of soul, argues that the soul retains memories of its bodily life even after its separation from the body.[120]

And so, when the Epicureans argued that the immortal soul or the regenerated body can have no memory, because memory depends upon sensation and sensation depends upon

---

[119] Gen. 2: 7. [120] *Enneades* IV, 3, 25ff.

body, and a body which has no interrupted existence, the Fathers would answer as follows: All this would indeed have to follow from the conception of soul held by your own school of thought. We, however, belong to another school of thought, a school of thought which claims discipleship of Plato, and according to this school of thought the soul itself is endowed with the power of memory, and it is the soul itself which remembers the past even when it is divested of its body during the state of its immortality, and it is also the soul itself which retains the memories of the past and in its state of existence when it is reclothed with its body at the time of its resurrection.

A third Epicurean argument against immortality is that the bodiless soul cannot experience any of the pleasures of life, for pleasure is based upon desire, and desire is based upon want, but a bodiless soul has no wants and hence no desire.[121] This argument, the Fathers must have felt, was also an argument against resurrection, inasmuch as the resurrected body, it is generally admitted by them, will not be subject to any of the desires of the body and hence will not experience any of the pleasures of the body. Though the Fathers have proved to their own satisfaction that the body resurrected to eternal life will have memory, they still felt the force of the argument that, without a constant renewal of experience, eternal life would be a life without pleasure. It would be the life of an eternal paralytic, who sees all and knows all and remembers all, but experiences nothing pleasurable.

In anticipation of this argument, the Fathers try to show how it will be possible for the resurrected saints to experience a kind of pleasure which is not based upon want and desire. And ironically enough, the pleasure without want and desire, by the assumption of which the Fathers seek to refute the Epicurean denial of the possibility of pleasure in the immortal souls, is a concept borrowed from the Epicureans'

[121] Lucretius, III, 894-901.

own philosophy. It is that kind of pleasure which the Epicureans describe as "static pleasure" (καταστηματικὴ ἡδονή) or "joy worth mentioning" (ἀξιόλογος χαρά) or "the highest and surest joy" (ἡ ἀκροτάτη χαρὰ καὶ βεβαιοτάτη) and which, according to them, is not based upon want and desire but rather upon "freedom from mental disturbance" (ἀταραξία) and "freedom from bodily pain" (ἀπονία).[122] With this Epicurean "freedom from mental disturbance" (ἀταραξία) the Fathers sometimes combine the Stoic impassibility (ἀπάθεια), either because they regarded the differences that there may be between the Epicureans and the Stoics on this point as irrelevant for their own purposes or because they regarded these differences between the Epicureans and the Stoics as a mere battle of words. What was significant for the Fathers was the fact that to both the Epicureans and the Stoics there was a kind of pleasure which was not based upon want and desire, but was purely of a negative nature, consisting in the absence of something which causes the opposite of pleasure, but yet, though negative, the mind was conscious and aware of it.

It is this kind of pleasure, the Epicurean "static pleasure" or "joy worth mentioning" or "the highest and purest joy" consisting in that which the Epicureans themselves describe as "freedom from mental disturbance" and "freedom from bodily pain" and in that which the Stoic describes as "impassibility," that the Fathers attribute to the resurrected saints. Tertullian, commenting upon the verse, "eternal pleasure (iocunditas) shall be upon their heads . . . and sorrow and sighing shall flee away," [123] takes the "eternal pleasure" to refer to the pleasure to be experienced by the saints after the resurrection, when "sorrow and sighing" will cease by "the cessation of their causes, that is to say, the afflictions of flesh and soul (laesurae carnis atque animae)." [124] Now the "cessation

---

[122] Cf. C. Bailey, *Epicurus*, Fragmenta 1 (p. 120), LXXXI (p. 118), 11 (p. 122).

[123] Isa. 35: 10.   [124] *De Resur. Carn.* 58.

of . . . the afflictions of body and soul" is nothing but the Epicurean *aponia* and *ataraxia*, that is to say, freedom from bodily pain and mental disturbance. Thus, again, speaking of the resurrected body, he says that, despite its being flesh and endowed with all the sensation of flesh, it will be "impassible" (*impassibilis*), inasmuch as it has been liberated by the Lord for the very end and purpose of being no longer capable of enduring suffering." [125] Here, again, the term "impassible" is nothing but the Stoic ἀπαθής. Similarly Augustine, speaking of the eternal felicity of the saints in the city of God after the resurrection, says: "True peace shall be there, where no one shall suffer (*patietur* = πείσεται) opposition either from himself or from any other." [126] The term peace here reflects the term peace (εἰρήνη) which together with joy (χαρά) is promised by Paul to prevail in the kingdom of God [127] and it is quite evidently taken by Augustine as the scriptural equivalent of the Epicurean *ataraxia* and *aponia* and the Stoic *apatheia*.

And so, when the Epicureans argued that an immortal soul or a regenerated body could experience no pleasure because pleasure is based upon desire and desire is based upon want, the Fathers would answer that the immortal souls and resurrected bodies will have exactly that kind of pleasure which the Epicureans themselves claim that man can have during his lifetime — a pleasure not based upon want and desire but one based upon freedom from both mental disturbance and bodily pain.

One of the essential characteristics of the Patristic conception of immortality and resurrection, as we have seen, is that they are acts of divine will. This, implying as it does that, if God willed, he could withhold them, implies also that, when God does will to bestow them upon man, He does so as a reward of righteousness. But any reward of God, as both the

[125] *Ibid.* 57.
[126] *De Civ. Dei* XXII, 30.   [127] Rom. 14: 17.

Old and the New Testament say, is rendered to "every man according to his work." [128] The Fathers, therefore, assume that there will be some difference in the rewards awaiting the righteous after the resurrection of their bodies or also during the state of the immortality of their souls. The difference of reward is expressed by some Fathers, such as Irenaeus,[129] Clement of Alexandria,[130] and Augustine,[131] as a difference in the "mansions" in which the righteous will abide, basing their view upon the verse, "In my Father's house are many mansions." [132] Though we are not told in the New Testament how many mansions there will be, Irenaeus and Clement of Alexandria supply us with the needed information. They tell us that there will be three such mansions, and in proof of this they quote from the parable of the sower the following verse: "But others fell into good ground and brought forth fruit, some an hundredfold, some sixtyfold, some thirty-fold." [133] These three mansions, or abiding places of the righteous, are described by Irenaeus as "the heavens" (οὐρα-νοί), "paradise" (παράδεισος) and "the city" (πόλις).[134] In the New Testament, it may be remarked, while these three terms occur as designations of the future abode of the righteous, there is no evidence that they are meant to designate three different places. Clement of Alexandria does not designate the three mansions by special names. He only says: "There are various mansions, according to the worth of those who have believed." The highest of these mansions, however, is described by him as that "where the Lord is." [135] It is interesting to note that Philo, who speaks only of immortality, but describes immortality in terms of resurrection,[136] similarly enumerates three places where the immortal souls abide. He describes these three abiding-places as follows: (1) heaven,

[128] Ps. 62: 13 (12); Matt, 16: 27; cf. Eph. 6: 8.
[129] *Adv. Haer.* V, 36, 2
[130] *Stromata* VI, 14.114 (PG 9, 337B).
[131] *In Joannis Evangelium* LXVII, 14, 2; *De Virginitate* 26.
[132] John 14:2.
[133] Matt. 13: 8.
[134] *Adv. Haer.* V, 36, 1.
[135] *Stromata* VI, 14.114 (PG 9, 337B).
[136] Cf. *Philo* I, 404–406.

the place of the angels; (2) the intelligible world, the place of the ideas; (3) above the intelligible world of ideas, described by him as the place where those who are immortal are stationed by God "near himself." [137] Clement's place "where the Lord is" would seem to correspond to Philo's place "near [God] himself." This is also, we may assume, what Irenaeus means when he describes the highest mansion as "the city," for the three mansions are described by him as the places where "God [138] [or the Lord Savior [139]] shall be seen according as they who see him shall be worthy," [140] and consequently the highest mansion or "the city" is the place which, in the language of Clement, is "where the Lord is" and, in the language of Philo, is "near [God] himself," that is to say, the place where the most righteous will have the highest vision of God.

The differences in the reward of the righteous are thus, as says Irenaeus, differences in their vision of God or in what is generally known as the beatific vision. Though the promise of the vision of God or the beatific vision is based upon scriptural texts, such as "They shall see God;" [141] "For now we see him in a mirror darkly, but then face to face;" [142] "We shall be like him, for we shall see him as he is," [143] it is treated by the Fathers philosophically, taken by them to refer to a direct knowledge of God in contradistinction to a knowledge of Him indirectly through His work in the world.[144] The vision of God or the beatific vision thus reflects what Plato calls the vision of the ideas,[145] what Philo calls the vision of God,[146] and what Plotinus calls the vision of the One,[147] except that with the Fathers this immediate knowledge of God is reserved for the saints in their immortal or resurrected state.

---

[137] *Sacr.* 3, 8; cf. *Philo* I, 403–404.   [138] So in the Latin version.

[139] So in the Greek fragment. See comment *ad loc.* in W. W. Harvey's edition of Irenaeus' *Adversus Haereses* (Vol. II, p. 428, n. 2).

[140] *Adv. Haer.* V, 36, 1 end.   [142] 1 Cor. 13: 12.

[141] Matt. 5: 8.   [143] 1 John 3: 2.

[144] Cf., for instance, Augustine, *De Civ. Dei* XXII, 29.

[145] *Republic* VII, 532 A–C.   [146] Cf. *Philo* II, 83ff.

[147] *Enneades* II, 9, 15; V, 5, 6; VI, 7, 31.

Immortality and resurrection are sometimes described as salvation, though salvation in Christianity has a wider meaning than resurrection. The question may therefore be raised whether such salvation is confined only to those who believed in Christ or whether others who do not believe in Christ, especially Jews who follow the Law and pagans who through philosophy gave up the worship of idols and lead a virtuous life, may also attain salvation.

The question is raised by the very first philosophic Church Father, Justin Martyr, in his *Dialogue with Trypho*.

Justin himself is represented there as a convert to Christianity who before his conversion was a Platonic philosopher and had given up the worship of idols and led an upright life. Trypho is represented as a Jew who has a vague and faulty knowledge of Christianity. He looks upon Christianity as a form of idolatry, the worship of a human being as God, and accordingly he regards Justin's conversion to Christianity as a relapse from a philosophic veneration of God to idol worship. He, therefore, says to Justin: "It would be better for you to follow Plato or any other philosopher . . . for, whilst you remained in that mode of philosophy and lived blamelessly (ἀμέμπτως), a hope for better destiny were left for you. But now that you have deserted God and placed your hope on a man, what means of salvation were left for you?" [148]

This statement of Trypho that, if Justin had remained a philosopher who had given up idolatry and led a blameless life, he would have had hope for a better destiny reflects a view which was common at that time among Jews, Hellenistic as well as Palestinian. In Philo it is expressed in his statements where he speaks of those among Greeks "who practice wisdom and live blamelessly (ἀνεπιλήπτως) and irreproachably (ἀνυπαιτίως)" [149] and where he applies the terms "wise and just and virtuous" not only to the Jewish Essenes but also to the seven wise men of Greece, the Magi among the Per-

[148] *Dial.* 8.   [149] *Spec.* II, 12, 44.

sians, and the Gymnosophists in India,[150] all of whom are regarded by him as what may be described as spiritual prose-
lytes.[151] Palestinian Judaism expresses itself on this point in
the Tannaitic saying that "pious gentiles have a portion in
the world to come." [152]

In his answer, Justin maintains that, after the advent of
Christ, salvation can come only through Christ,[153] which thus
excludes both Jews and gentile philosophers who do not believe in Christ. The same view is held by Clement of Alexandria, who maintains that Jews can be saved only by confessing faith in Jesus and pagan philosophers can be saved only
by both abandoning idolatry and confessing faith in Jesus.[154]
Augustine reaffirms this view succinctly in his statement that
"outside the true Church everything is possible except salvation (*extra ecclesiam catholicam totum potest praeter salu-
tem*)" [155] and, when the Pelagians were reported to him as
believing that "the Law leads to the kingdom of heaven," [156]
he exclaimed that while they "are not Jews in name, they become so by their error." [157]

With regard to those, however, who lived before the advent
of Christ, Justin Martyr declares that the righteous men in
the Old Testament before Moses and those who were righteous under the Law after Moses, but before Christ, will be
saved by Christ in his second coming.[158] Evidently this would
exclude pre-Christian pagan philosophers, seeing that whatever righteousness they may have had was not the kind of
righteousness described by Justin as being "under the Law."
In contradistinction to this, however, the mysterious author
known as The Ambrosiaster, in his comment on the words
"Nevertheless death reigned from Adam to Moses," [159] says

---

[150] *Probus* 11, 72–75.
[151] Cf. *Philo*, II, 372–374.
[152] *Tos. Sanhedrin* XIII, 2.
[153] *Dial.* 26.
[154] *Stromata* VI, 6.44.4 (PG 9, 205B); VI, 6.45.5–6 (PG 9, 268B).
[155] *Sermo ad Caesareensis Ecclesiae Plebem* 6 (PL 43, 695).
[156] *De Gestis Pelagii* 33; cf. *Epist.* 96, 1, 7.   [158] *Dial.* 44.
[157] *Epistolae* 96, 1, 7.   [159] Rom. 5: 14.

that over "those who have known God, either by tradition or by natural discovery, and have honored Him, imparting the honor due to His name to nobody else . . . death did not reign . . . for it reigned only over those who worshipped the devil under the form of idols." [160] According to The Ambrosiaster, then, pre-Christian pagan philosophers who had given up idolatry were entitled to salvation. But this mysterious author, it has been conjectured, was either a native born Jew who was first converted to Christianity and then reverted to Judaism or a native born Christian [161] whose mind may have been perverted by his unusual fund of knowledge of Judaism and of Jewish literature which he displays in his writings. In either case, he may be regarded as having subverted an old established Christian view. No wonder then, when in the 14th century the question was raised whether Aristotle would be saved, the answer was in the negative and, when later, in the 15th century, an attempt was made to answer in the affirmative, general opinion was against it.[162]

In their attempt to cite philosophic testimonials for immortality and resurrection,[163] the purpose of the Fathers, as we have seen, was not to explain why they believed in this twofold doctrine, but rather to show that it was not logically absurd. To them, the basis of this doctrine essentially was Scripture and tradition and the support of this doctrine logically was that it was a miraculous act, like all the miraculous acts of God, and miraculous acts of God, to them, were to be explained on the general principle that all things are possible

---

[160] *In Epistolam ad Romanos* V, 14 (PL 17, 99B).

[161] G. Morin, "L'Ambrosiaster et le Juif Converti Issac, Contemporain du Pape Damase," *Review d'Histoire et de Littérature Religieuses*, 4 (1899): 97–121; *id.*, "Hilarius L'Ambrosiaster," *Revue Bénédictine*, 20 (1903): 113–131.

[162] Cf. A. H. Chroust, "A Contribution to the Mediaeval Discussion: *Utrum Aristotelis sit Salvatus*," *Journal of the History of Ideas*, 6 (1945): 231–238.

[163] I have not dealt here with the analogies of resurrection drawn by the Fathers from the various natural phenomena of the vanishing and reappearance of things.

to God. Both Justin Martyr[164] and Tertullian [165] clinch their defense of the doctrine of resurrection by quoting the verse, "The things which are impossible with men are possible with God" [166] and Celsus reports that Christians defend their belief in resurrection by a paraphrase of that New Testament verse to the effect that "everything is possible to God." [167] Origen, in his reply to Celsus, does not deny the miraculous nature of resurrection as an act of the divine will [168] nor does he deny the defense thereof on the ground that "everything is possible to God;" what he does is only to qualify the term "everything" by excluding things that are "nonexistent" (τὰ ἀνύπαρκτα) or "inconceivable" (τὰ ἀδιανόητα) or "disgraceful" (αἰσχρά),[169] and to maintain that resurrection, especially as he understood it, is neither anything nonexistent nor anything inconceivable nor anything disgraceful.

This belief that everything is possible to God, traceable, of course, to the Old Testament teaching expressed in the verse, which in the Septuagint reads, "I know that Thou canst do all things, and that to Thee nothing is impossible," [170] is exactly the principle by which Philo justifies the miraculous power of God to change the laws of nature which He himself has implanted in the world.[171] No less than in four places in his writings does he repeat the statement that "all things are possible to God" [172] and in one of these places, almost in the words quoted from the New Testament, his statement reads: "The things which are impossible to every created being are possible to Him alone." [173] Indeed the Stoic Chrysippus, as quoted by Lactantius, in speaking of this theory of palingenesis or cycles, says: "But since this is so, it is evident that nothing is impossible (οὐδὲν ἀδύνατον), and that we, after our death, when certain periods of time have again come

---

[164] Apologia I, 19.
[165] De Resur. Carn. 57.
[166] Luke 18: 27; cf. Matt. 19: 26.
[167] Cont. Cels. V, 14.
[168] Ibid. V, 22.
[169] Ibid. V, 23.
[170] Job 42: 2.
[171] Cf. Philo, I, 325–356.
[172] Opif. 14, 46; Jos. 40, 244; Mos. I, 31, 174; Qu. in Gen. IV, 17
[173] Mos. I, 31, 174.

round, are restored to this state in which we are now." [174]
This universal negative proposition, "nothing is impossible,"
which is inferred by Chrysippus from the Stoic palingenesis
and which logically amounts to the same as the universal
affirmative proposition, "all things are possible," would at
first sight seem to have the same meaning as the scriptural
proposition "all things are possible to God" by which the
Fathers justify their belief in resurrection. However, it has
not the same meaning. What Chrysippus means by his
"nothing is impossible" is that nothing in the eternal succession of the generation and destruction of the world, with the
eternal succession of the birth and death of every individual
human being within the world, is to be thought of as impossible or can be rendered impossible, for these cycles in
the world's course are predetermined by fate or necessity or
nature. It does not mean that it is possible for anything to
happen which has not been predetermined by the eternal and
necessary order of nature, for, as says Chrysippus, in a passage quoted by Plutarch, "No particular thing, not even the
least, can be otherwise than according to common nature
and its reason," to which Plutarch adds that by "common
nature and its reason" Chrysippus means "fate." [175] To the
Fathers, however, the scriptural principle that "all things are
possible to God" means that God can change the laws of
nature which He himself has implanted in the world, and
resurrection is such a change in the laws of nature, whence
it is not an act of nature but an act of divine will.

Plato, to whom immortality was natural to the soul, said
that "immortality is in us." [176] Reflecting this sentiment and
restating it in terms of his own belief that immortality together with resurrection is a gift of God, Gregory of Nyssa
says that since one of the attributes of God is eternal existence, it was needful that we, who were created in the image

[174] *Div Inst.* VII, 23.
[175] Arnim, *S. V. F.*, II, 937.   [176] *Laws* IV, 713 E.

of God, should not be without the "gift of this attribute"
but that our nature "should have in itself the immortal" and
that it should "be possessed with a desire for divine and eternal life." [177] Augustine repeats this sentiment when he says
that "we are conscious in ourselves of having a desire" for
eternal life,[178] and he finds an intimation of this in Paul's
statement that we are "earnestly desiring to be clothed upon
with our house which is from heaven." [179]

With such a desire, I imagine we are all still possessed, and
we should, therefore, quite naturally like to know what meaning for us today have these views of the Fathers on immortality and resurrection — especially for those of us today who
think that we need a new kind of promise and a new kind
of hope for a new kind of fulfilment of this our innate desire
and longing for eternal life.

This kind of knowledge, I regret to say, I cannot supply.
I am the dragoman of the Fathers; I am not their neo-izer.
As one who for the past hour has acted the part of pure
historian, I should not like to perform before your very eyes
a feat of quick-change artistry and of a sudden turn myself
into theologian and preacher, and that kind of theologian and
preacher, too, who would make the Fathers talk latter-day beliefs and latter-day disbeliefs in the pious language of their
own old beliefs. But I think I shall not be stepping out of my
character as historian if I let the Fathers speak for themselves.

Let us then imagine that the Fathers are with us here now
in body, as I hope they are with us in spirit. Let us further
imagine that a bright young man, a student of divinity, came
up to tell them how sorry he was that he could not share with
them their belief in the resurrection of the body, seeing that
modern science is all against its possibility, but how glad he
was that he could share with them their belief in the immortality of the soul, seeing that respectable modern philosophers and even respectable modern scientists with a philo-

[177] *Oratio Catechetica Magna* 5 (PG 45, 21D).
[178] *De Peccatorum Meritis et Remissione* I, 2, 2.   [179] 2 Cor. 5: 2.

sophic turn of mind do occasionally give a nod of approval to immortality.

To this, I imagine, the Fathers would answer:

Young man, you are wrong on two counts.

You are wrong, first, in blaming your unwillingness to believe in resurrection upon modern science. The impossibility of resurrection and the fact of its being contrary to what is known as the laws of nature had already been proclaimed by the outmoded ancient science of our own time; modern science of your present time cannot make it more impossible. Still, if we, despite the science of our time, were willing to believe in resurrection and you, because of the science of your time, are unwilling to believe in it, your unwillingness to believe in it is not to be explained by the opposition of the science of your time. It is to be explained on other grounds, and there are other grounds by which it can be explained.

You are wrong, second, in distinguishing between immortality and resurrection, by assuming the former to be scientifically possible and the latter scientifically impossible. The kind of immortality in which we believe, immortality by the will of God, and even the kind of immortality in which Plato believed, immortality by nature, is discarded by science — — by the modern science of your time — just as is resurrection. The immortality which respectable philosophers and even respectable scientists with a philosophic turn of mind sometimes speak of approvingly is another kind of immortality; it is the Aristotelian conception of immortality, a spurious sort of immortality, an immortality not by the will of God nor by the necessity of nature but by the word of man. And let us tell you the story of Aristotle. He started as a disciple of Plato, with the belief that the soul, or rather one of the souls or one part of the soul, is separable from the body and is immortal. His works still contain reminiscences of this early belief of his, as when, for instance, he says of the intelligent part of the soul (νοῦς) that it may survive after death [180] or

---

[180] *Metaphysica* XII, 3, 1070a, 24–26.

that it is immortal and eternal.[181] But when later he found himself forced, by reason of his revised conception of soul, to deny the immortality of any part of the human soul, he held out as a consolation the immortality of the human race. Man as individual indeed dies, but the human race, of which the individual man is part, lives on forever.[182]

And here the Fathers would make their final remark: Dear young man, if you can find consolation in this verbal kind of immortality and if this verbal kind of immortality can serve you as an incentive to do good and shun evil, go and console yourself and sin no more, and mayhap the Lord in His mercy will reward you with true immortality, aye, and with resurrection, too.

And to this, and with this, we say, Amen.

[181] *De Anima* III, 5, 430a, 23.
[182] *Ibid.* II, 4, 415b, 6–7.

4

PHILOSOPHICAL IMPLICATIONS OF THE THEOLOGY OF CYRIL OF JERUSALEM *

CYRIL of Jerusalem, who flourished during the stormy years following the Council of Nicaea, is not counted among those Fathers whom we like to call philosophers. In his only complete work which is extant, the *Catecheses*, no philosophical discussions are introduced, either directly or indirectly, into his exposition of Christian doctrines. In fact, there is no mention of the term "philosophy" or of the name of any philosopher throughout that work. Only once is the term Aristotelian ('Αριστοτελικόν) mentioned,[1] but this, strangely enough, is used as a description of Scythianus, the reputed founder of Manichaeism. In one place, discussing erroneous views about God, he happens to mention two such views: first, that "God is the soul of the world"; second, that "His power reaches only to heaven, but not to the earth as well." [2] Philosophically-minded Fathers, such, for instance, as Tatian,[3] Athenagoras,[4] Clement of Alexandria,[5] Origen,[6] Lactantius,[7] and Augustine,[8] on quoting these two views, usually ascribe the former to Aristotle or the Stoics and the latter to Aristotle.[9] But Cyril refers both these views simply to the Greeks ("Ελληνες), a term which throughout his work he uses in the general sense of Gentiles or heathen, as, for instance, when

* Delivered at a Symposium on Christianity in "Palestine in the Byzantine Period" held at Dumbarton Oaks in April 1955, and published in *Dumbarton Oaks Papers*, No. 11 (1957), 1–19. Reprinted by permission of the Trustees for Harvard University, The Dumbarton Oaks Research Library and Collection, Washington, D.C.

[1] *Catecheses* VI, 22.   [3] *Orat. ed Graec.* 2.
[2] *Ibid.* VIII, 2.   [4] *Supplicatio ad Graecos* 6.
[5] *Protrepticus* 5.66 (PG 8, 169B; 172A); *Stromata* I, 11.88 (8, 149A); V, 14.51 (9, 129B); V, 14.90 (9, 132B). Section references here and in nn. below are to ed. Stählin.   [6] *Cont. Cels.* III, 75; II, 13.
[7] *Div. Inst.* I, 5 (PL 6, 135A).
[8] *De Civ. Dei* V, 12.
[9] Cf. my *Philosophy of the Church Fathers*, I (Cambridge, Mass., 1956), 85–88.

he speaks of those whom he calls "Greeks" as believing in "myths" [10] and as polytheists [11] and as worshippers of idols.[12] In another place, speaking of resurrection, he says: "Greeks contradict it." [13] The reference evidently is not to the Greeks mentioned in the New Testament as not believing in the resurrection of Jesus,[14] or to the casual remarks in Homer or Sophocles that the dead cannot be called back to life; [15] it is a reference rather to such denial of the Christian belief in eschatological resurrection as may be found in Celsus [16] and Plotinus,[17] for these "Greeks," he says, are to be answered "by reasonings ($\lambda o\gamma\iota\sigma\mu\hat{\omega}\nu$) and demonstrations ($\dot{\alpha}\pi o\delta\epsilon i-\xi\epsilon\omega\nu$)." [18] Philosophically-minded Fathers, again, would have said here "philosophers contradict it"; and, in fact, Augustine does attribute the denial of the Christian belief in eschatological resurrection to "gentile philosophers." [19] To Cyril, evidently, philosophers did not constitute a special class of men, with a special discipline of their own. They were to him simply heathen. He lumps them together with all those who believed in myths and in many gods, and who worshipped idols.

But still, like the famous unwitting prose-speaking gentleman of Molière's play, Cyril speaks philosophy without being aware of it. And how could he help it! Christian doctrine ever since the middle of the second century, beginning with the Apologists, was presented as a philosophy. The Apologists, and others after them, following the example of Philo in his treatment of Scripture, introduced new philosophical concepts and new philosophical terms into Christianity, and not only did they restore the few philosophical terms and concepts of the New Testament to their original meaning, they also gave a philosophical interpretation to old scriptural terms and old scriptural concepts. All these gradually

---

[10] *Catecheses* XII, 27; XIII, 37.
[11] *Ibid.* VI, 11 and 17.
[12] *Ibid.* VI, 10–11.
[13] *Ibid.* XVIII, 1.
[14] Acts 17:32; 26:24.
[15] *Iliad* XXIV, 551; *Electra* 137f.
[16] *Cont. Cels.* V, 14.
[17] *Enneades* III, 6, 6.
[18] *Catecheses* XVIII, 10.
[19] *Enarr. in Psalm.* 88, 5 (PL 37, 1134).

became part of Christian belief. Christian terminology and formulas became laden with deep philosophical meaning. All those who used them were thus unconsciously philosophers.

Such an unconscious philosopher also was Cyril of Jerusalem, which, in the course of this paper, I shall try to illustrate by two examples.

My first example is taken from his definition of faith.

"There is one sort of faith (πίστεως)," says Cyril, "the doctrinal, which implies an assent of the soul (συγκατάθεσιν τῆς ψυχῆς) concerning some particular things." [20]

This definition contains two terms, "faith" and "assent." Of these two terms, the term "faith" is used technically both as a religious term in Scripture and as an epistemological term in philosophy. As for the term "assent," however, while in philosophy it is used technically as the equivalent of the term "faith," in Scripture it is not used in any technical sense, though in a non-technical sense it occurs in the New Testament, once as a noun [21] and once as a verb. [22]

Let us then study the technical sense in which these two terms are used in philosophy, [23] and let us see whether that particular philosophical sense of these two terms is reflected in Cyril's definition of faith as an assent.

In Greek philosophy, the term "faith" has two technical meanings. First, in both Plato and Aristotle, it is used in the sense of a special kind of "opinion," or, as it is sometimes called, a "vehement assumption" (ὑπόληψις σθοδρά), in the general scheme of the division of knowledge into sensation (αἴσθησις), opinion (δόξα), and scientific knowledge (ἐπιστήμη). Second, in Aristotle, it is used, not only in the sense

---

[20] *Catecheses* V, 10.
[21] 2 Cor. 2:16.   [22] Luke 23:51.
[23] The various brief analyses of the historical background of Cyril's statements on faith, which are interspersed in the next few pages, are summarizations, with some additions, of my discussion of "Faith and Reason" in *The Philosophy of the Church Fathers*, I, 97–140.

of a particular kind of knowledge along with all the other kinds of knowledge, but also in the sense of a judgment of the truth of all the other kinds of knowledge, that is to say, as a judgment that the knowledge we have of a thing is self-consistent or that it corresponds to the reality of the thing —self-consistency and correspondence being, according to Aristotle, the two criteria of the truth of a thing. There is a certain faculty in our mind, he seems to say, by which we come to have faith and to become certain that the knowledge we possess is true. Taken in this sense, faith is said by Aristotle to be the judgment of the truth of both immediate knowledge, such as the primary premises, and of derivative knowledge, such as demonstrated conclusions. Thus, in one place he says that "things are true and primary which obtain faith ($\pi\iota\sigma\tau\iota\nu$), not on the strength of anything else, but of themselves," [24] and in another place he says that there is "faith" also "on the strength of reason ($\lambda\acute{o}\gamma o\upsilon$)," [25] or "from induction and syllogistic proof." [26]

In exactly the same sense as that in which Aristotle uses the term "faith" the Stoics use the term "assent ($\sigma\upsilon\gamma\kappa\alpha\tau\acute{\alpha}\theta\epsilon$-$\sigma\iota s$)." Assent is to them the judgment of the truth of our knowledge. And the knowledge of which assent is a judgment of its truth is, as in Aristotle, twofold in kind, either immediate knowledge or derivative knowledge. Thus with regard to immediate knowledge the Stoics are reported to have said that "all sensation is an assent" [27] or "cannot take place without assent," [28] and that "the notions (*notitiae*) of things . . . can have no existence without assent"; [29] with regard to derivative knowledge they are reported to have said that "all opinion ($\delta\acute{o}\xi\alpha$) and judgment ($\kappa\rho\acute{\iota}\sigma\iota s$) and assumption ($\upsilon\pi\acute{o}\lambda\eta\psi\iota s$) and learning ($\mu\acute{\alpha}\theta\eta\sigma\iota s$) . . . is an assent." [30]

---

[24] *Topica* I, 1, 100a, 30–100b, 18. [25] *Physica* VIII, 8, 262a, 18–19.
[26] *De Soph. Elench.* 4, 165b, 27–28; *Anal. Post.* II, 3, 90b, 14; *Topica* I, 8, 103b, 7. [28] *Ibid.*, II, 115; I, 61.
[27] Arnim, *S.V.F.*, II, 72. [29] *Ibid.*, II, 115.
[30] Clement of Alexandria, *Stromata* II, 12.55 (PG 8, 992C).

While "faith" in Aristotle and "assent" in the Stoics are thus used in the same sense, Aristotle never uses "assent" and the Stoics never use "faith" in this sense of the judgment of the truth of knowledge. In Aristotle the word "assent" occurs only once in its verb form (συγκαταθήσεται),[31] and it is used in the sense of a moral judgment as to the goodness of a thing, and not as an intellectual judgment as to the truth of a thing; in the Stoics the term "faith" does occur often, but always in the sense of a "strong assumption (ὑπόληψις ἰσχυρά)."[32] But then comes Clement of Alexandria who, combining these two terms, the Aristotelian "faith" and the Stoic "assent," defines "faith" as an "assent of the soul (ψυχῆς συγκατάθεσις)." And this "faith" which is "assent" is applied by him, as the one or the other of these terms is applied by Aristotle and the Stoics, to both immediate knowledge, which he describes by the Stoic, as well as the Epicurean, phrase as a "preconception (πρόληψις) of the mind,"[33] and derivative knowledge, which he describes by the Stoic terms quoted above as "opinion" and "judgment" and "assumption" and "learning."[34]

This is Clement's restatement in Stoic terms of Aristotle's philosophical definition of "faith" as an epistemological concept.

Then, transferring this philosophical definition of faith as an epistemological concept to the scriptural use of the term faith as a religious concept, he says that primarily faith is "obedience to commandments (τὸ πείθεσθαι ταῖς ἐντολαῖς),"[35] which reflects the scriptural expression "I have believed the commandments (ταῖς ἐντολαῖς ἐπίστευσα),"[36] and in which the term τὸ πείθεσθαι, as in Acts 5:36 and 5:40, is used by him in the sense of both "obedience" and "assent." This

---

[31] *Topica* III, 1, 116a, 11–12.
[32] Arnim, *S.V.F.*, III, 548 (p. 147, l. 11).
[33] *Stromata* II, 4.16 (PG 8, 948B).
[34] Cf. above n. 30.
[35] *Stromata* II, 11.48 (PG 8, 984C).
[36] Ps. 119:66.

obedience or assent to commandments, like the faith of Aristotle and the assent of the Stoics, he says, is twofold in kind. Either it is a grasping of the teachings of Scripture "by faith" as one grasps an "indemonstrable primary premise," inasmuch as the teachings of Scripture, being the voice of God, are "self-evidently true," [37] or it is like an assent to the conclusion of a valid demonstration, in which case, the faith is called "scientific faith" (ἐπιστημονικὴ πίστις)," [38] or "exact faith (ἀκριβὴς πίστις)" [39] or simply "gnosis." [40] But more than that, on the basis of scriptural proof-texts, he tries to show the permissibility as well as the usefulness of philosophy as a support of religious beliefs. "I call him truly learned," he says, "who brings everything to bear on the truth; so that, from geometry and music, and philosophy itself, culling what is useful, he guards the faith against assault." [41] Still he does not consider philosophically demonstrated faith superior to simple faith; both of them, according to him, are equally perfect and spiritual, for the teaching of Scripture, he argues, is "perfect and complete in itself," and therefore he "who knows what is perfect," whether he knows it with demonstration or without it, cannot be "imperfect"; [42] and, using the term "gnostic" as a description of those who possess demonstrated faith and the term "psychical" of those who possess simple faith, he maintains that "there are not in the same Word some gnostics and some psychical men; but all who have abandoned the desires of the flesh are equal and spiritual before God." [43]

In the light of this, when Cyril defines faith as that "which implies an assent of the soul concerning some particular thing," it reflects a definition of religious faith in terms of philosophy.

But here a question comes up. While Clement's definition of religious faith as an assent, that is, a voluntary obedience

[37] Stromata XII, 16.95 (PG 9, 532C).
[38] Stromata II, 11.49 (PG 8, 985A).
[39] Ibid. I, 6.33 (PG 8, 278B).
[40] Ibid. II, 11.48 (PG 8, 984C); VI, 17.155 (PG 9, 388A).
[41] Ibid. I, 9.43 (PG 8, 740C).
[42] Paedagogus I, 6.25 (PG 8, 280A); I, 6.29 (285A).
[43] Ibid. I, 6.31 (288AB).

to the teachings of Scripture, represents the generally accepted view among the Fathers of the Church, there were
differences of opinion among them with regard to the usefulness of philosophy as a support of faith, and also with regard to the equality between simple faith and philosophically
demonstrated faith. Clement himself speaks of those of his
own time whom he describes as the "multitude" as those who
"are frightened at the Hellenic philosophy, as children are
at masks, being afraid lest it lead them astray." [44] No names
are mentioned by him. But one of his contemporaries, Tertullian, writing in Latin and probably unknown to Clement,
shared in this denial of merit to philosophy as a support of
faith, though with some qualification. According to Tertullian, the search of philosophical demonstration for beliefs on
the part of a believing Christian implies either that he had
not really believed or that he ceased to believe, but to have
ceased to believe means a desertion of faith, and a desertion
of faith means a denial of faith. The search of philosophical
demonstration on the part of a believer, he therefore concludes, cannot pass with impunity, for "with impunity rambles
[only] he who deserts nothing." [45] From his own example,
however, it may be inferred that he saw no danger in the use
of philosophical demonstration for religious beliefs on the
part of one who had acquired a knowledge of philosophy
before he acquired faith. But in contrast to these two views,
the views of Clement and Tertullian, there is a third view,
the view of Origen. To Origen, faith demonstrated by reason
is superior to simple faith. "There is a great difference," he
says, "between knowledge conjoined with faith and faith
only," [46] for, he argues, "in agreement with the spirit of Christianity, it is of much more importance to give our assent
(συγκατατίθεσθαι) to doctrines upon grounds of reason and
wisdom than upon that of faith only." [47]

[44] *Stromata* VI, 10.80 (PG 9, 301A).
[45] *De Praescr. Haer.* 11.
[46] *In Joan.* XIX, 1 (PG 14, 529C); ed. Preuschen, XIX, 3, 20.
[47] *Cont. Cels.* I, 13.

Exactly what is meant by the equality or inequality of these two kinds of faith is not clearly stated by any of the Fathers who deal with this problem. In the case of Clement it can be shown that by the equality of these two kinds of faith he does not mean an equality of reward in the hereafter, for in a passage in which he identifies simple believers and philosophically-minded believers respectively with those who perform good work out of fear of God and those who perform good work out of love of God, he says that "their rewards are different." [48] Evidently what he means by the equality of these two kinds of faith is their equal ability to resist the seducement of false views. By the same token, when, in opposition to Clement, Origen maintains that philosophically demonstrated faith is superior to simple faith, he means thereby that the philosophically minded believer, whom, like Clement, he identifies with the lover of God as against the simple believer whom he identifies with the fearer of God,[49] is more strongly fortified against the seducements of false beliefs than the simple believer. This is also the meaning of Tertullian's statement, quoted above, that "with impunity rambles [only] he who deserts nothing," that is to say, only he who does not try to desert simple faith by the search for philosophical demonstration is without danger of falling into a denial of faith. And this, also, quite evidently, is the meaning of the term "merit" used by Thomas Aquinas [50] in his discussion of simple faith and philosophically demonstrated faith, for the expression "merit of faith" (*meritum fidei*) in that discussion is definitely not used by him in the sense of a difference in the "reward" (*praemium vel merces*) [51] of these two kinds of faith, but rather in the sense of a difference in the strength of the faith to resist false teachings.[52]

[48] *Stromata* IV, 18.113.5–114.1 (PG 8, 1321BC).
[49] *In Gen., Hom.* VII, 4 (PG 12, 201B).
[50] *Sum. Theol.* II–II, qu. 2.
[51] For "merit" in the sense of "reward," see *Sum. Theol.* I–II, 114, lc.
[52] *Ibid.*, II–II, 2, 10. The substance of this paragraph, by an oversight, was left out in my discussion of "Single Faith Theories" and "Double Faith Theory" in *The Philosophy of the Church Fathers*, I, 106–111, 120–127.

In the light of these differences of opinion, when Cyril defines faith as that "which implies an assent of the soul concerning some particular thing," the following questions may be raised: Is that particular thing to be assented to as an immediately perceived truth or as a demonstrated truth? Are the two kinds of faith yielded by the two kinds of assent equal or unequal? If the latter, is their inequality of the Tertullianic or of the Origenian kind? No direct answers to these questions are given by Cyril. Let us then see what we may gather indirectly from some of his statements which deal with faith.

To begin with, there is a statement wherein, referring to the articles of faith which he has taught to his catechumens, Cyril warns them as follows: "Guard them with reverence, lest perchance the enemy spoil (συλήσῃ) any of you who have been puffed up (χαυνοθέντας); lest some heretic pervert any of the truths delivered to you." [53]

This passage reflects Paul's warning: "Beware that any one spoil (μή τις . . . ὁ συλαγωγῶν) you through philosophy and vain deceit." [54]

Now it happens that this warning of Paul is interpreted by the Fathers in two ways. Tertullian takes it to mean that all philosophy is vain deceit; hence Paul's word is to him a warning against the use of philosophy even in support of the teachings of Scripture, and he exclaims: "What indeed has Athens to do with Jerusalem? What concord is there between the Academy and the Church? . . . Our instruction comes from 'the porch of Solomon' [Acts 3:11, 5:12], who had himself taught that 'the Lord should be sought in simplicity of heart' [Wisdom 1:1]. Away with all attempts to produce a mottled Christianity of Stoic, Platonic, and dialectic composition." [55] Origen, however, takes it to refer, not to all philosophy, but only to that kind of philosophy which is vain deceit, and this because of its containing views

[53] *Catecheses* V, 13.
[54] Col. 2:8.   [55] *De Praescr. Haer.* 7.

"which are plausible in the eyes of the many, but which represent falsehood as truth." [56] Later, Augustine similarly takes it to refer only to philosophy which is vain deceit, namely, that kind of philosophy which Paul himself describes as being "after the rudiments of the world"; and, as if he had Tertullian's statement in mind, he says that Paul's condemnation of "philosophy and vain deceit" does not include the philosophy of the Platonists, which, he says, leads to "the belief in God and His Word." [57]

In the light of these two kinds of interpretation of Paul's warning against "philosophy and vain deceit," the question arises as to what Cyril's interpretation of it was. It will be noticed that in his paraphrase of Paul's warning, the indefinite "any one" of Paul is changed to "the enemy" and to "some heretic." Now, in Paul the indefinite "any one" quite evidently refers to a philosopher, for that "any one" is described as one who might spoil them "through philosophy and vain deceit." Consequently "the enemy" and "some heretic" in Cyril's warning must refer to someone who is a philosopher. Consequently, too, Cyril's expression "any of you who have been puffed up (χαυνοθέντας)" is to be taken to mean being puffed up with philosophical knowledge, and thus, despite the difference in the Greek term used in it for being puffed up, it would reflect Paul's statement that "knowledge puffeth up (γνῶσις φυσιοῖ)," [58] for, according to Clement of Alexandria, the "knowledge" which "puffeth up" includes also the "knowledge of the philosophers of the Greeks." [59] But the question is, how did Cyril understand the warning of Paul upon which he based his own warning? Did he take it to mean, as did Tertullian, that all philosophy is vain deceit leading to heresy? In that case, by "the enemy" and "some heretic" he would mean every philosopher. Or, did he take it to mean, as did Origen, that only philosophy which is vain deceit leads to heresy? In that case, by "the enemy" and

---

[56] *Cont. Cels.* I, Praef. 5.
[57] *Confessiones* VIII, 2, 3.
[58] 1 Cor. 8:1.
[59] *Stromata* II, 11.48 (PG 8, 984B).

"some heretic" he would mean only the wrong kind of philosopher.

Then there is that mysterious strange woman, who, like the dark lady in the Sonnets, turns up occasionally in the pages of the Church Fathers.

In the works of Cyril, she turns up in the following passage:

"And the Greeks by their smooth tongue (εὐγλωττίας) draw you aside, 'for honey droppeth from the lips of a strange woman' [Prov. 5:3]." [60] In this passage, besides the direct quotation of the verse about the strange woman, the expression "the Greeks by their smooth tongue" contains also an allusion to the verse which says that wisdom "may keep thee from a strange and wicked woman, if she should make an attempt upon thee with pleasing words (λόγοις τοῖς πρὸς χάριν)." [61]

Now it happens that the "strange woman" in the Book of Proverbs is taken by some Fathers to refer to Greek philosophy. Thus Clement of Alexandria, in one passage,[62] raises the question whether or not the verses in the Book of Proverbs in which it is said that wisdom may "keep thee from a strange and wicked woman" [63] for from her lips "honey droppeth," [64] refer to "Hellenic culture" and "philosophy." His answer is that though they do so refer, they are not to be taken as a total condemnation of the use of Greek secular culture and philosophy, but admonish us only "not to linger and spend time with them." In another passage,[65] in an allusion to those who were opposed to philosophy, he quotes them as saying: "They know that, after lending their ears to Hellenic studies, they will never subsequently be able to retract their steps." The allusion here, again, is to the strange woman, concerning whom it is said in the Book of Proverbs that "none who go

---

[60] *Catecheses* IV, 2.
[61] Prov. 7:5 (LXX).
[62] *Stromata* I, 5.29 (PG 8, 720C–721A).
[63] Prov. 7:5 (LXX); cf. 5:2; 5:20.
[64] Prov. 5:3 (LXX).
[65] *Stromata* VI, 11.89 (PG 9, 309C).

unto her return again." [66] Similarly, when Gregory of Nyssa says that "secular knowledge is a spouse of foreign stock (ἡ ἐξ ἀλλοφύλων ὁμόζυγος)," [67] the reference is to that "strange (ἀλλοτρίας) woman" [68] from whom wisdom is said to keep one away, though it may include also a reference to Hagar, who in Philo is taken to symbolize secular knowledge as against wisdom, [69] and though, furthermore, it may also include a reference to the prohibition against marriage with heathen women lest their children might bring in heathen pollution. [70]

In the light of this interpretation of the "strange woman" as referring to philosophy, the question may be raised whether by the term "Greeks" in this passage Cyril means, as he does in other passages, heathen worshippers in general, or whether in this passage, because of his comparison of the "Greeks" to the "strange woman," he means, specifically, Greek philosophy. Moreover, on the assumption that he means philosophy, the question is whether the scriptural warning against the "strange woman" is taken by him, as by Clement of Alexandria, only as a warning against the excessive use of philosophy, or whether it is taken by him, as by those contemporaries referred to by Clement of Alexandria, as a prohibition against the use of philosophy altogether.

Whatever his attitude may have been on all these points, it is certain that he was opposed to Origen's view that philosophical speculation in religious matters is necessary for the strengthening of religious beliefs. In one passage, after stating that the teachings of Christianity rest upon Scripture alone, and are to be demonstrated only "with the proof from the Scriptures," he says that we must not "be drawn aside by mere plausibility and artifices of speech. . . . For this salvation which we believe depends not on ingenious reasoning, but on demonstration of the Holy Scriptures." [71] Here "mere

[66] Prov. 2:19.
[67] De Vita Moysis (PG 44, 336D–337A).
[68] Prov. 7:5.
[69] Congr. 27, 154.
[70] Exod. 34:15–16; Deut. 7:3–4.
[71] Catecheses IV, 17.

plausibility and artifices of speech" and "ingenious reasoning," which he contrasts with "demonstration of the Holy
Scriptures," quite evidently refer to what Origen would call
demonstration of philosophy. Having thus substituted the
"demonstration of the Holy Scriptures" for what Origen
would call the demonstration of philosophy, in another passage he then makes use of Origen's argument for attaching
merit to simple faith without the demonstration of philosophy
as a justification for his teaching to his catechumens a simple
faith based only upon dogmatic assertions without "demonstration of the Holy Scriptures."

The argument as given by Origen reads as follows: "If it
were possible for all to leave the business of life, and devote
themselves to philosophy, no other method ought to be
adopted by any one, but this alone. . . . But since the course
alluded to is impossible partly on account of the necessities
of life, partly on account of the weakness of men . . . what
better method could be devised with a view of assisting the
multitude, than that which was delivered by Jesus to the
heathen? . . . For it is manifest that [if we were to insist
upon faith arrived at through philosophy], all men, with very
few exceptions, would fail to obtain this [amelioration of
conduct] which they have obtained through a simple faith,
but would continue to remain in the practice of a wicked
life." [72]

The same argument as given by Cyril reads as follows:
"For since all cannot read the Scriptures, some being hindered
as to the knowledge of them by want of learning, and others
by want of leisure, in order that the soul may not perish from
ignorance, we comprise the whole doctrine of faith in a few
lines." [73]

Quite evidently the passage in Cyril is based upon the passage in Origen, and the change in the use of the same argument from its application to philosophical demonstration as
against simple faith, to an application to scriptural demonstra-

[72] *Cont. Cels.* I, 9.   [73] *Catecheses* V, 12.

tion as against undemonstrated articles of belief, is deliberate; and the reason for this change, it is quite evident,
is that to Cyril philosophical demonstration is not necessary
for the strengthening of religious beliefs.

And so Cyril's definition of faith as an assent, like that of
Clement and Origen, reflects a philosophical source. But while
it may be inferred from his writings that he did not recom-
mend philosophy and that he may even have condemned it, it
is not certain whether he condemned all philosophy or only
the wrong kind of philosophy.

My second example is taken from Cyril's discussion of the
Trinity.

On the whole, in his Trinitarian doctrine Cyril follows the
Nicene Creed in its most essential contention, namely, in its
rejection of Arianism, for while the name Arius or Arianism
is not mentioned by him, when he says that God "did not
bring forth the Son from non-existence into existence," [74] or
when he repudiates those "who dare to say that Christ was
brought into existence out of non-existence," [75] he definitely
rejects Arianism. In two things, however, he does not follow the Nicene Creed: he does not use the expression
"homoousios with the Father (ὁμοούσιον τῷ πατρί)" nor the
expression "begotten of the ousia (ἐκ τῆς οὐσίας) of the
Father." Instead, for the former expression he uses the expression "in all things like (homoion) to him that begot him
(τὸν ὅμοιον κατὰ πάντα τῷ γεννήσαντι)," [76] or some similar
expression in which the term homoios is used,[77] and for the
latter expression he uses the expression "begotten of the
Father (γεννηθεὶς ἐκ πατρός)." [78]

Now, as for the latter departure from the language of the
Nicene Creed, it can be easily explained. To begin with, the
Nicene Creed itself uses in its main formulation of the doc-

[74] Ibid. XI, 14.
[75] Ibid. XV, 9.
[76] Ibid. IV, 7.

[77] Ibid. VI, 7; XI, 4; XI, 9.
[78] Ibid. XI, 5.

trine the phrase *ek tou patros*, and it introduces the phrase
ek tes ousias tou patros only as an explanation of the former
phrase. Then, from Athanasius' defense of the Nicene Creed
we gather that the second phrase was introduced only in
order to remove a certain misunderstanding that might arise
with regard to the meaning of the original phrase.[79] So also
from Eusebius' account of the proceedings at Nicaea we
gather that the second phrase was not meant to add anything
new to the first phrase.[80] Moreover, the phrase *ek tes ousias
tou patros* never evoked widespread opposition, as did the
phrase *homoousion to patri*, and there were those who used
the former phrase, even though they were opposed to the use
of the latter.[81] Finally, from Basil's correspondence with Apollinaris we may gather that those who opposed *ousia* opposed it only "in order to leave no room for *homoousios*." [82]
Consequently, the omission by Cyril of the phrase containing
the term *ousia* does not mean a departure from the Nicene
Creed; it means, rather, the retention of only one phrase,
the main phrase, of the two used in the Nicene Creed.

But with regard to the phrase *homoousion to patri*, which
became a subject of long and bitter controversy, its omission by Cyril needs explanation. Undoubtedly the reason
for his omission of the phrase was based upon objections
raised against it by those who opposed the Nicene Creed.
But what were those objections, and is there any intimation
of any of these objections in Cyril?

One of the objections to the use of *homoousios* was the
rumor current at that time that the term had been used by
Paul of Samosata, and that it was, therefore, rejected by the
third Council of Antioch,[83] which had taken place about
sixty years before the Council of Nicaea. The rumor, it may

[79] *De Decret.* 19.
[80] *Eusebii Epistola ad Caesarienses* 5 (PG 20, 1540C–1541A).
[81] Cf. Newman's excursus to his English translation of the *Epistola
Eusebii* in *Nicene and Post-Nicene Fathers*, IV, 77ff.
[82] Basil, *Epistolae* 361.
[83] Athanasius, *De Synod.* 43.

be remarked, has so far not been substantiated.[84] Now it is quite possible that Cyril was influenced by this objection. Still, nowhere in his allusions to views which may be identified with those of Paul of Samosata, whom, by the way, he never mentions by name, does he give any intimation that he was aware of Paul's use of the term *homoousios*. The only inkling we can get as to what he thought was wrong with the Samosatene's conception of the Trinity is to be derived from his rejection of the view that the Word is unhypostatical (ἀνυπόστατος),[85] which would seem to refer to Paul of Samosata, for it agrees with the report that Paul of Samosata taught that the Word has no substance of its own,[86] and hence is unhypostatical.[87]

Another objection to the term *homoousios* was that it implied Sabellianism,[88] and it is this objection that is taken by Hefele [89] and Hagenbach [90] as the reason for the omission of the use of the term by Cyril. Here again it is quite possible that Cyril was influenced by this objection. But the fact is that in none of the passages in which he repudiates Sabellianism, in some of which he mentions Sabellius by name,[91] is any mention made of a connection between Sabellianism and the term *homoousios*. Moreover, the passage in Athanasius (*De Synod.* 12) upon which Hefele bases his statement contains no reference either to Sabellianism or to Cyril. Nor do the passages from Cyril cited by Hagenbach contain any reference to Sabellianism.

Still another objection was that the term *homoousios* does not occur in Scripture.[92] Here, too, it is quite possible that

---

[84] Cf. Hefele, *Conciliengeschichte* § 9, with Leclercq's additional notes in his French translation; G. Bardy, *Paul de Samosate* (1923), pp. 258ff.

[85] *Catecheses* IV, 8.

[86] Epiphanius, *Adv. Haer.* LXV, 1 (PG 42, 13A).

[87] *Ibid.* 5 (20B).

[88] Sozomen, *Hist. Eccl.* II, 18.

[89] *Conciliengeschichte*, § 82 (I, 712).

[90] *Lehrbuch der Dogmengeschichte*, § 92.

[91] *Catecheses* XVI, 4; XVII, 34.

[92] Athanasius, *De Decret.* I, 1; *De Synod.* 28; Basil, *Epistolae* 361.

Cyril was influenced by this objection. But the fact is that, while Cyril stresses the view that the Christian faith is based only upon Scripture, he nowhere says that none but scriptural language is to be used in the formulation of the creed. Bethune-Baker's statement that Cyril of Jerusalem "protests against terms of human contrivance" [93] is not borne out by the text to which he refers.[94] All that Cyril says in the passage which Bethune-Baker cites is that "the Articles of Faith were not composed at the good pleasure of men: but the most important points chosen from all Scripture, make up the one teaching of the Faith."

Moreover, if the reason for Cyril's not using *homoousios* was that this term is not scriptural, then why does he use the term *homoios*? There is no passage in Scripture in which it is explicitly stated that the Word, that is, the pre-existent Christ, is "like" (*homoios*) the Father. All we find in Scripture is a statement with regard to the born Christ, which reads: "The Son can do nothing of himself, but what he seeth the Father do . . . these also doeth the Son likewise (ὁμοίως)." [95] But the likeness spoken of is a likeness in operation and not a likeness in nature. If this statement was taken by him as a justification for his use of the term *homoios*, why should he not have taken as a justification for the use of *homoousion* the expression τὸν ἄρτον τὸν ἐπιούσιον,[96] where *ousion* in *epiousion* is used, according to him, in the same sense as *ousion* in *homoousion*, for this expression is taken by him, not in the sense of "daily bread," but rather in the sense of "supersubstantial bread," and is explained by him to mean bread "appointed for the *ousia* of the soul." [97]

Then, also, if Cyril meant to follow the language of Scripture, why did he not use the term ἴσος, for it is this term that is used by Paul when he says that the pre-existent Christ "thought it not robbery to be equal (ἴσα) with God," [98] and

[93] J. F. Bethune-Baker, *Introduction to the Early History of Christian Doctrine*, 8th ed. (1949), p. 192.   [96] Matt. 6:11.
[94] *Catecheses* V, 12.   [97] *Catecheses* XXIII, 15.
[95] John 5:19.   [98] Phil. 2:6.

it is this term, too, that is used by John when he says that
Jesus was accused of "making himself equal (ἴσον) with
God." [99]

Again, if the objection to *homoousios* was that the term
did not occur in Scripture, then why did Cyril use the term
ἐνυπόστατος as a description of both the Son [100] and the Holy
Spirit? [101] If you say that the term *enhypostatos* is based
upon the term *hypostasis*, a term which does occur in the
New Testament,[102] and which is used both in the Nicene
Creed and by Cyril himself,[103] then the question is why, on
the basis of the scriptural term *hypostasis*, and after the
analogy of the term *homoousios*, did he not coin the term
ὁμοϋπόστατος? The term *homohypostatos* would have been
a more suitable substitute for the objectionable *homoousios*
than the term *homoios*. Cyril did not hesitate to make use of,
or perhaps to coin, the term ὁμοιοπρόσωπος in the sense of
"of like face," [104] and there is no reason why he should not
have coined the term ὁμοϋπόστατος in the sense of "of the
same *hypostasis*." Since he did not coin the term *homohypostatos* to take the place of the objectionable *homoousios*,
he must have had some other objection to *homoousios*, an
objection that would apply equally to *homohypostatos*.

That objection, we shall try to show, is a philosophical
objection, which was bruited about ever after the term
homoousios was inserted in the Nicene Creed, and is reported by Athanasius and Basil. As reported by Athanasius
it reads: "Some . . . say" that "he who speaks of *homoousios* speaks of three, one *ousia* presubstratal (οὐσίαν τινὰ
προϋποκειμένην), and that those who are generated from him
are *homoousioi*; and they add, 'if then the Son be *homoousios*

---

[99] John 5:18.
[100] *Catecheses* XI, 10; XVII, 5.
[101] *Ibid*. XVII, 34.
[102] Heb. 1:3.
[103] *Catecheses* VI, 7 *et passim*.
[104] *Ibid*. XII, 14. The term ὁμοιοπρόσωπος occurs in Apollonius Dyscolus
(see latest edition of Liddell and Scott, s.v.,), but it is used by him in the
grammatical sense of "in the same person."

with the Father, then an *ousia* must have been presubstrated (προϋποκεῖσθαι), from which they have been generated.' " [105]

As reported by Basil, it reads as follows: "With regard to *homoousios* be so kind as to explain to us more fully . . . how it may be used with sound logic in matters wherein there is discerned neither a common superstratal genus (γένος κοινὸν ὑπερκείμενον) nor a substratal pre-existing material (ὑλικὸν ὑποκείμενον προϋπάρχον)." [106]

The philosophical considerations involved in these objections need explaining, and the best way to explain them is to give a brief account of the various meanings of the term *ousia* and *homoousios* as used in connection with the doctrine of the Trinity.[107]

Prior to the Nicene Creed the unity of the three persons of the Trinity was designated by two terms, one in Greek and one in Latin. The Greek term was *ousia*, and it was introduced by Origen. The Latin term was *substantia*, and it was introduced by Tertullian. The Greek term was used by Origen in the sense of Aristotle's second *ousia*, that is, in the sense of species or genus. Inasmuch as for Origen, as well as for all the Fathers, the persons of the Trinity were individual species rather than mere individuals, the term *ousia*, when it was used by him as a designation of their common unity, was used, not in the mere sense of species or in the mere sense of genus, but rather in the combined sense of specific genus, after the analogy of a combination of Aristotle's unity of species and unity of genus, illustrated respectively by the example of "man" in its relation to individual human beings, and by the example of "animal" in its relation to "horse, man, and dog." The Latin term *substantia* was used by Tertullian either as a translation of the Greek *hypostasis* in the sense of *hypokeimenon* or of the Greek

[105] *De Synod.* 51 (PG 26, 784BC).
[106] *Epistolae* 361 (PG 32, 1101).
[107] The brief analysis of the meanings of *ousia* and *homoousios* in the next few paragraphs is based upon my discussion of "The Mystery of the Trinity" in *The Philosophy of the Church Fathers*, I, 305–363.

ousia in its Stoic sense of matter, and hence as the equivalent of *hypokeimenon*. In either case it is used by Tertullian in the sense of substratum, after the analogy of Aristotle's unity of substratum, illustrated by the example of "water" in its relation to "oil and wine."

Corresponding to these two conceptions of the common unity of the Trinity, the one described by Origen with the term *ousia* and the other described by Tertullian with the term *substantia*, are the terms *homoousios* as it is actually used by Origen, and *homoousios*, in its Latin form *consubstantialis*, as it could have been used by Tertullian. When applied to the Father and the Son, for instance, Origen's *homoousios* would mean that the Father and the Son, each of them an individual species, are of the same specific genus, whereas Tertullian's *homoousios*, in its Latin translation, would mean that the Father and the Son, each of them, again, an individual species, are of the same substratum.

In the light of these two conceptions of the common unity of the Trinity, and also in the light of the corresponding two meanings of the term *homoousios*, the term *ousia*, as well as its equivalent *hypostasis*, which is used in the Nicene Creed as a description of the common unity of the Trinity, and similarly the term *homoousios* which is also used therein, would lend themselves to two possible interpretations, even though on the basis of internal evidence it can be shown that these terms are used in the Tertullianic sense of substratum. Consequently, when the opponents of the Nicene Creed began to raise objections against the use of the term *homoousios*, the objections were so phrased as to apply to both possible interpretations of the term.

It is against the interpretation of *homoousios* as meaning "of the same substratum" that the objection quoted by Athanasius argues that the term would imply a "presubstratal *ousia*," and it is against the interpretation of *homoousios* as meaning either "of the same specific genus" or "of the same substratum" that the objection quoted by Basil argues that the term would imply either a "common superstratal genus" or a "substratal pre-existing material."

The full meaning of the argument in its two alternative forms given by Basil may be unfolded as follows: Suppose, the argument starts in its first alternative form, you take *homoousios* to mean "of the same specific genus." But what is a species, and what is a genus, and what is a specific genus? Each is, of course, a universal. But what are universals: are they real or not? The Platonists say that universals are real; they are ideas which exist over and above and beyond individuals. Someone, therefore, who is a Platonist, would take the common *ousia* of the Father and the Son and the Holy Spirit as existing over and above and beyond the Father and the Son and the Holy Spirit. There would thus be an additional person, who is distinct from the Father and the Son and the Holy Spirit. Instead of a Trinity there would thus be a Quaternity. But suppose, the argument continues in its second alternative form, you take *homoousios* to mean "of the same substratum," after the analogy of water in its relation to oil and wine in Aristotle's example of the unity of substratum. But water has an existence prior to, and apart from, oil and wine. Some one, therefore, misled by the term *homoousios*, might take the *ousia* of the three persons of the Trinity to have an existence apart from the Father and the Son and the Holy Spirit. Again, instead of a Trinity there would thus be a Quaternity. Now this second form of the argument, directed against *homoousios* assumed to mean "of the same substratum," could also be used as an argument against the term *homohypostatos*, that is, "of the same hypostasis," inasmuch as sameness of *hypostasis*, in this case, would have the meaning of the sameness of substratum. It is for this reason, we may therefore conclude, that Cyril, on deciding not to use *homoousios*, decided also not to coin in its place the new term *homohypostatos*, but to use the expression *homoios kata panta* or *en pasin homoios*.

It is these philosophical arguments against the use of *homo-*

ousios, which, as we have tried to show, explain Cyril's failure to coin the new term *homohypostatos*, that also explain, we may assume, at least in part, why Cyril did not use the term *homoousios* in his exposition of the doctrine of the Trinity. So when reasons are sought for Cyril's failure to use the term *homoousios*, and mention is made of the alleged rejection of that term by the third Council of Antioch, or the Sabellian connotation of that term or its non-scriptural origin, mention should also be made of the philosophical arguments that were raised against it.

We have thus shown by two examples what philosophical implications are to be discerned in Cyril's theology. Cyril was not a professed philosopher: his task was to expound theological doctrines to simple believers, not to explain them to philosophers. But the doctrines which he tried to expound had, before they reached him, already gone through a process of philosophical reasoning; so whatever he says, as well as whatever he refrains from saying, reflects that background of philosophical reasoning. And so, to parody again a description of one of Molière's characters, Cyril was a philosopher in spite of himself.

PHILOSOPHICAL IMPLICATIONS OF
ARIANISM AND APOLLINARIANISM *

ARIANISM and Apollinarianism are two contrasting heresies of the fourth century. Arianism may be described as a leftist heresy: it denied the divinity of the pre-existent Christ, the Logos; and it also denied a divine nature in the born Christ, Jesus. Apollinarianism may be called a rightist heresy: it denied a human nature in the born Christ. Of the various phases of these controversies we have selected for discussion here one single phase, that of their philosophic implications.

Patristic opponents of Arianism as well as Patristic Church historians and heresiographers trace the Arian heresy to Aristotle. Thus Aristotle is mentioned as the source of the teaching of the various Arians by Basil,[1] Gregory of Nyssa,[2] Socrates Scholasticus,[3] and Epiphanius.[4] But when we study the passages in which Aristotle is mentioned as the source of this heresy, we are surprised to discover that the reference is not to any particular theory with which the name of Aristotle is generally associated, such, for instance, as his denial of Platonic ideas, his belief in the eternity of the world, his conception of God as only a prime mover, or his view that the soul is only a form of the body, but only to the Aristotelian method of reasoning. Thus they always speak in this connection of Aristotle's "syllogisms,"[5] or of Aristotle's "dialectics,"[6] or of Aristotle's "systematic treatment of the art

---

* Delivered at a Symposium on "The Cappadocian Fathers" held at Dumbarton Oaks in May 1956, and published in *Dumbarton Oaks Papers,* No. 12 (1958), 3–28. Reprinted by permission of the Trustees for Harvard University, The Dumbarton Oaks Research Library and Collection, Washington, D.C.   [2] *Cont. Eunom.* I (PG 45, 261D).

[1] *Adv. Eunom.* I, 5 (PG 29, 516B).   [3] *Hist. Eccl.* II, 35 (PG 67, 297).

[4] *Adv. Haer. Panar.* LXIX, 69 (PG 42, 316B).

[5] Basil, *loc. cit.*; Gregory of Nyssa, *loc. cit.*

[6] Epiphanius, *loc. cit.*

of reasoning" (τεχνολογία),[7] or of Aristotle's work on the *Categories*.[8] And when we examine these references to the Aristotelian method of reasoning as being the cause of the Arian heresy, we are further surprised to discover that they do not mean reasoning by the Aristotelian method from premises which are also Aristotelian, but rather the application of the Aristotelian method of reasoning to generally accepted Christian premises.

A good example of this is to be found in Socrates, who in his history of the Church tries to show how the Arian Aetius, under the influence of Aristotle's logic, and by his clumsy use of it, framed a fallacious argument against the orthodox Christian belief in the eternal generation of the Son, and how by the fallaciousness of his argument he proved himself to be "unable to comprehend how there could be an ingenerable generation and how that which is unbegotten can be co-eternal with him that begot."[9] The expression "ingenerable generation (ἀγέννητος γέννησις), the meaning of which Socrates charges Aetius with not having comprehended, is reminiscent of the expression "ingenerably generated" (ἀγεννητο-γεννής), which Alexander of Alexandria uses as the equivalent of the expression "eternally generated" (ἀειγεννής).[10] Now the expression "eternally generated" is used by Alexander of Alexandria in the same context, and also in the same sense, as the expression "begotten [or generated] of the Father without beginning (ἀνάρχως) and eternally (ἀϊδίως)" used by Athanasius.[11] The argument framed by Aetius may, therefore, have been directed either against the expression "ingenerably generated," or against the expression "eternally generated [or begotten]," or against the expression "generated [or begotten] without beginning." We are not told, however,

[7] Gregory of Nyssa, *Cont. Eunom.* VII (PG 42, 316B).
[8] Socrates Scholasticus, *loc. cit.*
[9] *Ibid.*
[10] In Theodoret of Cyrrhus, *Eccl. Hist.* I, 4 (PG 82, 912A); Epiphanius, *Adv. Haer. Panar.* LXIX, 6 (PG 42, 209D–212A).
[11] *Expositio Fidei* 1 (PG 25, 200–201A).

by Socrates how the argument was framed by Aetius, nor does he tell us why he branded the argument as fallacious. Let us then try to reconstruct the argument as well as the refutation by which it was shown to be fallacious.

Aetius, we may assume, started with the New Testament description of the pre-existent Christ as the "only begotten (μονογενὴς) Son" (John 1:18) and, having in mind the use of the expression "begotten [or generated] without beginning" as the equivalent of the expression "ingenerably generated," he framed his argument against it in the following syllogistic form:

Everything begotten has a beginning (ἀρχή);
The son is begotten;
Therefore, the Son has a beginning (ἀρχή).

The reason why Socrates branded this argument as fallacious was, we may assume, that he discovered in it some fallacy. The fallacy, we may further assume, was that of equivocation; for the term "beginning" (ἀρχή), he must have known, is used by Aristotle in many senses, of which two are that of "cause" and that of "not-eternal," [12] and Aetius, he must have noticed, uses the term "beginning" in his syllogism in these two different senses. When, in his proposition in the major premise, he says that "everything begotten has a beginning," he could have meant only that "everything begotten has a cause," for the proposition in the sense of "everything begotten is not-eternal" is yet to be proved. But when, in his conclusion, he says that "therefore, the Son has a beginning," he meant thereby that "therefore, the Son is not-eternal." Socrates' own contention that "that which was begotten can be coeternal with him who begot" is a restatement of the view generally accepted in catholic Christianity, namely, that the Son was eternally generated, which means that, though he was begotten and has a cause, he is still eternal.

---

[12] Cf., for instance, the two uses of the term in *Metaphysica* I, 2, 982b, 9, and *Physica* VI, 5, 236a, 14.

Thus it is the syllogistic method of reasoning from generally approved Christian premises that, according to the Fathers, has led to the Arian heresy.

When we study further those passages in which the Fathers trace the Arian heresy to the Aristotelian method of syllogistic reasoning, we note several other things.

First, the Fathers do not mean that only the Arian heresy, and no other, arises from the use of Aristotelian syllogistic reasoning. For we find that Eusebius quotes the non-extant *The Little Labyrinth*, now taken to be the work of Hippolytus, as saying in effect that some other heresies, such as those of Artemus or Artemon and of the Theodotians, were traceable to the fact that they apply syllogistic reasoning to scriptural beliefs.[13]

Second, the Fathers do not mean that only Aristotle, and no other philosopher, is responsible for the Arian heresy. For we find that Gregory of Nyssa himself, who so often blames Aristotle for the rise of Arianism, once at least blames Plato also."[14]

Third, they do not mean that if the Arians had not used the Aristotelian method of syllogism, but had used the Platonic method of division, they would not have arrived at their heretical and fallacious conclusion. For the Platonic method of division, as stated by Aristotle, is nothing but a weak syllogism,[15] its weakness being that, without the use of a middle term, it aims to arrive at the same conclusion as that at which the syllogism tries to arrive with the use of a middle term. So the Platonic method of division would not have prevented the Arians from arriving at the same heretical and fallacious conclusion.

Fourth, the Fathers do not mean that the syllogistic method is entirely fallacious and should never be employed in discussion of matters religious. For we sometimes find that the very same Fathers, such, for instance, as Basil and Gregory

---

[13] Eusebius, *Hist. Eccl.* V, 28, 13.
[14] *Cont. Eunom.* IX (PG 45, 813C).
[15] *Anal. Prior.* I, 31, 46a, 33.

of Nyssa, who blame the Aristotelian method of syllogistic reasoning for the rise of the Arian heresy, do themselves make use of this kind of reasoning in such investigations as those of the proofs of the existence of God and the creation of the world. In fact, Gregory of Nyssa openly admits that "subtle dialectic possesses a force that may be turned both ways, as well for the overthrow of truth as for the destruction of false-hood," [16] and consequently, though on the whole he prefers "a discussion which is in a naked unsyllogistic form," [17] still he asks, "With what, then, must we begin, so as to conduct our thinking by logical sequence to the proposed conclu-sion?," [18] and insists upon following what is philosophically considered to be good, logical reasoning.[19] In this their cau-tious use of the syllogistic method, the Fathers merely fol-lowed the example of Aristotle himself, who constantly warns those who use syllogistic reasoning to use it properly and to guard against certain fallacies, among them the fallacy of equivocation.[20]

From all this we may gather that, by their statements that the Arian heresy arose from the Aristotelian method of syl-logistic reasoning, the Fathers did not mean that only the Arian heresy was traceable to the Aristotelian syllogism, nor did they mean that only Aristotle was responsible for the Arian heresy, nor did they mean that the Platonic method of logical division could not have led to the Arian heresy, nor finally did they mean that all syllogistic reasoning was wrong and fallacious. What they meant was that the Arians, like all other heretics, were led astray by their wrong use of philoso-phy, especially of the Aristotelian method of syllogistic reasoning, which, as indicated by Aristotle's own warning, easily lends itself to misuse.

This, I believe, is a fair and accurate account of what the

---

[16] *De An. et Resur.* (PG 46, 52B).
[17] *Ibid.*
[18] *Oratio Catechetica Magna* 19 (PG 45, 56C).
[19] *Cont. Eunom.* 18 (PG 45, 316D).
[20] *De Sophist. Elench.* 4, 165b, 23–166b, 19.

Fathers meant when they blamed Aristotle for the heresy of Arianism.

But let us see what some modern historians have made of the statements of the Fathers. On the basis of these statements they try to make the struggle between Arianism and orthodoxy a battle between Aristotelianism and Platonism. This is how the controversy is presented by Baur.[21] And if we want to find out exactly what was the battle between Aristotelianism and Platonism, upon which the controversy between Arianism and orthodoxy is assumed to be based, we hear a great deal about how Aristotle derives concepts from concrete individual things in an empirical manner, referring always to experience, and how Plato, on the contrary, disregarding concrete things and empirical observation, deals with pure ideas. Out of such and similar contrasts, we are expected to derive all the theological controversies between Arianism and orthodoxy. Milman treats the controversy between Arianism and orthodoxy as a sort of War of the Roses, telling us how Aetius attached himself to the Aristotelian philosophy, and how "with him appears to have begun the long strife between Aristotelianism and Platonism in the Church." [22] Cardinal Newman, on the ground that Arianism had a "close connexion with the existing Aristotelic school," [23] sees in it a sort of Oxford Movement in reverse, and, because the Arians had a close connexion with the Aristotelic school, he calls them "The School of Sophists." [24]

But historians, as we know, do not always merely repeat one another; they are sometimes at variance with one another. So, while one school of historians identified Aristotle as the source of infection of the Arian heresy, another school identified Plato as the source of that infection. Chief ex-

[21] F. Ch. Baur, *Die christliche Lehre von der Dreieinigkeit und Menschenwerdung Gottes*, I (Tübingen, 1841), 389ff.

[22] H. H. Milman, *History of Christianity*, III (London, 1840), 43 n.

[23] J. H. Newman, *Arians of the Fourth Century*, 4th ed. (London, 1876), p. 29.

[24] *Ibid.*, p. 25.

ponent of this latter view is Ritter,[25] though before him a similar view had been expressed in a milder form by Baumgarten-Crusius.[26] Here is how Ritter finds a connection between Plato and Arius. Representing Arius as having transformed the eternally generated Logos of the orthodox Christians into a created being in order to provide God with an intermediary for the creation of the world, which He himself could not create directly, Ritter suggests that this view of Arius originated in Plato's *Timaeus*, where the Demiurge, after having created the "heavenly gods," addresses these traditional deities of mythology and delegates to them the creation of the mortal creatures, which he himself could not create directly.[27]

This representation of the view of Arius, as well as the explanation of its origin, is, to our mind, wrong on several grounds.

First, all that we know of the original teachings of Arius is that he reduced the Logos, who is described in John as he through whom all things were made by God and who in the orthodoxy of his time was considered an eternally generated being, to a created being. Among the reasons reported, in Arius' name, for his having introduced that change in the origin of the Logos there is no mention of the fact that it was out of a desire to provide God with an intermediary for the creation of the world, necessitated by reason of some inability on the part of God to create it directly. The view that the Logos was used as an intermediary in the creation of the world because of some inability on the part of God to create it directly was introduced by Asterius and adopted by Arius only after the Logos had already been transformed by them into a created being, and it was introduced only in answer to the question that, if the Logos was created by

[25] Heinrich Ritter, *Geschichte der Philosophie*, VI (Hamburg, 1841), 21–22.

[26] L. F. O. Baumgarten-Crusius, *Lehrbuch der christlichen Dogmengeschichte*, I (Jena, 1823), 262.

[27] *Timaeus* 40D–41D.

God *ex nihilo* in the same way as the world, "why then were not all things brought into being by God alone at the same command, at which the Son came into being?" [28]

Second, the Demiurge's address to the traditional gods in the *Timaeus* could not have been the source of Arius' transforming the Logos into a created being, for that address is couched by Plato in mythological language and the traditional gods are represented as "generated" rather than "created." Thus these traditional gods are described as "children (παῖδες) . . . born (ἐγενέσθην)," and in that passage the Demiurge describes himself as "he who begot (γεννήσας) this universe" and as "Father." [29] For be it remembered that Arius rejected not only the eternity of the generation of Logos out of the essence of God — the orthodox view of his time — but also the very concept of a generation out of the essence of God, even without its being eternal — the view held previously by the Apologists — substituting for it a creation out of nothing.

Third, this address of the Demiurge to the traditional deities in the *Timaeus* again could not have been the source of the Arians' explanation for the need of an intermediary in the creation of the world. In the *Timaeus*, the reason why mortal beings had to be created by an intermediary and not directly by the Demiurge was, in the words of the Demiurge himself, as follows: "If through me these came into existence and receive life, they would be equal to gods" [30] and hence immortal like them. The explanation as quoted in the name of the Arians reads that the created nature "could not participate (μετασχεῖν) in the unmixed (ἀκράτου) hand of the Father and in His workmanship" [31] or that "the other creatures could

---

[28] Cf. Athanasius, *Orat. cont. Arian.* II, 24 (PG 26, 200A): "This they not only have said, but they have dared to put in writing, namely, Eusebius, Arius, and Asterius who sacrificed"; *De Decret.* 8 (PG 25, 437A): "This is what Asterius the Sacrificer has written, and Arius has transcribed and bequeathed to his friends."

[29] *Timaeus* 40 E–41 A.

[30] *Ibid.* 41 C.

[31] *Orat. cont. Arian.* II, 24 (PG 26, 200A).

not endure (βαστάξαι) the work of the unmixed hand of the Ingenerate." [32] Neither in phraseology nor in content is there any similarity between the statement in the *Timaeus* and the Arian statements. With regard to phraseology, what is striking in the Arian statements is the expression which literally means "to participate in the . . . hand" and "to endure the . . . hand," and the description of the term "hand" by a term which literally means "unmixed." No suggestion of this phraseology is to be found in the statement in the *Timaeus*. With regard to content, the explanation implied in the Arian statements is that there was a certain unfitness or impropriety for the created natures, which are not unmixed or pure, to be, figuratively speaking, touched by the unmixed or pure hand of God, whereas the explanation given in the *Timaeus* is that the Demiurge did not want the created beings to be immortal like himself.

There is, however, a resemblance, both in phraseology and in content, between these Arian statements and a statement by Philo, in which the latter tries to explain why God had chosen to use ideas or powers as instruments in the creation or, rather, according to my own interpretation of the statement, in the preservation of the world.[33] The Philonic statement reads as follows: "When out of that [shapeless and qualityless matter] God produced all things, He did so without touching (ἐφα-πτόμενος) it himself, since it was not lawful for His nature, happy and blessed as it was, to touch (ψαύειν) indefinite and mixed up (πεφυρμένης) matter, but instead He made full use of the incorporeal powers, well denoted by their name of ideas, to enable each genus to take its appropriate shape." [34]

The resemblance between Philo's not "to touch" and the Arians' not "to participate in the . . . hand" or not "to endure . . . the hand" is quite obvious. Moreover, in the light of this passage of Philo, it may be suggested that the term

[32] *De Decret.* 8 (PG 25, 437A).
[33] Cf. my *Philo*, rev. ed. (Cambridge, Mass., 1948), I, 274ff.
[34] *Spec.* I, 60, 329.

βαστάξαι in the second quotation from Athanasius, which is usually translated by "endure" (Latin: *ferre*), was used in the sense of "touch," which is one of the common senses of that verb. Perhaps also the term μετασχεῖν in the first quotation from Athanasius, which usually means "participate in," was also used in the sense of "to touch," even though no such use of the term is recorded in lexicons, for if the term προσέχειν is sometimes used in the sense of "to touch," why should not also the term μετασχεῖν? There is, too, a resemblance between the statement that it would be unfit and improper for the impure created natures to be touched by the pure hand of God, which is implied in the Arian passages, and the statement that it would be unlawful that God should touch impure matter, which is explicitly expressed in the Philonic passage. Both these statements, that of Philo directly and that of the Arians indirectly, through Philo, reflect the many passages in the Old Testament that make it unlawful for the clean and the holy to touch the unclean and for the unclean to touch the clean and the holy.[35]

As for the meaning of these statements about the unfitness or impropriety or unlawfulness that God should do certain things, we have shown how Philo, with his known conception of God as all-powerful, for whom nothing is impossible, could not have meant by these statements that God, because He was unable to create the world directly, needed intermediaries, and how he could only have meant that God, who to him was not only the creator of the world, but the pedagogue of mankind, by not touching gross matter, wished to set an example before men and to teach them not to defile themselves by anything gross and unclean.[36] This, also, we may assume, is the meaning of the Arian statements.

There are some historians who, indeed, object to these methods of treating the controversy between Arianism and orthodoxy as having its origin in Aristotle or Plato. Thus

[35] Cf. *Philo*, I, 280–281.
[36] Cf. *ibid.*, 280–286, 271–274; II, 128.

Dorner objects to aligning Arians and their opponents as Aristotelians against strict Platonists. He does so, he says, only on the ground that "amongst the teachers of the Church also there were some who received an Aristotelian training." He admits, however, that "the Arians were trained in the Aristotelian dialectic," and that, "on the ground of the empirical feature common to both [Aristotelianism and Arianism]," he recognizes "a relationship between them." [37] Hefele, without discussing whether Arianism had its origin in Aristotle or in Plato, volunteers the opinion that "Philonism . . . seems to have exercised some influence over the development of Arianism," but the Philonic influence which he finds in Arianism is the same as that which Ritter discovered in Plato's *Timaeus*, for he represents Philo as having an exaggerated notion of "the distinction between God and the world," and as considering "the supreme God much too sublime to enter into direct relation with the world and the world . . . too low to bear any direct action of God" and as having, therefore, introduced the Logos for the purpose of serving, "like the created gods of Plato," as an intermediary in the creation of the world.[38] This is a misrepresentation of Philo.

On the whole, it is not historically correct to arrange the Fathers into groups, to dress them up in the uniform of the Academy or Lyceum or the Porch, to march them under the school banner of Plato or of Aristotle or of the Stoics, and to make them sing their school song. The Fathers did not regard themselves as followers of the various schools of Greek thought. They did not think in terms of contrasts between the different systems within philosophy; they thought only in terms of a contrast between Scripture and philosophy. Within philosophy itself there were to them only right doctrines, which were in agreement with Scripture, and wrong

[37] I. A. Dorner, *The Person of Christ*, I, 2 (Edinburgh, 1859), note 50, pp. 499–500; (German, I, Stuttgart, 1845, 859). Cf. Heinrich Voigt, *Die Lehre des Athanasius von Alexandrien* (Bremen-Leipzig, 1861), p. 193 n.

[38] K. J. von Hefele, *Conciliengeschichte*, §19.

doctrines, which were in disagreement with Scripture, though on certain doctrines they found some philosophers were more often in agreement with Scripture than others. In battling with each other, the Fathers did not battle as partisans of certain opposing schools of Greek philosophy; they battled only as advocates of opposing interpretations of Scripture. Their opposing interpretations of Scripture, however, were sometimes influenced by philosophic considerations or supported by philosophic arguments, and in this way, therefore, it happens that the Fathers are found occasionally to have aligned themselves with certain philosophic attitudes on certain particular problems. In the case of the Arian controversy, the difference of opinion, in so far as it indirectly reflects philosophic considerations, reflects not the controversy between Plato and Aristotle, but a difference in the interpretation of the Platonic theory of ideas. Directly and primarily it is a difference in the interpretation of texts in the New Testament.[39]

The main New Testament texts involved in this controversy are the opening verses in the Gospel According to John, "In the beginning was the Logos, and the Logos was with God, and the Logos was God . . . All things were made through him." [40] It is not necessary for us to reopen here the discussion of whether or not John follows Philo, or of whether or not he understood Philo properly, or of whether or not, if he understood him properly, he deliberately differed with him. Suffice it to say that beginning with the Apologists, in the middle of the second century, the Fathers began to fill out the skeleton-like outline of the Logos as found in the Prologue of John with details borrowed from the writings of Philo.

Two main points characterize this interpretation. First, the Logos, as in Philo, became the place of an intelligible world,

[39] Certain parts of the discussion which follows have been dealt with by me more fully in *The Philosophy of the Church Fathers*, I (Cambridge, Mass., 1956), to be referred to henceforth as *Church Fathers*.

[40] John I: 1–3.

consisting of ideas and constituting a plan by which the world was created, and, accordingly, John's statement that "all things were made through him" assumed that meaning or that additional meaning. In the New Testament itself there is no indication that the Logos or the pre-existent Christ, which is meant by the Logos, reflected, even remotely, the Platonic ideas. Second, the Logos had two stages of existence, first from eternity as a thought of God; then beginning with the creation of the world, and prior to it, prior, of course, not in a temporal sense, as a real personal being existing with God and by the side of God, as it were. This twofold-stage theory may be considered as an attempt on the part of Philo to harmonize in Plato those statements where the ideas are spoken of as eternal with those where the ideas are spoken of as having been made by God.

But, while following Philo on these two points, the Fathers from the very beginning differed with him on two other points. First, the Logos to them came into being not, as in Philo, by an act of creation out of nothing, but rather by a process of generation out of the essence of God. He was begotten, not made or created. Second, the Logos was not, as in Philo, merely divine, but he was God, equal with God in divinity. This latter belief followed as a corollary from the conception of the Logos as begotten of God, and is based on the philosophical principle that in natural generation the progeny is of the same species as the begetter, which is expressed by Aristotle in his statement that "man begets man." [41] This explanation, which may already have been in the mind of the philosophically trained Apologists, is explicitly advanced later by Augustine in a passage where, arguing against the Arian Maximinus in support of the traditional belief in the divinity of the Logos, he quotes Aristotle's statement that "man begets man," adding thereto his own words, "and dog dog." [42] But these Apologists, though they all believed in the twofold-stage

[41] *Metaphysica* VII, 7, 1032a, 23–24; cf. IX, 8, 1049b, 27–29.
[42] *Cont. Maximin.* II, 6.

theory of the Logos, still differed among themselves as to the interpretation of John's words, "In the beginning was the Logos . . . and the Logos was with God." Some took it to refer to the first stage of existence, and interpreted the verse to mean that from eternity the Logos was in the thought of God and then was generated and hence was with God. Others interpreted it to mean that in the beginning, when God was about to create heaven and earth, the Logos came into being and was with God. Incidentally, it means that in this latter interpretation the Greek term ἦν in John was taken not in the sense of "was," but rather in the sense of "became" (ἐγένετο) or "came to be," a sense which could be justified as a Hebraized term.[43] In the Septuagint the Greek word "to be" (εἶναι) also means "to become," "to be made" (fieri).

This conception of the Logos was held consistently and uniformly by all the Fathers until Irenaeus and Origen. Those two Fathers rejected the twofold-stage theory and substituted for it a single-stage theory. The Logos was eternally generated by God. Irenaeus introduced it out of pure opposition to the Gnostics. Origen introduced it on philosophic grounds. It happened that Origen was a disciple of Ammonius Saccas, whose teachings we may presume are those we find in the work of another of his disciples, Plotinus. Now Ammonius was born a Christian. We may therefore assume that originally, like all Christians of his time, he followed Philo's interpretation of Platonic ideas, and believed in a twofold-stage theory. Then, when he gave up Christianity, he abandoned the twofold-stage theory of the Logos as well as the use of the term Logos, substituting for it the conception of an eternally generated Nous. Neoplatonism, as we find it in the *Enneads*, is thus to be regarded as a paganized version of Philonic philosophy. As in this new version of Philonism, Nous, which takes the place of the Logos in Philo, was eternally generated from God, the Logos, which, being a Christian term, was retained by Origen, was made by him eternally

[43] Cf. *Church Fathers*, pp. 197–198.

generated from God, for an eternally generated Logos appealed to him as being more compatible with the Christian conception of the Logos as God. The transition from the Apologists to Origen in Christianity thus corresponds to the transition from the Philonic to the Plotinian interpretation of Plato in the general history of philosophy. But though Irenaeus and Origen had introduced the single-stage theory, certain Fathers still continued to believe for some time in the twofold-stage theory. In the fourth century these two theories still existed side by side.

This is the status of the doctrine of the Trinity, among the orthodox Fathers by the time of Arius. Two theories, the single-stage and twofold-stage theories, existed side by side. Both recognized the principle of generation. To both theories the Logos was generated out of the essence of God, though to only the single-stage theory was it eternally generated, and to both theories the Logos was God.

It is here that Arius comes in with his new view. The starting point is his adoption of Philo's twofold-stage theory of the Logos. The manner in which he expresses himself in favor of the twofold-stage theory is strongly reminiscent of the language of Philo and the Apologists. He begins by saying: "God was alone ($\mu\acute{o}\nu os$), and the Word as yet was not." [44] This reflects two sources. First, it reflects Philo's comment upon the verse, "It is not good that man should be alone," [45] as meaning that it is good that God should be alone, thus establishing the principle of the unity of God.[46] Second, it reflects Hippolytus' further interpretation of the same verse as meaning that, before the generation of the Logos, God was alone, thus establishing the twofold-stage theory.[47]

Then Arius continues: "When wishing ($\theta\epsilon\lambda\acute{\eta}\sigma as$) to create ($\delta\eta\mu\iota o\nu\rho\gamma\hat{\eta}\sigma a\iota$) us, He made a certain one, and named him

[44] Athanasius, *Orat. cont. Arian.* I, 5 (PG 26, 21A).
[45] Gen. 2:18.
[46] *Leg. All.* II, 1, 1–2.
[47] *Cont. Haer. Noeti* 10.

Word and Wisdom and Son, that he might form us by means of Him." [48] This reflects Philo's statement that "When God willed (βουληθεὶς) to create this visible world, he first modelled (προεξετύπου) the intelligible world," [49] which has "no other place than the divine Logos," [50] and by the Logos he created the world. The Logos thus to Arius, as to Philo, entered upon its second stage of existence.

These two stages of existence are described by Arius as two Wisdoms or Logoi. The Logos or Wisdom of the first stage is further described as being proper (ἰδίαν) to God and coexistent with Him"; the Logos or Wisdom in the second stage is described by him primarily as "the Son" and is said to be named "Wisdom and Logos" only because of its participation in the Wisdom or the Logos of the first stage.[51] This corresponds exactly to the Philonic view, according to which the Logos, and the powers or ideas it contains, is, in its first stage, only a property of God, and becomes a real being, called "the first-born Son of God," only upon its entrance into its second stage.[52] Then, of course, following both Philo and John, who described the Logos as an instrument by which God created the world, Arius says that "the Unoriginate made the Son an origin of the things generated." [53]

The terms used by Arius as a description of the Logos' coming into existence are, as quoted by Athanasius from his *Thalia*, various forms of the term γίνομαι, "to become," "to be born," and ποιέω, "to make." [54] Arius himself in his letter to Eusebius, Bishop of Nicomedia, describes his conception of the Son's coming into existence indiscriminately by such terms as "he was begotten (γεννηθῇ), or created (κτισθῇ), or singled out (ὁρισθῇ), or established (θεμελιωθῇ)." [55] And

[48] Athanasius, *Orat. cont. Arian.* I, 5 (PG 26, 21A).
[49] *Opif.* 2, 16.
[50] *Ibid.* 5, 20.
[51] Athanasius, *Orat. cont. Arian.* I, 5 (PG 26, 21A,B).
[52] Cf. *Philo*, I, 231, 234; II, 126ff.
[53] Athanasius, *De Synod.* 15 (PG 26, 705D).
[54] Athanasius, *Orat. cont. Arian.* I, 5.
[55] Theodoret, *Hist. Eccl.* I, 4 (PG 82, 912B); ed. L. Parmentier: I, 5, 4.

the Logos himself, because he is he through whom all things were made, is described by Arius as "under-worker (ὑπουργός) and assistant (βοηθός)," [56] or as "co-worker (συνεργός) or under-worker." [57] This reflects Philo's use of the term συνεργοί, "co-workers," as a description of the powers, contained in the Logos, in their capacity of agents commissioned by God to create the body and the irrational soul of man.[58]

In the description of Arianism so far there is nothing with which fault could be found on the ground or orthodoxy. By itself the twofold-stage theory of the Logos, which was adopted by Arius, would not have been regarded by his contemporaries as heretical. The Apologists held the twofold-stage theory and were never attacked for it.[59] Zeno of Verona, toward the end of the fourth century, reasserted the twofold-stage theory, without ever being declared unorthodox.[60] In fact, while the twofold-stage theory somehow disappeared, it was never anathematized.[61] Neither would Arius' failure to use the term "generated" or "begotten" exclusively as a description of the Logos' coming into existence have been, by itself, heretical, for the orthodox Fathers, too, at that time had not used the term "generated" or "begotten" exclusively.[62] Nor, again, was there in Arius' statement that, when God was alone, "the Word as yet was not," if taken by itself, anything that could have aroused opposition, for a similar statement was made also by Tertullian,[63] and it aroused no opposition.

Similarly Arius' use of the term ὑπουργός, "under-worker," or βοηθός, "assistant," or συνεργός, "co-worker," as a description of the Logos, would not by itself have been considered by his contemporaries as heretical. The term ὑπουργός has been used by Theophilus as a description of the Logos,[64] with-

---

[56] De Decret. 8 (PG 25, 437A).

[57] Athanasius, Orat. cont. Arian. II, 29 (PG 26, 208B).

[58] Opif. 24, 75; Conf. 35, 179; De Fuga 13, 68–70; cf. Philo, I, 269–270, 272–274.

[59] Cf. Church Fathers, pp. 192–198.

[60] Ibid., p. 197.

[61] Ibid., pp. 217–219.

[62] Ibid., pp. 252–253.

[63] Ibid., pp. 195, 217, 586 n. 53.

[64] Ad. Autol. II, 10.

out causing any damage to his reputation. Then there is a term similar to those three terms used by Arius, namely, the term σύμβουλος, "counsellor," which was used by both Theophilus [65] and Clement of Alexandria,[66] without, again, causing any damage to their reputations. Even Athanasius himself, who attacks the Arians for the use of these terms,[67] describes the Logos as a "living counsel (ζῶσα βουλή),"[68] though it would seem to be in direct opposition to the verse, "For who hath known the mind of the Lord, or who hath been his counsellor?"[69] But, as we have suggested,[70] the Logos or the preexistent Christ was called "co-worker" or "under-worker" or "assistant" or "counsellor" or "counsel" not in the sense that God was in need of his help or counsel, but in the sense that he was initiated in the knowledge of God and was called by God to cooperate with Him in His work of creation. Philo himself, who describes the powers as "co-workers," found in his use of this term no opposition to his statement that God created the world "without any helper (παράκλητος)."[71] In Philo, the use of "co-workers" was for the purpose of setting an example to mankind.

It is, therefore, not his adoption of the twofold-stage theory, nor his use of the term "created" by the side of the term "generated," nor his use of the expression "the Word as yet was not," nor his description of the Logos as "underworker" or "assistant" or "co-worker," but rather what he meant by all this, that has brought about his anathematization. What he meant by all this is quite explicitly expressed by him in his statement that the Logos came into existence "out of things that were not (ἐξ οὐκ ὄντων)."[72] This was the gravamen of his theory: the Logos was not generated from the es-

[65] Ibid. II, 22.
[66] Stromata VII, 2.7 (PG 9, 412A).
[67] Cf. De Decret. 8; Orat. cont. Arian II, 29.
[68] Orat. cont. Arian. II, 64 (PG 26, 457B).
[69] Rom. 11:34, quoting Isa. 40:13 (LXX).
[70] Cf. Church Fathers, p. 193 n. 12.
[71] Opif. 6, 23.
[72] Athanasius, Orat. cont. Arian. I, 5 (PG 26, 21A).

sence of God, but was created *ex nihilo*. As a corollary of this view, the Son or Logos was no longer God; he was only divine. This is what roused opposition. And the opposition expressed itself in the statements in the Nicene creed that maintain that the pre-existent Christ was "begotten (γεννη-θέντα) of the Father"; "of the substance (οὐσίας) of the Father"; "begotten (γεννηθέντα), not made (ποιηθέντα)." It also expresses itself in the anathematism of those who say "Before He was begotten (γεννηθῆναι) He was not" and "He came into existence (ἐγένετο) out of things that were not (ἐξ οὐκ ὄντων)." Note the indiscriminate use of the terms γεννη-θῆναι and ἐγένετο, by which it describes the view of those who say that the Son was created out of nothing. Note also that, in its positive statement, the Creed insists only that the generation was out of the essence of God; it does not insist, that is to say, openly, that the generation itself was an eternal process. There is no anathema here, as there never was afterwards, of the twofold-stage theory of the Apologists, though the conception of eternal generation was tacitly adopted as the general Christian view.[73]

But what was the motive behind this Arian adoption of the Philonic conception of the Logos?

Primarily it was a religious motive. It was an attempt to preserve two principles which Arius thought were fundamental to Christianity.

First, it was the principle of the unity of God in its absolute sense as defined by Philo on behalf of Judaism. This principle of the unity of God, as proclaimed in the Old Testament in the verse, "Hear, O Israel: the Lord our God, the Lord is one," is reaffirmed by Jesus, when he said that it constituted the first of all commandments.[74] It is reaffirmed also by Paul in his oft-repeated statements that "there is no God but one." [75] Now in the Old Testament the unity of God means only an external, numerical unity. It is in opposition to polytheism.

---

[73] Cf. *Church Fathers*, pp. 217–218.
[74] Mark 12:19.   [75] I Cor. 8:4; cf. 8:5; Eph. 4:3–6.

There is no speculation there about what philosophers would call internal unity, logical or metaphysical unity. But Philo extended and deepened the scriptural meaning of the unity of God; it was to exclude any kind of logical or metaphysical divisibility, such as divisibility into two substances, even when inseparable from each other, or divisibility into matter and form, or divisibility into genus and species. The unity of God meant absolute unity.

Christianity rejected this Philonic conception of the unity of God. God indeed is one, but one only in an external or numerical unity. Internally God consisted of three inseparable individual substances, called hypostases or persons. And the philosophers among the Fathers tried to justify this interpretation of the unity of God on philosophic grounds. The entire problem of the Trinity was a search to find a philosophic interpretation of this relative conception of the unity of God. Arius, like many other Christians before him, was dissatisfied with this revised conception of the unity of God. He, therefore, readopted the Philonic conception.

This is the first religious principle which led him to his heresy.

The second religious principle is the biblical, and especially the post-biblical, Jewish conception of God in his relation to the world, and the fulness thereof, as an artisan and not as a begetter. Early Semitic mythology, like Greek mythology and all other mythologies, conceived of God as begetter, bringing other gods and men, and the world as a whole, into existence after the manner of animal procreation. Traces of this mythological conception of God as begetter have survived in the Hebrew Scripture. But the entire history of the religion of Israel as depicted in Scripture itself is an attempt to eradicate all mythological conceptions of God. God is a creator of things; He is not a begetter of things. The few references in the Hebrew Scripture to angels as "the sons of God" [76] may be survivals of this old Semitic mythology. But in the

[76] Gen. 6:2,4; Job 1:6, 38:7; Dan. 3:25 (Son of God).

Hebrew Scripture they came to be used in the sense of "heavenly" or "unearthly" or "supernal" beings, and in post-biblical Jewish literature, Apocalyptic as well as rabbinic, angels are explicitly described as created by God, like anything else. And in Philo the Logos, ideas, intelligible world, and powers are all described as made and created, not begotten by God.

Christianity restored the conception of God as begetter. This is emphasized with great clearness by every one of the Fathers, beginning with Justin. One of the Fathers, Theophilus, even uses the expression "within His own bowels" [77] as a description of the Logos before its generation.

What Arius did was to return to the original Scriptural and post-Scriptural Jewish conception of God as artisan.

But there is also a philosophic aspect to the problem. This controversy between Arianism and catholic Christianity as to whether God is an artisan or a begetter has its parallel in two contrasting conceptions of God in Greek philosophy. The four theistic systems in Greek philosophy, the Platonic, the Aristotelian, the Stoic, and the Neoplatonic, fall into two groups. The Platonic and Aristotelian theism is anti-mythological, considering God as artisan, for Plato, whenever he expresses himself in his own language, speaks of God as handicraftsman ($\delta\eta\mu\iota\upsilon\rho\gamma\acute{o}s$),[78] as a maker ($\pi o\iota\eta\tau\acute{\eta}s$),[79] or as a maker of something natural ($\phi\upsilon\tau o\upsilon\rho\gamma\acute{o}s$),[80] and Aristotle speaks of God only as the cause of the motion of the world.[81] The Stoic and the Neoplatonic theism is mythological, that is to say, a rationalization of mythology, conceiving of God as a begetter. Philosophically, therefore, the Arian theism is of the Platonico-Aristotelian type, whereas the orthodox theism is of the Stoico-Neoplatonic type.

This is as much as we have to say on the pre-existent Christ or Logos of Arius.

[77] Theophilus, *Ad Autol.* II, 10.
[78] *Timaeus* 41 A.
[79] *Republic* X, 597 D.
[80] *Ibid.*
[81] *Physica* VIII, 1, 252b, 5–6; 4, 256a 2–3; *Metaphysica* XII, 7.

Let us now take up the Christology of Arius.

With his denial of the divinity of the Logos, it was only logical for Arius to deny that in Jesus there was a divine nature beside a human nature. The Logos, indeed, was made or became flesh, and this being made or becoming flesh is the incarnation of the Logos in the man Jesus, but since the Logos was not God there was no divine nature in Jesus. We should, therefore, expect him to say that Jesus was "a man" or "a mere man" or "a man akin to all" or "an ordinary man" — descriptions used by Theodotus of Byzantium [82] and Paul of Samosata [83] in expressing their denial of the divinity of the born Christ. No such descriptions, however, are reported in the name of Arius. But a description similar to these is attributed to him and to one of his followers. The so-called "Easterns" in their criticism of Cyril of Alexandria refer to Arius and Eunomius as believing in "one nature," [84] that is to say, as believing that in Jesus there was only a human nature, which is the same as believing that Jesus was a mere man.

Now the expression "one nature," which the Arians themselves did not use, but could have used, was actually used by the Apollinarians, though in a different sense, for, while to Arius the one nature was the human nature, to Apollinaris the one nature was the divine nature. And so this difference between Arius and Apollinaris may serve us here as a point of transition from our discussion of Arianism to a discussion of Apollinarianism.

In his conception of the pre-existent Christ, Apollinaris is orthodox and shares with orthodoxy in the opposition to Arianism. The Logos is generated and not created; and it is eternally generated, and is equal with God the Father in divinity. But in his Christology, in his conception of the born Christ,

---

[82] Hippolytus, *Refut. Omn. Haer.* VII, 35, 2; X, 23, 1; Philaster, *Liber de Haeresibus* L.

[83] Eusebius, *Hist. Eccl.* V, 27, 2; Theodore of Raythu, *De Incarnatione* (PG 91, 1485D).

[84] *Apologeticus pro XII Capitibus contra Orientales* IV, (PG 76, 333B).

he is opposed to orthodoxy. As against orthodoxy, he maintains, like Arianism, that Jesus had only one nature; not two natures. But then, against Arianism, he maintains that that one nature was a divine nature.

The origin of his denial of a human nature to Jesus, as explained by Apollinaris himself, is based upon his own application of rational investigation or logical reasoning to what he considered fundamental Christian principals — the very same method which, as may be recalled, the Arians have been accused of using and of having been led thereby into heresy. The old traditional view of two natures in Jesus, which he was combating, was regarded by him as being based only on faith, and, like all doctrines which are based only on faith, he maintains, must be examined by reason to see whether it is consistent with fundamental Christian principles, for there is always the danger, he says, that certain beliefs, which are accepted without examination, have been adulterated by heathenish or Jewish opinions.[85] The fundamental Christian principles with which, according to him, one is to start his investigation in the doctrine of the person of Christ, and from which one is to derive, by the method of logical reasoning, a true and valid conclusion are two: first, God alone can be a savior; second, Jesus was sent down to be a savior. Both these principles he undoubtedly assumed to be genuinely Christian principles, without any mixture of false heathenish opinion or of wrong contemporary Jewish opinion. In support of the principle that only God can be a savior, he would undoubtedly have pointed to a combination of such Old Testament verses as, "A just God and a savior; there is none beside me," [86] and "I am the Lord thy God . . . and beside me there is no savior," [87] and such New Testament verses as, "My spirit hath rejoiced in God my savior," [88] "By the commandment

---

[85] Gregory of Nyssa, *Adv. Apollinarium, Antirrheticus* 4 (PG 45, 1130C). Cf. A. Neander, *Allgemeine Geschichte der christlichen Religion und Kirche*, II, 2 (Hamburg, 1829), pp. 912–915 (Eng. tr., 12th Am. ed., II, 484–486).
[86] Isa. 45:21.
[87] Hos. 13:4.
[88] Luke 1:47.

of God our savior," [89] "The living God, who is the savior of all men," [90] and "To the only wise God our savior." [91] In support of the principle that Jesus was sent down as savior he would have pointed to the many New Testament verses where Jesus is spoken of as savior, such as, for instance, "For unto you is born this day in the city of David a Savior, which is Christ the Lord"; [92] "For we know that this is indeed the Savior of the world." [93]

The rational investigation or logical method of reasoning by which he seeks to establish on the basis of these two Christian principles that Jesus has only one nature, the same as the nature of God, may be set down in the form of a syllogism as follows:

> None is a savior but who is God;
> Jesus is a savior;
> Therefore, Jesus is God.

And so Apollinaris came to describe Jesus as having only "one nature," a divine nature.

Besides the expression "one nature," which is used by both Arius and Apollinaris, though in different senses, there is another view which they share. Both of them deny that Jesus had a rational soul, but, more than that, both of them started also with a denial that Jesus had an irrational soul, then changed their minds and endowed him with an irrational soul, denying him only a rational soul. The question before us, therefore, is twofold: First, why did they deny Jesus a rational soul? Second, why did they first deny him also an irrational soul and then change their minds about it?

Various explanations have been given, both on behalf of the Arians and on behalf of the Apollinarians, for their denial of a rational soul to Jesus. We shall forgo a discussion of any of these explanations, and shall try to suggest, on behalf of

---

[89] 1 Tim. 1: 1; cf. 2:3; Tit. 1:3, 2:10, 3:4.
[90] 1 Tim. 4:10.
[91] Jude 25.

[92] Luke 2:11.
[93] John 4:42.

the Arians as well as on behalf of the Apollinarians, explanations which involve certain philosophic considerations.

On behalf of the Arians, we suggest that their denial of a
rational soul in Jesus was a logical consequence of their adoption of the Philonic conception of the Logos as a being created
by God, and hence as not being God.

In Philo, the pre-existent Logos is a sort of incorporeal
rational soul like the Holy Spirit,[94] and it is sometimes called
by him "the mind above us," just as the human rational soul
is called by him "the mind within us." [95] But, unlike the Holy
Spirit, which, according to Philo, occasionally enters the
body of man as in the case of the prophet during his prophetic
experience,[96] the Logos, according to him, never enters the
body of man, though it enters the body of the physical world
as a whole as an immanent Logos, corresponding to what
Plato and the Stoics call the soul or mind of the world, terms
which Philo never applies to his immanent Logos.[97] But, while
the Logos itself does not enter the body of man, it is represented in the body of man by its copy, namely, the rational
soul in man; for the rational soul in man, or the human mind,
is a copy of the idea of the mind contained in the Logos or,
as Philo sometimes says, a copy of the Logos; wherefore, in
contrast to "the archetypal Logos above us," he describes the
rational soul as "the copy of it which we possess." [98]

But Arius, though he accepted the Philonic conception of
the pre-existent Logos and also the Philonic conception of the
rational soul in man as being a copy of the Logos, still clung
to the Christian conception of the incarnation of the Logos
in Jesus. Thus, the Logos itself, according to Arius, entered
into the body of Jesus, just as according to Philo, it entered
into the body of the world; so, since the Logos itself was in
the body of Jesus, there was no need for its copy, the rational
soul, to be there. The position of the Logos in Jesus, according

[94] Cf. *Philo*, II, 31–32, 45–46.
[95] *Heres*. 48, 236.
[96] Cf. *Philo*, II, 32–33.
[97] Cf. *ibid*. I, 324–332.
[98] *Heres*. 48, 230 and 233.

to Arius, is analogous to the position of the Holy Spirit in the prophet, according to Philo. To Philo, the Holy Spirit in the prophet takes the place of the rational soul; [99] to Arius, the Logos in Jesus similarly takes the place of the rational soul.

On behalf of Apollinaris, we suggest that his denial of a rational soul in Jesus is due to what he himself would describe as the application of logical reasoning to what he believed to be a fundamental Christian principle. The fundamental Christian principle with which he started was the belief, which he has already established to his own satisfaction, that in Jesus there was no human nature; there was in him only one nature, a divine nature. The logical reasoning which he applied to this fundamental Christian principle started with another principle, which he again considered fundamentally Christian, namely, that the rational soul of every human being, like the rational soul of Adam, is created by God and is breathed by God, like a "breath of life," into every human being, who, like Adam, is in his body "dust of the ground," and it is this combination of the "dust of the ground" and the rational soul, called "breath of life," that constitutes the human nature in man, which is called in Scripture "a living soul"; [100] all of which means that anybody without a human nature is without a rational soul. Combining these two principles, considered by him to be fundamental Christian principles, he reasoned logically as follows:

All those who are without a human nature
    are without a rational soul;
Jesus is without a human nature;
Therefore, Jesus is without a rational soul.

This is how we may explain on behalf of both Arius and Apollinaris why they denied a rational soul in Jesus.

No explanation, however, has so far been given, on behalf of either Arius or Apollinaris, as to why each changed his mind by first denying in Jesus both an irrational and rational

[99] Cf. *Philo*, II, 28–30.   [100] Cf. Gen. 2:7.

soul and then denying in him only a rational soul, and it seems strange that such a change should have taken place in the minds of both of them. Had they any reason for first denying to Jesus an irrational soul and then granting him one? Or are we to assume that they had no reason for their change of mind, but acted only as if they were shopping for a Christmas present for the holy child Jesus, and, after debating with themselves whether or not he could use an irrational soul, for no reason at all first decided he could get along without one, then bethought themselves further and decided to get him one anyhow? But no student of the history of Christianity, to our mind, should assume that those who were engaged in the formulation of its doctrines — especially the Fathers of the Church — ever said anything without good reason; consequently, when no reason for what they happened to say is furnished by the Fathers themselves, we must try to see whether we cannot discover one.

In the matter before us, we may suggest, the reason is to be found in the philosophic problem whether the irrational faculties in man have their origin in an irrational soul, which is corporeal in its essence and inseparable from the human body, or whether they emerge out of the rational, incorporeal, and separable soul in the course of its degeneration as a result of its union with the body. I shall not here go into the history of the problem, which I discuss fully in the as yet unpublished Volume II of *The Philosophy of the Church Fathers*. Suffice it to say here that the problem was one of which the Fathers were conscious, and which was debated by them. Now if we assume that there is an irrational soul, apart from the rational soul, one that is inseparable from the body, then, of course, even if it be assumed that Jesus had no rational soul, he would still have an irrational soul. On the other hand, if we assume that there is no irrational soul apart from a soul which is rational, then, with the denial of a rational soul in Jesus, there would also be a denial of an irrational soul in him. The debate which both Arius and Apollinaris seem to have had with themselves as to whether or not Jesus had an irrational soul, and their change of mind from a denial to an affirmation of an irrational soul in him, was therefore a vacillation between two philosophic positions on the question of the nature of the irrational soul. Thus their change of mind was really a change from one philosophic position to another. Philosophers, as we know, have a right to vacillate and to change their minds.

There is one more topic which I should like to discuss in connection with Apollinaris. By his denial to Jesus of a rational soul, which constitutes the human nature, Apollinaris concluded that Jesus had no human nature. Thus we should expect that by his ultimate decision to endow Jesus with an irrational soul, which constitutes the animal nature, he would endow him with an animal nature. The question may therefore be raised whether by denying in Jesus a human nature he meant also to deny in him an animal nature, which is part of the human nature, or whether he meant thereby to deny in him only a human nature, and not an animal nature. The question is not discussed by Apollinaris directly and, as far as I know, it has never been raised by students of Apollinarianism. But in at least nine passages in the fragments of his writings, Apollinaris happens to deal with the irrationally animate body of Jesus. In two of these passages he seems purposely to avoid ascribing to the irrationally animate body of Jesus a "nature." In one passage, however, he does ascribe to it a "nature," and in another an "ousia" which has the same meaning as "nature." But this is offset by still another passage, where he says that it has "not a proper nature" and "not a nature by itself." What he does quite clearly ascribe to the irrationally animate body of Jesus is a "quality" or "property." [101] The general conclusion one may derive from these passages is that, while the irrationally animate body of Jesus has no "nature," it has a "quality" or "property."

What is the basis of this distinction between "nature" and

[101] Cf. *Church Fathers*, pp. 440–441.

"quality" or "property"? The basis, I think, is again to be found in ancient Greek philosophy, or rather in ancient Greek chemistry — a science drawn upon by all the Fathers in their discussion of the Incarnation.[102]

In ancient Greek philosophy or chemistry the following question is raised. What happens when two or more things, whether solids or liquids or gases, are combined? Aristotle, the Stoics, and Alexander Aphrodisiensis discuss this question. We shall use here only Aristotle, who says that it all depends upon the nature of the combination. Sometimes the combination is only a composition (σύνθεσις), in which the component parts remain unchanged. Sometimes it is a mixture (μίξις, κρᾶσις), in which the resultant is a tertium quid, something new, unlike either one of the constituent parts; but these constituent parts are not destroyed: the resultant is resolvable into them. The Stoics add another kind of combination, which they call confusion (σύγχυσις), illustrated by the example of the tetrapharmacon, which consists of wax, fat, pitch, and resin. The resultant in a confusion is something new, which is not resolvable into its constituent parts.

But then Aristotle describes a combination, which is neither composition, nor mixtures, nor confusion — a combination of two things of unequal power, one of which is active and the other passive. It is illustrated by the example of the combination of a drop of wine with 10,000 gallons of water, or of tin with bronze. In this kind of combination, says Aristotle, the stronger element remains intact, whereas the weaker element is changed. It is, however, not destroyed. What survives of the weaker element is, he says, some quantity, in the case of the wine, or some quality, in the case of the tin. Aristotle uses no special term to describe this kind of combination. In fact, the Greeks have no word for it. But, on the basis of Aristotle's statement that in this kind of combination the weaker element "changes into that which predominates (εἰς τὸ κρατοῦν)," [103] I have coined the term "predominance," as counterpart to the

[102] Cf. ibid., pp. 372ff.   [103] De Gen. et Corr. I, 10, 328a, 26.

terms "composition," "mixture," and "confusion," and describe this kind of combination as a "union of predominance." [104] It is this Aristotelian conception of "predominance" that, I believe, is reflected in Apollinaris' contention that in the union of the irrational soul with the Logos, the Logos retains its nature, but the irrational soul does not retain its nature; it retains only its quality or property. That is to say, while indeed Jesus had only one nature, the divine nature, the nature of the Logos which was incarnate in him, his body still retained the property of its irrational animal soul in that it could experience the suffering common to all bodies that have animal souls. If I am right in this interpretation of Apollinaris, we have in him an answer to an objection raised by certain Fathers against his doctrine. Both Gregory of Nazianzus [105] and Gregory of Nyssa [106] argued that Apollinaris' denial of a human nature would lead to Theopaschitism, that is, to the view that God himself suffered in the crucifixion of Jesus. To this Apollinaris, I imagine, would have answered that by his denial of a human nature in Jesus he did not deny in him an animal property, and it was this animal property in him, and not the divine nature, that experienced the passion of Jesus.

Let us now sum up our conclusions.

Without going into a search for philosophic parallels of single expressions or terms in the fragments of the Arian and Apollinarian writings, we confined ourselves to the philosophical implications of the main issues in their theological systems. We have found that primarily the motive underlying the main issues was religious, but indirectly it involved certain philosophic views.

In the Arian controversy, the question whether the Logos was created *ex nihilo* after it had never been or whether it

[104] Cf. *Church Fathers*, p. 379.
[105] *Epistolae* 202 (PG 37, 333A).
[106] *Adv. Apollinarium, Antirrheticus* 5 (PG 45, 1132B).

was eternally generated from the essence of God, with its resultant question whether the Logos was only divine or whether it was God, involved two philosophic problems: (1) whether to follow the Philonic interpretation of the Platonic ideas, or the interpretation of the Platonic ideas that is identified with the name of Plotinus; (2) whether God's should be conceived of as an efficient cause, after the analogy of an artisan, or whether He should be conceived of also as a material cause after the analogy of a begetter.

In the Apollinarian controversy, Apollinaris' contention that Jesus had only a divine nature was due to his application of logical reasoning to what he considered to be a fundamental Christian principle, namely, that only a God could be a savior.

In both the Arian and the Apollinarian controversy, the denial by both Arius and Apollinaris of a rational soul in Jesus had also a philosophic implication. In the case of Arius, it was a logical consequence of his adoption of Philo's conception of the human mind as a copy of the Logos, coupled with his retention of the Christian doctrine of the incarnation of the Logos. In the case of Apollinaris, it was, again, his application of logical reasoning to what he considered two fundamental Christian principles, namely, (1) the aforementioned principle that only a God could be a savior; (2) that the rational soul constitutes the human nature.

Finally, the vacillation on the part of both Arius and Apollinaris between the denial and the affirmation of an irrational soul in Jesus had its basis in the philosophic problem whether the irrational soul in man is a distinct soul second to the rational soul or whether it is an exuviation of the rational soul.

Arianism was accused by its opponents among the Fathers of being tainted with Jewish monotheism.[107] This is a valid accusation, for Arianism was a revival of the Philonic conception of the absolute unity of God. Arianism was also ac-

---

[107] Cf. Epistle of Alexander of Alexandria in Theodoret of Cyrrhus, *Eccl. Hist.* I, 3 (PG 82, 889B; PG 18, 549B).

cused of being tainted with heathenish polytheism.[108] This
accusation is valid only if aimed at those Arians who, out of
regard for John's statement that "the Logos was God," named
the Logos God, even though it was to them only a created
being.[109] Arius himself, however, interpreted the statement
that "the Logos was God" to mean only that it was divine.[110]
Apollinarianism, as far as I know, was never called by its opponents either a Judaistic heresy or a heathenish heresy. There
is no assurance, however, I imagine, that historians who see in
every mention of the term "savior" in the New Testament the
influence of pagan mysteries may not someday raise the question whether in Apollinarianism, with its insistence that only
a god can be a savior, there is not the recrudescence of that
old pagan influence. But this would not be a subject for historical investigation; it would be a subject for metahistorical
speculation.

[108] *Ibid.*
[109] Cf. Athanasius, *Orat. cont. Arian.* III, 16 (PG 26, 353C).
[110] *Ibid.* I, 6 (21Df).

6

ST. AUGUSTINE AND THE PELAGIAN CONTROVERSY *

OF the many problems involved in the controversy between Augustine and Pelagius in the early part of the fifth century I shall deal here this morning only with one problem, the problem of free will, and of the several aspects of this problem I shall deal only with one, its philosophical aspect.

To Greek philosophers, human action is the resultant of a conflict of forces. Man is conceived by them as being constantly pulled by two opposite forces, called emotion and reason, and at every turn of his life man is faced with the problem of deciding whether to follow the one or the other. But the decision is not his. It is made for him by the relative strength of these two forces, and the strength of these forces is determined by nature, for man is part of nature and is governed by its laws. But what are the laws of nature? Greek philosophers, because of their belief in the inexorableness of these laws, described them by the mythological term fate. Thus Plato in his *Timaeus* (41e) refers to them as the "fated laws" (νόμοι εἱμαρμένοι) which the Demiurge declared to constitute the nature of the universe, Aristotle in his *Physics* (V, 6, 230a, 32), by implication, refers to generation according to nature (κατὰ φύσιν) as generation determined by fate (εἱμαρμένη), and the Stoics, through many of the fragments which have preserved their teachings, use "nature," and "fate" as synonymous terms.[1] And it was the Stoics who in their doctrine of palingenesis have given the ultimate expression to this conception of human action, for according to this doctrine of an eternally recurrent world-process we are all bound

* Delivered in part at the autumn meeting of the American Philosophical Society, 1958, and in a more expanded form as one of the three Walter Turner Candler Lectures at Emory University, 1959. Published in the *Proceedings of the American Philosophical Society*, 103 (1959): 554–562.
[1] Cf. *Index Verborum* to Arnim's *S.V.F.*, under εἱμαρμένη.

to do what infinite predecessors had done in an infinite succession of worlds before us.

Still all these philosophers speak of freedom of the will and in their discussion of legal responsibility and moral virtue they distinguish between actions done voluntarily and involuntary actions. But free will or choice, according to them, does not mean man's absolutely unlimited power to choose between several alternative actions; it means to them only man's power to choose between alternative actions without external compulsion, even though by his internal nature he has already been determined from eternity to act only in one single way. A man's act is called by them free even if it could not be otherwise, provided only that he was not compelled to do it by some force external to him. Freedom means to act by the necessity of one's own nature, a nature which itself is prefated and predetermined.

This is the relative conception of freedom.

In Palestinian Judaism at the time of the rise of Christianity man was also conceived as being constantly drawn by two opposite forces. These forces were called the good impulse and the evil impulse. But Hellenistic Judaism, through its spokesman Philo, identified these good and evil impulses with what the philosophers called emotion and reason. To both Palestinian and Hellenistic Judaism, however, human action was not the resultant of these two forces; it was the result of the unrestrained choice of the human will. Man indeed is a part of nature, and as a part of nature it often happens that one of these two forces is the stronger. Still it is not always the stronger force that prevails. Man can decide in favor of the weaker force. As expressed by Philo, God has endowed man with part of His own power and freedom, and, just as God who implanted in the world the laws of nature has reserved for himself the right to override these laws of nature and work what is called miracles, so also man has the miraculous power to override the laws of his own nature. Moreover, even when man, because he is part of nature, finds himself powerless to fight the evil force within him, if he only makes an honest effort to do so, he may receive help from God. This is what is called divine grace, a merited or auxiliary kind of grace. Man is therefore asked to pray for this divine help or grace. It is this kind of grace, a merited or auxiliary kind of grace, that was meant when the rabbis prayed that the evil impulse might not have sway over them and that their souls might pursue the divine commandment, or when Philo urged people to offer a prayer to God, petitioning for assistance in their effort to do good. It is also this kind of merited or auxiliary grace that was meant when Jesus instructed his disciples to pray to God to deliver them from "evil" or rather "the evil one" (Matthew 6:13, Luke 11:4), that is, the evil impulse. It was a prayer for divine assistance or grace to overcome the evil impulse, without any implication that by their own effort they had no freedom to overcome him.

This is the conception of absolute freedom of the will.[2]

It is these two conceptions of freedom that the Fathers of the Church were confronted with. Though the earliest Church Fathers, from Aristides to Clement of Alexandria, were all converts to Christianity, coming from a pagan background and trained in pagan philosophy, they all chose to follow the Philonic conception of absolute freedom.

Let us sketch briefly the salient points in their discussion of the problem of freedom. Following Jewish tradition, both Hellenistic and Palestinian, they all begin with the statement that God created Adam free and master over his own will and actions. And because Adam was a free agent, when he fell, it was by his own free will that he fell. Then they all begin to debate whether there were any consequences of that fall. From Jewish tradition they inherited the question whether physical death was a consequence of that fall or not. Most of them said yes, some said no — a difference of opinion the like of which existed also in Judaism. Then, without any

[2] See chapter on "Free Will" in my *Philo*, rev. ed. (Cambridge, Mass., 1948), I, 424–462.

support from Jewish tradition, but as an interpretation of a statement by Paul, there was introduced the view that the sin of Adam itself was transmitted to his descendants. This is the doctrine of original sin. Then, again, from Jewish tradition there was introduced the view that the fall of Adam left a taint or corruption upon the moral character of his descendants. This is the doctrine of original corruption. These two doctrines are sometimes combined by the Church Fathers or identified, but, as they each have a different origin, they should be distinguished from each other and, in fact, some Church Fathers treat of them as if they were two distinct doctrines. What the Fathers before Augustine meant by the original corruption, as may be gathered from their statements about it, is that, by his fall, Adam's own power, as well as the power of his descendants, to resist the evil impulse within them was weakened, so that they became more in need of divine assistance to overcome it. With none of the Fathers did it mean a complete loss of the power of freedom. Man was still free and he was free in two senses. In the struggle between the spirit and the flesh, he still had the power to resist the flesh, even though he was now in greater need of divine grace. And if divine grace was extended to him, he still had the power to resist that grace. When, therefore, the Fathers repeated the Lord's prayer, petitioning God to deliver them from evil or from the evil one, they only asked to help them to make the right choice and to carry out into action the choice they have made by their own free will. Freedom of the will was still absolute.

This was the situation toward the end of the fourth century.

But in 400, Augustine's *Confessions* appeared, which contained the following prayer: "Give what thou commandest, and command what thou wilt." [3] Five years later, as Augustine himself informs us, a Bishop in Rome recited it in the presence of Pelagius.[4] Now, by itself, out of its context, this prayer

[3] *Confessiones* X, 29, 40.   [4] *De Dono Perseverentiae* 20, 53.

could be taken only as a prayer for divine auxiliary grace, without any implication of a denial of free will. But it happens that in the *Confessions*, immediately after the prayer, Augustine wrote his own commentary on it. In that commentary he made it clear that grace did not follow free will, as something merited and auxiliary, but preceded it and created it. A similar view was expressed by him in another work [5] which had appeared about three years prior to the appearance of the *Confessions*. Pelagius evidently knew the true meaning of the prayer, and so the Pelagian controversy started.

In this controversy, Pelagius maintained that there was no loss of free will in the descendants of Adam as a result of the fall. Accordingly, in every man today, as in Adam before the fall, there still abide two impulses, the good and the evil, and every man today, again as Adam before the fall, is free to choose between the two impulses, even when one of them happens to be dominant, for, as he is reported to have said, "newborn infants are in the same condition as Adam was before the fall." [6] Philo similarly had taught that "the soul of an infant . . . has no share in either vice or virtue" [7] or that "by nature all we men, before the reason in us is fully grown, lie in the borderline between vice and virtue, without ever inclining as yet to either side." [8] This is the prevailing view among the Fathers before Augustine, both Greek and Latin.

Defining freedom of choice (*libertas arbitrii*) as consisting "in the capacity (*possibilitas*) of abstaining from sin," [9] Pelagius conceives of this freedom as absolute. Like Philo, who maintains that, even though free will is the "most peculiar possession of God," by His having bestowed it upon His rational creatures, man "has been made to resemble Him," [10]

---

[5] *De Diversis Quaestionibus ad Simplicianum* I, 7 (PL 40, 115).
[6] Augustine, *De Gestis Pelagii* 24 (PL 44, 334).
[7] *Leg. All.* II, 15, 53.
[8] *De Praemiis* 11, 62.
[9] *Contra Julianum Opus Imperfectum* I, 78 (PL 45, 1102).
[10] *Immut.* 10, 47–48.

Pelagius maintains that, even though free will "properly belongs to God," God "has bestowed it upon His creatures" [11] and thereby man has become "emancipated from God." [12] This was also the prevailing view among the Fathers before Augustine. For the purpose of illustration we may cite here a Latin Father, Tertullian. "I find," he says, "that man was by God constituted free master of his own will and power," for "in nothing else does man show more the image and likeness of God" than "in that essence which he derived from God himself, the spiritual, which answered to the form of God, and in the freedom and power of his will," [13] and in support of his belief in free will, like Philo,[14] he quotes the Old Testament verses, "See I have placed before thee this day life and good, and death and evil . . . therefore choose life" (Deut. 30:15,19).

By the same token, man also has absolute power to do good. But as in Philo and the rabbis and the Church Fathers before him, Pelagius draws a distinction between man's freedom of doing evil and his freedom of doing good. In both cases the choice of his will is absolutely free. But in the effectuation of his choice there is a difference. Once man has chosen to do evil, he is left to himself to carry out the decision of his will. God will neither help him nor hinder him. But once man has chosen to do good, and meets with difficulty in carrying out the good decision of his will, God will come to his help. This is Pelagius' conception of grace — a grace which is merited and only auxiliary. As reported in his name by Augustine: "Pelagius says that what is good is more easily (*facilius*) fulfilled if grace assists." [15]

In contradistinction to all this, Augustine maintains that as a result of the corruption produced by the fall of Adam and inherited by his descendants that freedom consisting of the ability to sin or not sin which was possessed by Adam before

[11] *De Gratia Christi* I, 4, 5 (PL 44, 362).
[12] *Contra Julianum Opus Imperfectum* I, 78.
[13] *Adversus Marcionem* II, 5.   [14] *Immut.* 10, 49–50.
[15] *Contra Duas Epistolas Pelagianorum* II, 8, 17 (PL 44, 583).

his fall is no longer possessed by his descendants. Whatever man today does he does it not by his own free choice but by necessity. This view is expressed by him in a variety of ways. In one place, he raises the question, "By what means is it brought about that man is with sin — by the necessity of nature, or by the freedom of choice?" In answer to this he says: "It came by freedom of choice that man was with sin; but a penal corruption (*vitiositas*) closely followed thereon, and out of liberty produced necessity," [16] so that "because the will has sinned, the hard necessity of having sin has pursued the sinner." [17] In another place, he raises again the question, "Can men do anything by the free determination of their own will?" and again his answer is: "Far be it, for it was by the evil use of his free will that man destroyed both it and himself." [18] Man thus both sins and does good not by freedom of choice but by necessity. This necessity is described by Augustine by two terms, one applied to the necessity by which one sins and the other to the necessity by which one refrains from sinning and acts righteously.

As to the necessity by which one sins, Augustine describes it by the term concupiscence, which he identifies with sexual desire and considers it as the source of all sin. He is uncertain whether concupiscence in this sense existed in Adam before the fall or did not exist in him, but he is certain that, if it did exist in him before the fall, it existed in him then in some innocent form and only later was it corrupted by the fall.[19] He is also certain that, as a result of the fall, concupiscence in the descendants of Adam is "a corruption" (*vitium*), which, "like a bad state of health is implanted in man from a corrupt origin, by which corruption," and here Augustine quotes from the New Testament (Gal. 5:17) the words, " 'the flesh lusteth (*concupiscit*, ἐπιθυμεῖ) against the spirit.' " [20] Moreover, this

---

[16] *De Perfectione Institiae Hominis* 4, 9 (PL 44, 295).
[17] *Ibid.* (296).
[18] *Enchiridion* 30 (PL 40, 246).
[19] *Contra Julianum Opus Imperfectum* VI, 22 (PL 45, 1553).
[20] *Contra Julianum* VI, 18, 55 (PL 44, 855).

lusting of the flesh against the spirit cannot be resisted by man, for, he maintains, "the power of good living . . . is not given save by God's grace" [21] and by grace, he goes on to explain, he does not mean merely God's helping man to carry out the decisions of his free will.[22]

There is no statement by any of the Fathers prior to Augustine in which the corruption transmitted by Adam to his descendants as a result of the fall is called concupiscence; unless it be the statement in the *Apocalypse of Moses* that the "poison" (ἰός) with which the serpent infected Eve, and was evidently transmitted to future generations, is called ἐπιθυμία, "concupiscence." [23] But there is no evidence that this statement existed before the time of Augustine or that it was known to him. Nor is there any statement by any of the Fathers before Augustine which identifies the inherited corruption exclusively with sexual desire described by some other term. In fact, Augustine himself does not always use the term concupiscence in a bad sense and in the exclusive sense of sexual desire, for on the basis of such verses as "My soul hath coveted (*concupivit*, ἐπεπόθησεν) to long (*desiderare*, ἐπιθυμῆσαι) for thy justifications, at all times" (Ps. 118/9:20) and "The desire (*concupiscentia*, ἐπιθυμία) of wisdom bringeth to a kingdom" (Wisdom 6:20) and "Thou shalt not covet (*concupisces*, ἐπιθυμήσεις)" (Exod. 20:17) he infers that concupiscences may be either laudable or condemnable.[24] Moreover, of condemnable concupiscences, on the basis of the verse, "For all that is in the world, is the concupiscence of the flesh, the concupiscence of the eyes, and the pride of life, which is not of the Father, but is of the world" (I John 2:16), he infers that the pleasure of the flesh, curiosity, and pride include all sins,[25] and he explicitly explains that "concupiscence of the flesh" in the verse quoted refers to "food" [26] and he

---

[21] *Contra Duas Epistolas Pelagianorum* I, 2, 5 (PL 44, 552).
[22] *Ibid.* I, 2, 6.
[23] Cf. C. Tischendorf, *Apocalypses Apocryphae*, 10–11.
[24] *Enarr. in Psalm.*, Ps. 118, Sermo 8, No. 3.
[25] *Ibid.*, Ps. 8, No. 13 (PL 36, 115).   [26] *Ibid.* (116).

also explicitly uses the expression "the concupiscence of eating and drinking." [27] The reduction of all bad concupiscences to the concupiscence of sex and the identification of sexual concupiscence with the inherited corruption is something new introduced by Augustine into Christian theology.

Still this theological innovation is not without its philosophical background. *Concupiscentia* is one of the Latin terms by which the Greek term ἐπιθυμία is translated in philosophical literature, the other Latin terms being *libido* [28] and *cupiditas*.[29] In Plato the underlying Greek term is used as a description of one of his three parts of the soul and as the opposite of the rational soul.[30] In Aristotle it is used in the technical sense of an irrational appetite.[31] Among the Stoics it is one of the four primary emotions and is again an irrational appetite.[32] Then, in Plato there are the statements that "the concupiscent soul" is the largest part of our soul and "contains bodily pleasures" [33] and that "pleasure is the strongest allurement to evil." [34] In Aristotle there is the statement that "concupiscence is the appetite for what is pleasurable" [35] and also the statement that "the pleasure of coition is more vehement (σφοδροτέρα) [36] than other pleasures, which is reflected in Philo's statement that the pleasures connected with coition are "the most vehement (σφοδρόταται)." [37] All these must have created in the minds of students of philosophy the view that the concupiscence for the most vehement of pleasures, namely, the sexual pleasure, is the strongest allurement to evil. This, we may assume, is how Augustine arrived at his

---

[27] *Confessiones* X, 31, 47.

[28] Cf., for instance, Cicero's Latin translation of the Stoic four principal emotions (*Tusc. Disp.* III, 11, 24; IV, 7, 14; *De Finibus* III, 10, 35).

[29] Cf., for instance, Augustine's Latin translation of the Stoic four principal emotions (*De Civ. Dei* XIV, 5).

[30] *Republic* IV, 435 E–439 E.

[31] *De Anima* III, 10, 433a, 25–26.

[32] Diogenes Laertius, VII, 113.   [34] *Timaeus* 69 D.

[33] *Republic* IV, 442 A.   [35] *De Anima* II, 3, 414b, 5–6.

[36] *De Gen. Animal.* I, 18, 723b, 33, according to the reading in MS. Vat. 261 recorded in Bekker. Other MSS, read σφοδρὰ (cf. I, 17, 721b, 15).

[37] *Leg. All.* II, 18, 74.

identification of concupiscence with sexual desire and at his description of that desire as the source of all evil.

How Augustine arrived at the belief in the irresistibility of concupiscence is explained by himself. Early in his life, he reminisces, even though in himself he did not find the power to overcome his sexual concupiscence, he still believed that continency was in our power.[38] But a verse in the Latin translation of the Wisdom of Solomon convinced him that continency was not in the power of man. The verse in question (8:21) reads: *Et ut scivi quoniam aliter non possem esse continens, nisi Deus det*, which was taken by Augustine to mean: "And as I knew that I could not otherwise be continent, except God gave [it]." If this is really what has led Augustine to the belief in the irresistibility of concupiscence, and it would seem to be so, for he quotes this verse twenty-odd times in his works in support of it, then this belief of his has its origin in a misunderstanding of the meaning of the verse. In the original Greek, the verse quite unmistakably refers to wisdom, which is mentioned previously, and it reads: "And as I knew that I could not otherwise obtain (ἐγκρατὴς) [it], except God gave [it]." This is undoubtedly what the Latin translation also meant, for in two other places it uses the term *continens* as a translation of the Greek ἐγκρατὴς, namely, in Ecclesiasticus 6:27/8 and 15:1, and in both these places there can be no doubt that the term *continens* is used in the sense of "obtaining" or "possessing." [39] What happened here, then, is that Augustine misunderstood the meaning of the term *continens*, taking it in the sense of "continent," and thus derived therefrom his belief in the powerlessness of man to abstain from sin. A similar misunderstanding of the same verse in its Latin translation seems to be found also in Tertullian,[40] but Tertullian does not derive from it the same belief as Augustine.

---

[38] *Confessiones* VI, 11, 20.
[39] Cf. W. J. Deane's note in his edition of *The Book of Wisdom, ad loc.*
[40] *De Virginibus Velandis*, 13.

The necessity by which man can refrain from sin and act righteously is divine grace, which alone, as said by him in the passages quoted above, can resist concupiscence. Then Augustine goes on to maintain that, just as man is powerless to resist his concupiscence, so he is also powerless to resist the grace bestowed upon him by God; and consequently, just as by the necessity of his concupiscence man must sin, so by the necessity of grace man must refrain from sinning and act righteously. This irresistibility of grace is expressed by him in passages wherein he speaks of the human will as being "indeclinably (*indeclinabiliter*) and invincibly (*insuperabiliter*) influenced by divine grace" [41] and of God as He "whom no man's will resists when He wills to give salvation." [42] The irresistibility of grace is also suggested in the statement that of "whomsoever He has mercy, He calls him in a manner which He knows would befit him that he would not reject Him who called him." [43] Since man has no power of his own to resist concupiscence, or even to will to resist it, the grace bestowed upon him by God could not be a merited grace or an auxiliary grace; it must be a free gift of God which creates in man not only the will to resist concupiscence but also the power to carry out the decision of the will which He himself has created in man. Augustine formally distinguishes between these two aspects of grace, the former being described by him as prevenient or operative grace and the latter as subsequent or cooperative grace. [44] Both these two aspects of grace are free grace, for according to him there is no other kind of grace. "Grace," he lays it down as general principle, "is not rendered for any merits, but is given *gratis*, on account of which it is called grace (*gratia*)." [45] From this he is led to say that "no man ought, even when he begins to possess good

[41] *De Correptione et Gratia* 12, 38 (PL 44, 940).

[42] *Ibid.* 14, 43 (942).

[43] *De Diversis Quaestionibus ad Simplicianum* I, 7 (PL 40, 115).

[44] *Enchiridion* 32 (PL 40, 248); *De Gratia et Libero Arbitrio* 17, 33 (PL 44, 901).

[45] *De Natura et Gratia* 4, 4 (PL 44, 249).

merits, to attribute them to himself and not to God." [46] Augustine, of course, knew that men were instructed to pray to God to deliver them from evil or from the evil one, and this would seem to imply that God's help in delivering men from evil, which comes as an answer to prayer, is a merited grace. But, in anticipation of such reasoning, Augustine maintains that even God's answer to man's prayer cannot be considered a merited grace, for the will to pray as well as the act of praying does not come from man but from God. Thus, referring to those "who think that our seeking, asking, knocking is of ourselves, and is not given to us," he says that "they are mistaken" and that they do not understand "that this is also of the divine gift, that we pray; that is, that we ask, seek, and knock." [47]

The debate between Augustine and Pelagius ran the normal course of all religious debates. They quoted Scripture against each other. They hurled ancient authorities at each other. They spun arguments against each other. Then, as so often happens in theological discussions, they began to call each other names. Said Augustine to Pelagius: You are a Jew in all but name.[48] Said Pelagius to Augustine: You are a fatalist; you assert fate under the name of grace.[49] And both of them shouted at each other: You are a Manichaean.[50] We do not know what Pelagius' answer would have been, and I shall not try to reconstruct on the basis of what we know of his views what his answer would have been, though it could be done. But Augustine answered it in many places of his works and in many different ways. I shall try to give a brief analysis of his answer.

Quoting a passage from Seneca, he derives therefrom the Stoic definition of fate. Fate, according to the Stoics, he says,

[46] *De Gratia et Libero Arbitrio* 6, 13 (PL 44, 889).
[47] *De Dono Perseverantiae* 23, 64 (PL 45, 1032).
[48] *Epistolae* 196, 1, 7 (PL 33, 893).
[49] Augustine, *Contra Duas Epistolas Pelagianorum* II, 5, 10 (PL 44, 577).
[50] Augustine to Pelagians: *ibid.* IV, 4, 6 (613). Pelagians to Augustine: *ibid.* I, 2, 4 (552); *Contra Julianum* I, 3, 5, (PL 44, 643).

contains among others the following points: (1) There is an order and connection of causes which makes everything become what it does become. (2) This order and connection of causes is traceable to the will and power of God. (3) This will and power of God "extends itself irresistibly through all things." [51]

With this view, that there is an order of nature predetermined by an irresistible will of God, Augustine agrees.[52] He would be even willing to use the term "fate" as a description of this predetermination of the will of God, for, etymologically, he argues, the Latin *fatum*, "fate," means "that which is spoken," and Scripture describes the determination of God's will by the expression, "God hath spoken once" (Ps. 62/1:12).[53] Still he is reluctant to use the term fate, and this because in popular language the term "fate" means the belief in "the influence of that particular position of the stars which may exist at the time one is born or conceived," [54] and so, he says, "if any one," like the Stoics, "calls the will of God or the power of God itself by the name of fate, let him keep his opinion but correct his language." [55] Still he considers the whole matter as "a merely verbal controversy." [56]

But despite all this, Augustine maintains that man is free. If he sins, he sins freely, even though his sinning is predetermined by his irresistible concupiscence. Thus answering to the charge that he believed that "by the sin of the first man, that is, of Adam, free will perished; and that no one has now the power of living well, but that all are constrained to sin by the necessity of the flesh," [57] he exclaims: "For who of us can say that by the sin of the first man free will perished from the human race?" and proceeds to explain that only the freedom enjoyed by Adam in Paradise, the freedom "to live well and righteously," was lost, but not the freedom by which all

---

[51] *De Civ. Dei* V, 8.
[52] *Ibid.*
[53] *Ibid.* V, 9.
[54] *Ibid.* V, 1.
[55] *Ibid.*
[56] *Ibid.* V, 8.
[57] *Contra Duas Epistolas Pelagianorum* I, 2, 4 (PL 44, 552).

sin, "especially they who sin with delight (*delectatione*) and with love (*amore*) of sin; they will what pleases them." [58]

Similarly, if man does good, he does good also freely, even though his doing of good was predetermined by an irresistible grace. Thus, while on the one hand, he describes divine grace as being indeclinable and invincible and the divine will to give salvation as irresistible, he still says that "to yield our consent, indeed, to God's summons, or to withhold it, belongs to our will" [59] and that "we know that those who with their own heart believe in God, do this with their will and with their free choice." [60] But when he was asked how the two statements could be reconciled, all he answered is this: "The reason, however, why in doing a right action there is no bondage of necessity, is that liberty comes from charity (*charitatis*)." [61]

It is obvious then that Augustine himself believed that even under the power of concupiscence or of grace man acts not by necessity but by free will and the reason given by him why man, who can only act in one predetermined way, is still said to act by free will is that when man sins he sins "with delight (*delectatione*) and love (*amore*) and when he does a right action his action comes from charity (*charitatis*)." But this is hardly an explanation on the basis of what we know to have been Augustine's view on the nature of "delight" and "love" and "charity." According to Augustine, delight in the pleasures of this world is to be called a "delight of concupiscence" (*delectatio concupiscentiae*) [62] and similarly the love with which one sins is to be called *cupiditas* or *libido* [63] — terms which are synonymous with the term *concupiscentia* as translations of the Greek ἐπιθυμία.[64] And

---

[58] *Ibid.* I, 2, 5 (PL 44, 552).

[59] *De Spiritu et Littera* 34, 60 (PL 44, 240).

[60] *Epistolae* 217, 5, 16 (PL 33, 985).

[61] *De Natura et Gratia* 65, 78 (PL 44, 386).

[62] *Sermo* 153, 8 (PL 38, 830).

[63] *Enarr. in Psalm.* Ps. 9, No. 15 (PL 36, 124); cf. Ps. 31, Enarr. 2, No. 5 (260).

[64] Cf. above at n. 28.

so also with regard to charity by which one does right actions, Augustine repeatedly says that "charity" (*charitas*), like grace, is a free gift from God.[65] How then could Augustine offer "delight" and "love" and "charity" as explanations of why certain actions are actions of free will and not of necessity, when he himself ascribes "delight" and "love" to "concupiscence" and "charity" to a sort of "divine grace," and "concupiscence" and "grace" themselves are according to him, irresistible and render all actions proceeding from them necessary? Since Augustine does offer these terms as an explanation of actions which are voluntary and not necessary and since he expects his opponents to be satisfied with this explanation without any further elucidations on his part, he undoubtedly must have touched here upon some distinction between the terms voluntary and necessary which was well known to students of philosophy of his time, so that he could be confident that only by alluding to it the matter would be clear to them without the need of any further elucidation.

What then is that well-known distinction alluded to here by Augustine?

That distinction, we shall try to show, is based upon two passages in Aristotle. In one of these passages, Aristotle distinguishes between two usages of the term necessary (ἀναγκαῖον), one in the sense of that which is compelled (τὸ βίαιον) by something external to itself, and the other in the sense of that which cannot be otherwise, as, for instance, a demonstration is said to be a necessary thing, because the conclusion cannot be otherwise, not because it is compelled by something external to itself, but because it is the nature of the first premise that that particular conclusion must proceed from it by necessity.[66] In the other passage, using the term necessary in the sense of being compelled by an external cause, he contrasts with it any action caused by an internal tendency (ὁρμή), such as appetite (ὄρεξις), concupis-

---

[65] Cf. *Contra Julianum Opus Imperfectum* III, 114 (PL 45, 1296).
[66] *Metaphysica* V, 5.

cence (ἐπιθυμία), and reason (λόγος) in animate beings, and this kind of action he describes as voluntary (ἑκούσιος).[67] From a combination of these two passages it would be possible for one to form the opinion that necessary in the true sense of the term is to be applied only for that which is compelled by an external force, and that any action in animate beings caused by an internal tendency and not by an external force, even if it is necessary in the sense that it cannot be otherwise, may be described as voluntary. Such a use of the terms necessary and voluntary had in fact already become common among the Church Fathers long before Augustine. Thus the generation of the Logos from God, which was eternal and could not be otherwise, was described by the early Church Fathers as a voluntary act on the part of God, voluntary as used of that which is not necessary in the sense of being compelled by an external force. It was only when Arius used the term voluntary to imply that the Logos was created *ex nihilo* that the Fathers rejected that term and substituted for it the term natural,[68] using it, again, as the opposite of necessary in its use as that which is compelled by an external force — a sense in which the term natural is also used by Aristotle.[69] Augustine himself follows this usage of the term natural in the case of the generation of the Logos.[70] Moreover, the internal tendency, called by Aristotle nature, by which the simple elements have their uncompelled motion, is called by Augustine love (*amor*).[71] And so when Augustine argues that man sins or acts righteously not by necessity but by will on the ground that he sins by delight and love and acts righteously by charity, he means thereby that when man sins or acts righteously not by the necessity of an external

---

[67] *Ethica Eudemia* II, 8, 1224a, 9ff.

[68] Cf. my *Philosophy of the Church Fathers*, I (Cambridge, Mass., 1956), 223–232.

[69] *Physica* VIII, 4, 255a, 28–29.

[70] *De Trinitate* XV, 20, 38. Later, in order to express the view that Jesus acted without external compulsion, Maximus Confessor describes Jesus as acting both by will and by nature (cf. *The Philosophy of the Church Fathers*, I, 485–486). [71] *De Civ. Dei* XI, 28.

force but by the necessity of an internal tendency, his action may be described as voluntary, even if it could not be otherwise. In other words, the free will which Augustine grants to man is not absolute free will but only relative free will.

This conception of relative free will is more clearly brought out by Augustine in two passages.

In one of these passages, a Pelagian opponent of Augustine argues that necessity and free will are mutually exclusive terms, and so Augustine is wrong in maintaining that sin is both necessary and voluntary. To this Augustine's answer is as follows: "If you knew what you were saying, you would not make the statement that necessity and will could not exist simultaneously. Death is a necessity, and yet would any one dare deny that it could also be an object of voluntary desire?" [72] What Augustine means to say is that natural death, coming as it does not by external but by internal causes and is inevitable and cannot be otherwise, may still be described as something voluntary, as when, for instance, the dying person, for some reason or other, happens to welcome death.

In another passage,[73] Augustine tries to show that, if necessity is defined as that "according to which we say that it is necessary that anything be of such and such a nature or be done in such and such a manner," then that kind of necessity does not take away "the freedom of our will," that is, it does not make us act by compulsion. He illustrates it by such a proposition as "God is immortal" or "God is infallible," which, he argues, does not mean that because God must live forever and cannot die or because He must foreknow all things and cannot be wrong that He has life and foreknowledge by compulsion. By the same token, he also argues, man's action, whether sinning or acting righteously, is not to be described as compelled because of the fact that man could not but sin under concupiscence and could not but act righteously under grace. What Augustine means to say is quite evident.

[72] *Contra Julianum Opus Imperfectum* IV, 103 (PL 45, 1398).
[73] *De Civ. Dei* V, 10.

Man's action, though always determined either by concupiscence or by grace and could never be otherwise, is still to be described as voluntary on the ground that concupiscence and grace are within man himself, so that man's action, when only so determined, flows from his own nature and is not compelled by any force external to it.

Freedom thus to Augustine does not mean the choice to act one way or the other, for there is no such freedom; everything is determined to act only one way. Freedom is only relative, and it means to act according to one's own nature, without external compulsion. It is in this sense that man is free either to sin or to act righteously, for each man has a determinate nature either to sin or to act righteously. Men, according to Augustine, are not all of one nature. There are two kinds of human beings and correspondingly two kinds of human natures, and each man belongs either to the one or to the other. For Augustine, the old definition of man as a rational animal would not do; for him, some men are concupiscent rational animals and some are grace-endowed rational animals. And he has a theological explanation for this division of mankind. Prior to the creation of the world, God in His infinite wisdom, for reasons unknown to us, had elected out of the future sinful lump of humanity a certain number of persons whom He "predestined to grace" [74] or to "everlasting life" [75] or "to reign eternally with God." [76] They are those whom Augustine calls by the New Testament term (Rom. 8:33) "the elect" (ἐκλεκτοί, electi). These are governed by grace, and grace constitutes their nature. For them to do good is to act by the necessity of their own nature, and without external compulsion. They are thus free. Those who were not elected for grace or for everlasting life or for eternal reign with God are called by the New Testament term (II Cor. 13:5) "the reprobate" (ἀδόκιμοι, reprobi), that is, the not-approved, the rejected, the castaway, and are de-

---

[74] *Enchiridion* 100.
[75] *De Anima et Ejus Origine* IV, 11, 16.   [76] *De Civ. Dei.* XV, 1, 1.

scribed by Augustine as those "predestined to eternal punishment" or "to condemnation." These are governed by concupiscence, and concupiscence constitutes their nature. For
them to sin, is, again, to act by the necessity of their own
nature, and not by external compulsion. They are thus also
free. And in support of such a restricted conception of freedom he quotes the Stoics, though not without a grumble
against their particular classification of causes.

These are some of the philosophical implications of one of
the problems involved in the Pelagian controversy. I have
stated the problem in the form of a thesis and presented it
in its bare outline, with only partial documentation and without discussing different interpretations of passages cited and
recalcitrant passages not cited.[77]

And let us now add one concluding remark. The name-
calling, especially with regard to Pelagius, is still a favorite
pastime among some historians of dogma. Pelagius is still
called a pagan, a Stoic, a follower of the New Academy,
and, in fact, everything in the history of philosophy disliked
by the particular historian dealing with him. Augustine is
represented as the exponent of true Christianity and his concupiscence is being heralded as an anticipation of the Freudian
libido. In our judgment, Pelagius, on the problem of freedom, represents the original Christian belief. It was Augustine
who introduced something new from without. On the showing of his own statements, his doctrine of grace is only a
Christianization of the pagan Stoic doctrine of fate. As for
his concupiscence, it is not clear whether it is based upon his
own personal experience before his conversion or whether
it is based upon a misunderstanding of the Latin translation
of a Greek verse in the Book of the Wisdom of Solomon.

[77] This paper is based upon a longer, more fully documented, and differently constructed study of the same subject to be included as a chapter
in Volume II of my *Philosophy of the Church Fathers.*

7

IBN KHALDŪN ON ATTRIBUTES AND PREDESTINATION*

IBN KHALDŪN opens his sketch of the "science of the Kalam" with a discussion of two topics, the unity of God and the power of God. His purpose is to show that the belief in the unity of God is not incompatible with the belief that attributes are real incorporeal beings, eternally subsisting in God, and that the belief in the power of God, that is, in predestination, is not incompatible with divine justice in its holding man responsible for his actions. These were two distinct problems in Muslim religious philosophy. He combines these two problems and tries to solve them by one common argument.

The one common argument by which he tries to solve these two problems may be briefly stated. Throughout the history of philosophy, the unity and power of God were treated as corollaries deducible from the proofs of the existence of God. So Ibn Khaldūn says to himself: Let us examine the proofs for the existence of God and see what kind of unity of God and what kind of power of God are established thereby, and then let us see whether that kind of unity is compatible with divine attributes and whether that kind of power is compatible with divine justice. Accordingly, at the very beginning of his discussion of the Kalam, after stating that the "unity" of God is the core of the articles of faith and after declaring that he was going to prove the unity of God in a method and manner which is "most direct," [1] he proceeds to prove not the unity of God but the existence of God.

Let us study Ibn Khaldūn's proof of the existence of God.

* Reprinted by permission of The Mediaeval Academy of America from *Speculum*, 34 (1959): 585–597.

[1] *Muqaddimah*, III, 27, ll. 4–6. Quotations from the *Muqaddimah* are from its English translation by Franz Rosenthal (New York, 1958), except for occasional deviations in the case of technical terms. Page and line references are to Quatremère's edition (Paris, 1858).

In Arabic philosophy, by the time of Ibn Khaldūn (1332–1406), the proofs used for the existence of God were mainly of two types. Both of these types were of the cosmological kind. We may characterize them, with reference to their ultimate philosophical origin, as the Platonic type of argument and the Aristotelian type of argument. The Platonic type of argument starts with the assumption that the world came to be (γιγνόμενον) after it had not been,[2] or as the Muslim theologians have come to express this view, the world was created (makhlūq). Then, adding the principle that everything created must have a creator, it directly infers that there must be a Creator. The Aristotelian type of argument starts with the assumption that the world is eternal. Then, by an empirical study of the world, it arrives at the conclusion, first, that every form of coming into being within the world is effected by a cause and, second, that since the world is eternal, the series of causes and effects would have to be infinite. Then, adding the principle that an infinite regress of causes is impossible, it arrives at the conclusion that there is a first beginning for all causes.[3]

When we examine, however, the proof for the existence of God used by Ibn Khaldūn, we find that it is neither a purely Platonic type of proof nor a purely Aristotelian type; it is a combination of the two. As in the Aristotelian type of proof, Ibn Khaldūn starts with the empirical observation that "the things which come into being in the world of existing things . . . require appropriate causes which are prior to their coming into being" and that "each one of these causes . . . requires other causes."[4] But he does not go on to say, as does Aristotle, that the causes and effects would form an infinite series and that an infinite series of causes and effects is impossible. As in the Platonic type of proof, he assumes that the world was created and that consequently the series

[2] *Timaeus* 28 A.
[3] *Metaphysica* II, 2, 994a, 1ff.
[4] *Muqaddimah*, III, 27, ll. 7–11.

of causes and effects within it is finite. From the combination of these two types of proof he then arrives at the existence of God, whom he describes in terms borrowed from both these two types of proof, as Cause and as Creator. His conclusion thus significantly reads: "Causes continue to follow upon causes in an ascending order, until they reach the Causer of causes, Him who is the Author of their existence and their Creator." [5]

But, having started his argument with the empirical observation that things within the world are causally connected with each other, Ibn Khaldūn became conscious of a difficulty. It was well for Aristotle and for Avicenna and for all other philosophers to speak of the existence of causes in the world and of causes requiring other causes, for they all believed that God is a "Causer of causes" only in the sense that He is a Prime Cause or a Remote and Ultimate Cause, who acts upon the world through intermediate causes, so that there is a real causal nexus in the world. But Ibn Khaldūn, as a follower of the orthodox Kalam, did not believe in causality. To him the world was a succession of events, each of which was created directly by God. The sequence in this order of events which is observed is due to what the Mutakallimūn describe by the term "custom" ('adah).[6] So Ibn Khaldūn, after stating that "the things that come into being in the world of existing things . . . require appropriate causes which are prior to them," [7] immediately corrects himself by adding with regard to those causes that "by them the things that come into being fall into the realm of custom (al-'adah)." [8] This may be taken as a general explanation of all other places where he speaks of "nexuses (rubuṭ) between causes and things caused" [9] or "the dependence (tawaqquf)

---

[5] *Ibid.*, ll. 12–14. For the expression "Causer of causes" (*musabbib al-isbāb*), see Ghazālī, *Tahāfut al-Falāsifah*, I (ed. Bouyges), §78, p. 65, l. 4. It is the equivalent of the expression *'illah al-'ilal* in *Liber de Causis* (ed. Bardenhewer), §17, p. 92, l. 11.

[6] Cf. Ghazālī, *Tahāfut al-Falāsifah*, VII, §§1–7.

[7] *Muqaddimah*, III, 27, ll. 8–10.

[8] *Ibid.*, ll. 10–11.   [9] *Ibid.*, I, 173, l. 6.

of things upon each other." [10] By all these expressions he means only a conception of causality due to "custom."

What he means by "custom" is explained by him subsequently in his statement that the causes "are known only through [persistence of] [11] custom (*bil-'adah*) and through logical conclusions (*al-iqtirān*) [12] which attest to [the existence] of an apparent [causal] relationship." [13] A similar explanation is given by him in his statement that "the faculty of cogitation (*al-fikr*) perceives the order that exists among things that come into being," [14] that is to say, it is our thinking that sees a causal nexus between things which we are accustomed to see following each other in orderly succession. This corresponds to one of the three possible explanations of "custom" suggested by Averroes. As this explanation is phrased by Averroes, "custom" means "our custom of forming a judgment (*al-ḥukm*) concerning existing things" [15] which is "an act of the mind (*al-'aql*)." [16] In reality, as Ibn Khaldūn says, "all these things are connected with the divine power," [17] that is to say, all things which through "custom" are seen to be causally connected with each other are in reality connected with God as their direct cause.

But, as we have seen, Ibn Khaldūn, by his own declaration, had set out to prove not the existence of God but the unity of God. Therefore, immediately after he has shown that there is a God, he adds: "There is no God but Him." [18] How the unity of God follows from his proof for His existence is ex-

[10] *Ibid.*, II, 366, ll. 16–17.

[11] Cf. the expression *istimrār al-'adah* in Ghazālī's *Tahāfut al-Falāsifah*, XVII, §13, p. 285, l. 11.

[12] The Arabic *iqtirān* is a literal translation of the Greek συναγωγή, a *bringing together, a collection*, which is used technically in the sense of the conclusion in a syllogism.

[13] *Muqaddimah*, III, 29, ll. 3–4.

[14] *Ibid.*, II, 366, l. 1. On the technical meaning of *fikr*, see my paper "The Internal Senses in Latin, Arabic, and Hebrew Philosophic Texts," *Harvard Theological Review*, 27 (1935): 69–135.

[15] Averroes, *Tahāfut al-Tahāfut*, I (XVI) (ed. Bouyges), §10, p. 523, l. 4.

[16] *Ibid.*, l. 12. Cf. Ghazālī's statement in *Tahāfut al-Falāsifah*, VII, §13, p. 285, ll. 11–12.

[17] *Muqaddimah*, II, 365, l. 16.   [18] *Ibid.*, III, 27, l. 14.

plained by him later briefly that "otherwise, the creation [of the world] could not have materialized, on account of mutual antagonism" [19] or, as he phrases it elsewhere, the world "would have been destroyed." [20] This refers to a well-known Kalam proof, based upon the philosophic as well as Koranic conception of one world, which argues that two deities could not cooperate in creating the world or, having created it, could not cooperate in keeping it in existence.[21]

With this proof for the existence of God and His unity, Ibn Khaldūn, in the course of his discussion, takes up the problem of attributes. He mentions three views. First, there was the view of those who "sank deep into anthropomorphism," [22] believing that God has hands, feet, and face,[23] and that He extends in different directions and is sitting and descending and has a voice and sound.[24] Second, there was the view of the Mu'tazilites, who denied not only anthropomorphism but also "decided to deny attributes in the form of abstract nouns ($sifāt$ $al-ma'āniyy$), such as knowledge, power, will, life, in addition to denying what follows from them," [25] that is to say, in addition to denying attributes in the form of adjectives derived from abstract nouns ($sifāt$ $ma'nawiyyah$), such as living, knowing, willing, powerful.[26] Third, there was the view of those whom he calls "the Early Muslims," who "knew that anthropomorphism is absurd" [27] but "affirmed of God the possession of the attributes of divinity and per-

[19] *Ibid.*, III, 27, l. 1.

[20] *Ibid.*, I, 348, ll. 13–14.

[21] Cf. Averroes, *Kitāb al-Kashf 'an Manāhij* (ed. M. J. Müller), p. 47, l. 4ff.   [22] *Muqaddimah*, III, 37, l. 8.   [23] *Ibid.*, l. 9.

[24] *Ibid.*, 38, ll. 1–2.   [25] *Ibid.*, ll. 8–9.

[26] For this interpretation of the expression "what follows from them" see the distinction made in the Creed of al-Faḍālī between $sifāt$ $al-ma'āniyy$ and $sifāt$ $ma'nawiyyah$ (cf. *Kifāyat al-'awamm min 'Ilm al-Kalām*, with Commentary of al Bājūrī, Cairo, A.H. 1315, p. 60, ll. 9ff.; cf. English translation in D. B. Macdonald's *Muslim Theology*, New York, 1903, p. 337). A similar contrast is implied in Ibn Khaldūn's statement later, p. 39, ll. 12–13, that al-Ash'arī "recognized four $sifāt$ $ma'nawiyyah$ [that is, living, knowing, willing, powerful] as well as audition ($al-sam'$), vision ($al-basar$), and speech ($al-kalām$)." The last three he would describe as $sifāt$ $al-ma'aniyy$.

[27] *Muqaddimah*, III, 37, ll. 1–3.

fection." [28] This view of the Early Muslims is identified by him with the view of Ash'arī, which he describes as mediating between the view of the Anthropomorphists and the view of the Mu'tazilites.[29]

Now it happens that Ibn Ḥazm reports two views in the name of Ash'arī, taken from two different books written by him. According to one of these views "one is not to say of the attribute of knowledge [and for that matter of any other attribute] that it is God nor that it is other than God." [30] According to the other view, "God's knowledge is other than God and different from God, yet in spite of this it is uncreated and ceaseless." [31] Evidently these two views were held by him at different periods in his life. What the difference is between these two views does not concern us now. I shall discuss it in my work *The Philosophy of the Kalam*. But it is interesting to note that these two views are represented among the followers of Ash'arī. Thus Bāqillānī [32] and one group of Ash'arites [33] adopted the view that attributes are other than God, whereas another group of Ash'arites [34] adopted the view that attributes are neither God nor other than God. Consequently, when Ibn Khaldūn identifies the view of the Early Muslims with that of Ash'arī, we may ask ourselves, with which of these two reported views of Ash'arī does he identify the view of the Early Muslims? An answer to this question is furnished by Ibn Khaldūn himself, when, commenting on the Mu'tazilite argument that the belief in real attributes is tantamount to a belief in many gods, he says: "This argument is refuted by the view that the attributes are neither identical with the essence nor other than it." [35]

---

[28] *Ibid.*, p. 48, ll. 8–9.   [29] *Ibid.*, p. 39, ll. 9–14.
[30] Ibn Ḥazm, *Kitāb al-Fiṣal fī al-Milal*, II (Cairo, A.H. 1317–1337), 126, ll. 21–22.
[31] *Ibid.*, ll. 22–24. Cf. Ash'arī, *al-Lumaʿ* (ed. R. J. McCarthy), §25, p. 14, ll. 11–12.   [32] *Fiṣal fī al-Milal*, IV, 207, l. 8.
[33] Shahrastānī, *Nihāyat al-Iqdām* (ed. A. Guillaume), p. 181, ll. 1–4.
[34] Cf. The Creed of Al-Nasafī and al-Taftāzānī's comment on it in the latter's commentary (Cairo, A.H. 1335), p. 71, l. 1, and p. 72, l. 10; E. E. Elder's translation, pp. 48, 53, 53 n. 9.   [35] *Muqaddimah*, III, 38, ll. 16–17.

Thus the Ash'arite view, which he identifies with that of the Early Muslims, is that which held that the attributes of God are neither God nor other than God, and it is this view which Ibn Khaldūn approves of and recommends as a view which is compatible with the oneness of God.

But here another question must have arisen in the mind of Ibn Khaldūn. The formula that attributes are neither identical with the essence of God nor other than His essence was used by Abū Hāshim, a contemporary of Ash'arī, in the sense of what he calls "modes" (aḥwāl) and was attacked by Abū Hāshim's father, al-Jubbā'ī, and others,[36] among them Ash'arī himself, evidently after his conversion to orthodoxy.[37] It was found by all of them to be contrary to the Law of Excluded Middle, which requires that of two contradictories a subject must be either the one or the other. How, then, could Ibn Khaldūn approve a formula which Ash'arī himself, after having accepted it, rejected on the ground that it was in violation of a fundamental law of thought? Ibn Khaldūn does not discuss this difficulty. But I am going to show that he anticipated it and provided an answer for it.

Let us go back to his proof of the unity of God, or rather to his proof of the existence of God of which the proof of unity is a corollary.

In that proof, after showing how we can arrive at a knowledge of the existence and unity of God from an observation of the sequence of causes and effects in the world, Ibn Khaldūn dwells at great length on the scantiness and inadequacy of our knowledge of these causes. To begin with, though the causes in the created and finite world must have been taken by Ibn Khaldūn to be finite in number, still he says: "The intellect becomes confused in an attempt to perceive and enumerate them. Only a comprehensive knowledge can encompass them all." [38] In making this statement, he must have

[36] Shahrastānī, Milal (ed. Cureton), p. 56, ll. 13ff.; Nihāyat, p. 134, ll. 12ff.

[37] Ash'arī, al-Luma' §26; Shahrastānī, Milal, p. 67, ll. 2–3.

[38] Muqaddimah, III, 27, ll. 15–16.

had in mind the Koranic verse that God, and evidently God only, "counteth all things by number" (Surah 72:28). Second, though Ibn Khaldūn believed that all events in the world are directly created by God and that the causal nexus which appears to exist between them is only a matter of "custom," he still wonders whether in the succession of such events directly created by God earlier events may not have, by the mysteriousness of God's action, some influence upon later events, and so he says that "What that influence really is and how it takes place is unknown." [39] And since we are ignorant of the nature of the causes in the world, by which we arrive at the knowledge of the one Causer of causes, we are also ignorant of the nature of the Causer of causes. All we know about Him is the fact of His existence. He therefore concludes: "The intellect should not be used to weigh such matters as the oneness of God" [40] and "the real character of divine attributes," [41] for "it cannot comprehend God and His attributes." [42] In this assertion of the unknowability of God, Ibn Khaldūn was re-echoing a widely current view which was first introduced into philosophy by Philo.[43]

This, then, is the answer provided by Ibn Khaldūn for any difficulty arising with regard to the oneness of God and attributes. We are to believe in the unity of God; we are also to believe in the reality of attributes. These attributes, though real, are neither identical with God nor other than He. There appears to us to be a difficulty here, but there is really no difficulty. How this apparent difficulty can be solved is unknowable to us, for our intellect cannot comprehend the unity of God and His attributes. And why should we expect to comprehend God's unity in its relation to His attributes, he tries to tell us, when even the world of our observation and experience, from which we derive our knowledge of the unity of God, is not fully comprehended by us. One must,

---

[39] *Ibid.*, p. 29, ll. 4–5.
[40] *Ibid.*, p. 30, l. 17.
[41] *Ibid.*, l. 18.
[42] *Ibid.*, p. 31, l. 2.
[43] Cf. my *Philo*, rev. ed. (Cambridge, 1948), II, 94ff.

therefore, accept such truths as given by revelation, without seeking to demonstrate them by reason.

Let us now take up Ibn Khaldūn's view on predestination. In his proof of the existence of God, which we have analyzed, within his opening statement that "the things that come into being in the world of existing things . . . require appropriate causes which are prior to them," after the words "in the world of existing things," he adds the explanatory statement: "whether they belong to bodies (*al-dhawāt*) [44] or to either human or animal actions." [45] The purpose of this additional statement is to enable him to use this proof of the existence of God from creation also as a proof of the power of God over all human actions. The argument by which he tries to prove the power of God is based upon Aristotle's explanation of the psychology of action, which in its essential features is as follows: Human action is caused by will (βού-λησις), which consists of appetite (ὄρεξις) and intelligence (νοῦς), or that special kind of intelligence described as thought (νόησις) or reason (λογισμός) or practical thought (διάνοια πρακτική), which calculates the means to an end, [46] and thought (τὸ νοεῖν) includes imagination (φαντασία). [47] Animal action, however, is caused by desire (ἐπιθυμία), which, again, consists

---

[44] I take the term *al-dhawāt* 'essences,' used here in contrast to human and animal "actions," to refer to what Ibn Khaldūn describes elsewhere as "pure essences" (*dhawāt maḥḍah*), such as the elements . . . and the three things that come into being from the elements, namely, minerals, plants, and animals" (II, 365, ll. 14–16). The expression *dhawāt maḥḍah*, I take it, is used by Ibn Khaldūn as the equivalent of the expression *ajsām mabsūṭah*, which, as a translation of Aristotle's ἁπλᾶ σώματα, "simple (i.e., unmixed and hence pure) bodies," is used in the sense of "elements." The substitution by Ibn Khaldūn of the term *dhawāt* 'essences,' for *ajsām* 'bodies,' is to be explained on the ground that both *dhāt* and *jauhar* are translations of the Greek *ousia*, and in Aristotle there is a statement, upon which the statement quoted from Ibn Khaldūn is evidently based, which reads: "*Ousia* means the simple bodies, as e.g., earth, fire, water, and the like, and in general bodies and the things composed of them, both animals and divine beings, and the parts of these" (*Metaphysica* V, 8, 1017b, 10–13).

[45] *Muqaddimah*, III, 27, ll. 8–9.
[46] *De Anima* III, 10, 433a, 9–25.
[47] *Ibid*. III, 3, 427b, 27–28.

of appetite and intelligence, but that special kind of intelligence which is described as imagination.[48]

With this in the back of his mind, Ibn Khaldūn says with regard to "human and animal actions" that "among their causes there evidently belong intentions and desires, since no action can take place without desire (*irādah*) and intention (*qaṣd*)."[49] The term *qaṣd* 'intention', I take it, is used by him here quite evidently in the sense of rational human desire, as the equivalent of βούλησις in Aristotle, which is the equivalent of προαίρεσις, *ikhtiyār* 'choice', and the term *irādah* is used by him here, I take it, either in the narrow sense of irrational animal desire, as the equivalent of ἐπιθυμία in Aristotle, or in the general sense of both irrational and rational desire, as the equivalent of ὄρεξις in Aristotle.[50] Again, with Aristotle in the back of his mind, he says: "Intentions and desires are functions (*umūr*, literally: things) of the soul, originating ordinarily from previous consecutive representations (*taṣawwurāt*)."[51] The term *taṣawwurāt*, which I have translated here by "representations," is used by him here, as the term is generally used in Arabic philosophical literature, in the general sense of both representations of the imagination and representations of the intellect.[52] Then, dropping the actions of animals and confining himself to human actions, he continues: "These representations are the causes of the intention to act and the causes of these representations are other representations."[53] As he goes on, he explains that of these representations, which are the causes of human actions, some take place

[48] *Ibid*. III, 10, 433a, 25–27.

[49] *Muqaddimah*, III, 27, ll. 17–18.

[50] On these two meanings of *irādah*, cf. Alfārābī, '*Uyūn al-Masa'il*, 31, p. 98, ll. 20–23 (ed. Fr. Dieterici, in his *Alfarabi's philosophische Abhandlungen*, 1890).

[51] *Muqaddimah*, III, 28, ll. 1–2.

[52] Cf. Goichon, *Lexique de la langue philosophique d'Ibn Sina*, §374. For *taṣawwur* as used by Ibn Khaldūn in its logical sense as contrasted with *taṣdiq* (III, 87, l. 8, *et passim*), see my paper, "The Terms *taṣawwur* and *taṣdiq* in Arabic Philosophy and their Greek, Latin, and Hebrew Equivalents," *The Moslem World*, 33 (1943): 114–128.

[53] *Muqaddimah*, III, 28, ll. 2–4.

in the soul (*nafs*),[54] whereas others belong to the intellect (*'aql*).[55]

The term "soul," used here by Ibn Khaldūn in contrast to the term "intellect," corresponds to what in another place he describes as the first [56] and second [57] degrees (*marātib*) of the cogitative power (*al-fikr*) of the soul, as contrasted with its third degree.[58] It also corresponds to what in still another place he describes as the first of the three kinds (*aṣnāf*) of human souls, as contrasted with the second kind.[59] The first two degrees of the cogitative power are called by him respectively "the discriminating intellect" (*al-'aql al-tam-yīziyy*) [60] and "the empirical intellect" (*al-'aql al-tajribiyy*),[61] and the first kind of human soul corresponding to them is described by him as moving "downwards toward the perceptions of the senses and imagination." [62] The third degree of the cogitative power is called by him "pure intellect" (*'aql maḥḍ*),[63] and its corresponding second kind of human soul is described by him as that "which moves in the direction of spiritual intellection (*ta'aqqul*) and type of perception that does not need the organs of the body" [64] and "it proceeds to a state of actuality in its intellection [65] by assimilating itself to highest spiritual host of angels (*mala*)," [66] that is, assimilating itself to what Ibn Khaldūn describes as the third kind of human soul, which he calls "angelicality" (*malakiyyah*).[67] It is his first two degrees of the cogitative power of the soul, which correspond to his first of the three kinds of human

[54] *Ibid.*, p. 28, l. 4.
[55] *Ibid.*, l. 11.
[56] *Ibid.*, II, 364, l. 18.
[57] *Ibid.*, p. 365, l. 2.
[58] *Ibid.*, l. 5.
[59] *Ibid.*, I, 176, l. 18; p. 177, l, 15.
[60] *Ibid.*, II, 365, l. 1.
[61] *Ibid.*, p. 365, l. 5. Cf. Aristotle, *Anal. Post.* II, 19, 100a, 5: ἐμπειρία, tajrībah (ed. Badawi, p. 464, l. 1).
[62] *Ibid.*, I, 177, ll. 1–2.
[63] *Ibid.*, II, 365, l. 11.
[64] *Ibid.*, I, 177, ll. 9–10; cf. p. 176, ll. 10ff.
[65] I take the expression *al-fi'l fī ta'aqquliha* to reflect the expression *al-'aql bil-fi'l*, νοῦς ἐνεργείᾳ, 'intellect in actuality', rather than the expression *al-'aql al-fa''āl*, νοῦς ποιητικός, 'active intellect.' Hence my use here of "actuality in its intellection" instead of Rosenthal's "active intellection."
[66] *Muqaddimah*, I, 176, l. 13.
[67] *Ibid.*, p. 177, l. 16.

souls, that Ibn Khaldūn had in mind when he speaks here of some of the representations as taking place in the "soul," and it is the third degree of the cogitative power, which corresponds to his second of the three kinds of human souls, that he had in mind when he speaks of some other representations as taking place in the "intellect."

Finally, Ibn Khaldūn arrives at the conclusion that this series of representations which cause human action in this created world of ours must culminate at a Causer or Creator. This conclusion is expressed by him in the following statement: "The representations are functions (ashyā', literally "things") which God puts into the cogitative faculty of the soul (al-fikr) and of which one follows the other in succession." [68] The term "causes" throughout this statement must, of course, be taken in accordance with his own previous explanation as meaning things that come into being in "the realm of custom."

Having proved that God has power over all human actions, he presents in the course of his subsequent discussion, the various opinions held by Muslims as to God's power in relation to human action. He reproduces two views. First, he reproduces the view of the Mu'tazilites as denying "predestination" (al-qadar) [69] and as considering "man as the creator of his own actions, the latter having nothing to do with the divine power." [70] Second, he reproduces the view of the Early Muslims as maintaining that "God predetermines the action of each being," [71] of which he himself approves in his warning to the reader not to think that it is "in your own power or in your own choice" to stop doing anything or to resume the doing of anything.[72] This view of the Early Muslims is later identified by him with the view of Ash'arī, whom he describes as mediating between extreme views on all controversial problems, including the problems of attributes and

[68] Ibid., III, p. 28, ll. 6–7.
[69] Ibid., p. 38, l. 18.
[70] Ibid., p. 48, ll. 12–13.
[71] Ibid., p. 35, l. 12; p. 36, ll. 3–4.
[72] Ibid., p. 28, ll. 18–19.

predestination.[73] But, while, with regard to attributes, he tells us, as we have seen,[74] what the two extreme views were, with regard to predestination, he mentions only one extreme view, that of the Mu'tazilites;[75] but no mention is made by him of the other extreme. We know, however, that the other extreme view, which was in direct opposition to the view of the Mu'tazilites is the view of the Jabarites, who believed that man is compelled with regard to his action, and we know also that between these two extreme views was the view which maintained that man has the power of "acquisition" (*kasb*, *iktisāb*).[76] We know furthermore that Averroes described the Ash'arites as follows: "The Ash'arites try to find a view which is a mean between these two extreme views, by maintaining that man has acquisition (*kasb*) but that which is acquired through it (*al-muktasab bihi*) and that which causes the acquisition (*al-muksib*) are both created by God."[77] From ash'arī's own work it may be further gathered that he regarded acquisition as an "originated power" (*qudrah muḥdathah*),[78] that is to say, a power "which God created (*yakhluquhu*) for man,"[79] but that he still referred to that power as the power of the man for whom it is an aquisition.[80]

From all this we may conclude that the other extreme view is the view of the Jabarites and that the mediating view approved of and adapted by Ibn Khaldūn is the view of acquisition, which Ash'arī has described as being the power of the man for whom it is an acquisition. The power of acquisition is thus that modicum of freedom possessed by man in his action. But, inasmuch as according to Ibn Khaldūn that which immediately precedes human action is "intention," we have reason to assume that man's power of acquisition is connected with man's intention.

[73] *Ibid.*, p. 39, ll. 7–16.
[74] Cf. above at nn. 22–26.   [75] *Muqaddimah*, III, 38, ll. 17–18.
[76] Baghdādī, *Farq* (Cairo, A.H. 1328), pp. 327, l. 14–328, l. 10; Shahrastānī, *Milal*, p. 59, ll. 15–18; cf. W. M. Watt, *Free Will and Predestination in Early Islam* (London, 1948), pp. 96ff.
[77] *Kashf*, p. 105, ll. 18–20.   [79] *Ibid.*, p. 552, l. 8.
[78] *Maqālāt* (ed. Ritter), p. 542, l. 8.   [80] *Ibid.*, p. 542, l. 9.

An allusion to this power of acquisition as a power created by God in man to act with a certain amount of freedom is to be found in his statement that "cogitation (*al-fikr*) is a special nature (*ṭabī‘ah*) which God created exactly as He created all His other creatures," that it is "a power" (*quwwah*), and that "at times, it is the beginning of orderly and well-arranged human actions and, at other times, it is the beginning of the knowledge of something that had not been hitherto available."[81] Now, it will be noticed, he does not say that each act of cogitation is directly created in man by God. He only says that God created in man "a special nature" or a "power" to cogitate, and that thereby man is led to planned or orderly action or to the discovery of new knowledge by logical reasoning. Here, again, the orderly action and the new knowledge is not said to be directly created by God in man. There is in all this the implication that there is a certain element of freedom in man, known as "acquisition," and that kind of freedom is sufficient to vindicate divine justice in its holding man responsible for his actions.

Here again a question must have arisen in the mind of Ibn Khaldūn. The theory of acquisition has been criticized by Averroes as being "meaningless," on the ground that "if," as Ash‘arī says, "the acquisition (*al-iktisāb*) and that which is acquired are created by God, then man is inevitably compelled with regard to his acquisition."[82] And, again, as in the case of unity and attributes, there is no discussion of this difficulty and no open attempt to solve it. But, we shall try to show that, as in the case of unity and attributes, and by the very same device, he has provided an answer in anticipation of the difficulty.

As previously in dealing with the succession of causes so now in dealing with the succession of representations, though he has said that God puts each of these representations in the human soul, he still assumes that there is some connection between them, and so he asks himself, How

---

[81] *Muqaddimah*, III, 254, ll. 11–16.   [82] *Kashf*, p. 105, ll. 20–21.

to think of as a causal series, connected with each other? To quote: "With regard to the representations which take place in the soul, their cause is unknown, since no one is able to know the beginnings of the functions (*al-umūr*, literally: the things) of the soul nor their ends." [83] This protestation of our ignorance of the internal causes that lead man to action, we take it, is meant to be an answer to any difficulty that may be raised against any attempt to mediate between God's power and human freedom. What Ibn Khaldūn wants to say by this protestation of human ignorance is this. It is true that God is the determining cause of all human action, even his power of acquisition. It is also true that man cannot initiate action by himself. But man acts by a succession of what we are accustomed to call causes, namely, representations of the internal senses, which lead to intentions, which in turn lead to action. But we do not know how these internal causes, the representations of the internal senses, are causally related to the external causes which precede them, nor do we know how they are related to each other and how they are related to the intentions which follow them, nor again, do we know how actions are causally related to intentions. All we know is that God is their creator, but how He is their Creator we do not know. It is all a mystery, and within that mystery, Ibn Khaldūn seems to suggest, there may be another mystery, one which allows a certain amount of inexplicable free action, so that somehow man is responsible for his actions, even though he has been predestined so to act; and somehow also God is just in holding man responsible for his actions, even though He himself has predestined man so to act.

This tacit admission of a certain degree of human freedom, which in some inexplicable manner is reconcilable with God's absolute power, is subtly indicated by him in still another way. The successive stages of events in the soul leading to action mentioned by him, as we have seen, are two: representations

[83] *Muqaddimah*, III, 28, ll. 4–7.

and intentions. But it will be noticed that, while he explicitly says that "intentions" originate from "previous consecutive representations" [84] and while he also explicitly says that the consecutive representations are put by God into the cogitative faculty of the soul,[85] he does not say that also the intentions are put by God into that faculty of the soul. The omission, I take it, is deliberate, and it is significant. The "intention" to Ibn Khaldūn is an "acquisition," and acquisition is a "power," which, though created in man by God, is man's own power. The two somehow are reconcilable, though how they are reconcilable we do not know, for we are ignorant of the interconnection of events in the human mind.

Such an ignorance of the interconnection of events, as we have seen, is maintained by Ibn Khaldūn to exist also with regard to the external order of nature.[86] Still, he takes care to point out, there is a difference between these two kinds of ignorance.

With regard to the nature of the external world about us, he says: "As a rule, man is able to comprehend the causes that are external to us in nature and are apparent to the eye and present themselves to our perception in an orderly and well-arranged manner, because nature is encompassed by the soul and on a lower level than it." [87] A similar view is expressed by him in his statement that "knowledge of things that come into being, or opinion about them, can only result from knowledge of all their [four] causes, that is, the efficient cause, the material cause, the formal cause, and the final cause." [88] All this reflects the view of Ghazālī, who, while denying causality and making every event dependent directly upon God, to whom all things are possible, argues that this does not mean that we could not know beforehand that a youth left at home would not be changed into a dog or that a stone would be changed into god and similar changes con-

---

[84] Cf. above at n. 51.
[85] Cf. above at n. 68.
[86] Cf. above at nn. 38–39.
[87] *Muqaddimah*, III, 28, ll. 8–10.
[88] *Ibid.*, p. 223, ll. 2–4.

sidered impossible by experience, for, he says, that, though we believe that all these things are possible, "God created in us a knowledge that He would not do these possible things." [89] But ultimately this view is traceable to Philo, who, while admitting that God can upset the order of nature and create miracles, finds in the Hebrew scripture an assurance by God that the order of nature established by Him in the world will not be upset by Him unnecessarily.[90]

With regard, however, to the psychological causes within man, namely, the imaginational and intellectual representations, Ibn Khaldūn says that "inasmuch as the representations and the order in which they are arranged exceed the perceptive power of the soul, because they [partly] belong to the intellect (*'aql*), which is on a higher level than the soul, the soul can scarcely perceive very many of them, let alone all of them." [91] Human action, therefore, is less predictable than action in the external order of nature.

This conception of an inexplicable element of freedom despite his belief in the omnipotence of God runs throughout the course of his explanation of the development of human society, its beliefs and its institutions. Throughout his delineation of the history of beliefs and institutions, he works on the assumption that civilization is the result of an interplay between the external world and human nature. Human nature is depicted by him as flexible and as subject to the influence of external causes and as always being guided by reason. All this would seem to be contrary to Ibn Khaldūn's openly avowed belief that God predetermines all human action. Of this contradictory attitude Ibn Khaldūn himself every once in a while seems to become aware, and to assuage his theological conscience he quotes appropriate verses glorifying the power of God. Accordingly his exposition of the development of human beliefs and institutions as a natural process determined by external causes is rhythmically punctuated by such

[89] Ghazālī, *Tahāfut al-Falāsifah*, XVII, § 13, p. 285, ll. 9–10; cf. §§ 11–12.
[90] Cf. my *Philo*, I, 347ff.   [91] *Muqaddimah*, III, 28, ll. 10–12.

Koranic verses as "God decides, and no one can change His decision" (13:41),[92] "God leads astray whomever He wants to lead astray, and He guides whomever He wants to guide" (16:95),[93] "God gives kingdom to whomever He wants to give it" (2:248);[94] "When we want to destroy a city, we order those of its inhabitants who live in luxury to act wickedly therein, so that the sentence against them is justified, and we do destroy it" (17:17).[95]

This, then, is the answer provided by Ibn Khaldūn for the apparent conflict between predestination and divine justice. As in the case of the oneness of God and His attributes, he declares that the conflict is only apparent. In reality, the two beliefs are reconcilable, even though we do not know how they are reconcilable, and they are reconcilable because in some inexplicable manner there is some free play in the internal, psychological causes of human action.

The answer provided by Ibn Khaldūn for both these difficulties is not altogether new. It is only the adoption of an old answer given by Muslim theologians whenever they found themselves committed to two contradictory beliefs — an answer expressed by the Arabic words bi-lā kayfa, which, freely translated, means, "we know the contradiction can be reconciled, but ask us not how." The significance of this bi-lā kayfa answer by Ibn Khaldūn is to be found in his own account of its history. According to Ibn Khaldūn, the bi-lā kayfa answer was commonly used by the Early Muslims [96] as well as by the Ḥanbalites,[97] but fell into disuse with the appearance of Sunnite Mutakallimūn (al-mutakallimūn al-sunniyyah), the first of whom was Ash'arī,[98] and more so with the appearance of "the method of recent theologians"

[92] Ibid., I, 284, ll. 1–2; II, 233, ll. 13–14; III, 264, l. 15.
[93] Ibid., I, 364, l. 5.
[94] Ibid., p. 282, ll. 12–13.
[95] Ibid., p. 261, ll. 12–14.
[96] Ibid., III, 37, ll. 2–7.
[97] Ibid., p. 51, ll. 4–6.
[98] Ibid., p. 52, ll. 16–17; p. 53, l. 10; p. 39, l. 9.

(*tariqah al-muta'khkhirin*),[99] the first exponent of which was Ghazālī.[100] With Ash'arī there began what Ibn Khaldūn describes as "intellectual evidence in defense of the articles of faith" [101] and with Ghazālī this intellectual evidence began to be couched in the "technical" (*mustalah*) terminology of the philosophers,[102] resulting in what Ibn Khaldūn deploringly describes as a confusion of theology and philosophy.[103] Now, while these new types of theologians have found rational solutions for all the difficulties that could be raised against the belief in attributes and in predestination, Ibn Khaldūn would have none of them. For him the old *bi-lā kayfa* was good enough. The rational arguments of Ash'arī and Ghazālī and their followers served a good purpose in refuting the arguments of heretics, when heresy was rampant in Islam. But Islam, thank Allah, has long since been purged of heresy, and so Ibn Khaldūn felt that for students of his own time there was no need of the rational kind of justification of religious doctrines. Faithful believers know that the doctrines of their religion are true, and whatever objections may be raised against them are not real objections; and so why bother to answer them. And in support of this attitude, Ibn Khaldūn quotes a maxim by al-Junayd to the following effect: "The denial that there is anything wrong, when we know that it is impossible that there should be anything wrong, is itself wrong." [104] Or, perhaps, he was not so simple-minded as he appears. Perhaps in the age-old struggle between orthodoxy and rationalism in religion he saw nothing but a struggle between the suspension of reason and the perversion of reason and, like a goodly number of non-quibblers of every religion, he chose to suspend reason rather than to pervert it.

[99] *Ibid.*, p. 41, l. 12.
[100] *Ibid.*, l. 15.
[101] *Ibid.*, p. 39, ll. 7–9.
[102] *Ibid.*, p. 41, l. 11.
[103] *Ibid.*, ll. 17–19.
[104] *Ibid.*, p. 43, ll. 15–16; I, 38, ll. 9–10.

8

CAUSALITY AND FREEDOM IN DESCARTES, LEIBNIZ, AND HUME*

Two theories of completely undetermined freedom of the will were advanced in Greek philosophy in opposition to the rationalized conception of fate which prevailed in the philosophies of Plato, Aristotle, and the Stoics. One of these theories, the Epicurean, was based upon the denial of causality, maintaining that the rise of the world as well as the occurrence of everything within it was due to chance. The other, the Philonic,[1] was based upon the belief in the possibility of the suspension of causality, maintaining that God, who in His working of miracles intermits the process of causation which He himself implanted in the world, has endowed the human will with a similar miraculous power enabling it to act in a free and undetermined manner.

In the general history of the philosophy of religion, whether Christian, Muslim, or Jewish, it is the Philonic conception of freedom that prevailed, though sometimes with certain modifications. One of the modifications was that of denying that God has endowed created beings with the power of causality, which meant the denial of any causality in the world apart from that exercised directly by God. The appearance of this modified form of the Philonic theory was not altogether without the influence of Epicureanism, but primarily it was due to a desire to maintain with greater strictness the Philonic doctrine that God is the sole creative being. The full story of this modified form of Philonism, or, as we shall refer to it here, Neophilonism, will be told in my work *The Philosophy of the*

---

* Reprinted by permission of Cornell University from *Freedom and Experience: Essays Presented to Horace M. Kallen,* edited by Sidney Hook and Milton R. Konvitz (Cornell University Press, 1947), pp. 97–114.

[1] See my discussion of this theory in *Philo,* rev. ed. (Cambridge, Mass., 1948), I, 424–462; or in "Philo on Free Will," *Harvard Theological Review,* 35 (1942): 131–169.

Kalam. Briefly stated it is this. Things in the world are, as in the Epicurean theory, not causally connected. But they do not happen by chance. They have the will of God as their immediate cause. The succession of events in the world is accordingly described in Neophilonism as a continuous creation of God. Though at its first appearance Neophilonism was held to be incompatible with free will, theologians soon found that the belief in the miraculous free working of the human will in a world governed directly by the will of God, while indeed involving difficulties, is not more difficult than the belief in the working of such a will in a world governed by God indirectly through causes subordinate to His will.

The difficulties involved in the assumption of the freedom of the human will were those arising out of its obvious conflict with the various phases of God's omnipotence, such as His pre-ordination, His foreknowledge, and their like. Solutions were offered, but every solution was met with a refutation, every refutation was countered by a rebuttal, and every rebuttal was again met with a refutation; and so the debate went on, without any one side yielding to the other. In the heat of the debate opponents accused one another of infringing either on human freedom or on some of the phases of divine omnipotence. But in all such controversies, one must not take a doctrine at the evaluation of its opponents. With the exception of one Muslim sect, an unorthodox sect, which openly declared itself against free will, all religious philosophers, including Calvinists, were vying with one another in showing how they all had the proper conception of freedom. At least all of them contended that man's will could be free from the determination of natural causes.

And so on the eve of the new period in its history, philosophy had at its disposal two theories for undetermined free will, the Epicurean and the Philonic, each of which could be expressed in a general formula. The formula for the Epicurean theory would be: given a world in which there was no causality, one could logically maintain the undetermined freedom of the human will. The formula for the Philonic theories would be: given a world in which God is either the remote or the immediate cause of all that happens, and given also a God who in a miraculous manner sometimes either breaks the chain of secondary causes or deviates from the continuity of His own direct creation, one could logically maintain that man's will was endowed by God with part of His own miraculous power to act in a manner free and undetermined.

In the light of these two formulas we shall discuss the treatment of causality and freedom in Descartes, Leibniz, and Hume.

I

When Descartes, in his opposition to the generally accepted Aristotelian conception of man as an organic being, shocked his contemporaries by his announcement that man is but a machine,[2] he immediately compensated by putting into that machine a Platonic soul, one which was created by God as something distinct from body and as something separable from it. This soul, he admitted after much debating with himself, though having no community with the body, still, in the course of its connection with it, is somehow acted upon by it and also acts upon it. It is acted upon by it insofar as the motions of the body may transform the actions of the soul into passions and thereby corrupt its thinking into error and its willing into sin. It acts upon it insofar as by a certain freedom possessed by its will it may overcome the passions induced into it by the body.

The freedom with which Descartes endows man's will is the Philonic, miraculous kind of freedom. He repeatedly speaks of it as something which we "have received from God"[3] or as something which God "has given"[4] to us. The

[2] *L'Homme* (*Oeuvres*, ed. Adam et Tannery, Paris, 1897–1910, XI, 120, l. 15ff.).
[3] *Meditationes de Prima Philosophia* IV (VII, 58, ll. 14–15).
[4] *Ibid.* (p. 60, ll. 20–21; p. 61, ll. 4–5).

purpose for which God has given it to us is, as in the Philonic theory, to help man in his uneven struggle with the powers of nature. For the smaller machine, the human body, is made out of matter, that universal matter out of which is also made the larger machine, the world; the actions of the body are part of those universal motions which God has implanted in matter at the time of the creation of the world; and, while God did not impart to created things the power of causation — for Descartes follows the medieval tradition of Neophilonism — He continuously creates things in the human body as well as in the world as a whole in accordance with certain universal laws of nature which He had conceived in His mind at the time of the creation of the world. Faced by the force of the actions of his own body upon his own soul, which are determined by God as part of His universal plan for the world, man, by the mere native powers of his soul, would be helpless. God therefore equipped the human will with the power of freedom by which in a miraculous way man can overcome the natural forces of his body.[5]

But, then, in addition to the general power of the freedom of the will given by God to all men to enable them to resist error and sin, Descartes also speaks of a divine grace by which God aids certain individual human beings in the attainment of a knowledge of the true and the good. This is not altogether a new doctrine; it is part of the original Philonic doctrine of freedom; it has also been used in a variety of senses in the history of Christian theology; and there is a variety of doubtful phases in Descartes's use of it. But for the purpose of our present discussion there is only one phase of the problem of divine grace which is of importance, and that is the problem as to whether man's will is free to resist divine grace.

In Christian theology at the time of Descartes there were two views on this problem. According to one view, generally described as Thomistic, which had just at that time

[5] *Ibid.* (p. 60, l. 31; p. 61, l. 26).

come to be known also as Jansenistic, divine grace could not
be resisted by man. Man was free only insofar as he could
act without forcible compulsion. Such a freedom was described as being without indifference. According to another
theory, generally described as Molinistic, divine grace could
be resisted by man, and man's will was free even in the sense
that it was undetermined. Such a freedom was described as
freedom of indifference.

Of these two views, Descartes at first followed the one and
then changed to the other.[6] In the *Meditations*, published in
1641, he maintained that the freedom which God has given
us is a freedom of indifference only as long as He has not by
His grace disposed our inward thoughts to acts which are
true and good.[7] But once God by this grace has disposed us
to true and good actions, that divine grace cannot be resisted. This latter kind of freedom given to us by divine grace
is no longer a freedom of indifference; and if it is called freedom it is only because freedom means acting without being
conscious "that any outside force constrains us in doing so,
for in order that I should be free it is not necessary that I
should be indifferent as to the choice of one or the other of
two contraries." [8] Later, however, at about the time of the
publication of the *Principles*, in 1644, in answer to objections
raised by one of his correspondents, Descartes himself gives
another interpretation of his words. He admits that by freedom he means more than the mere absence of external re-
straint; [9] he also admits that there is an element of indifference
even in the freedom that is determined by divine grace; [10]
and he makes the outright declaration that "grace does not
completely abolish indifference." [11] And the same view is

[6] A full account of this change is given by E. Gilson in *La Liberté chez
Descartes et la théologie* (Paris, 1913), pp. 286–432; cf. also A. B. Gibson,
The Philosophy of Descartes (London, 1932), pp. 329ff.

[7] *Medit.* IV (VII, 60, l. 26ff.; cf. p. 58, ll. 5–10).

[8] *Ibid.* (p. 57, ll. 26ff.). See above, "St. Augustine and the Pelagian Controversy," pp. 159, 170–176.

[9] Lettre CCCXLVII (IV, 117, ll. 1–5).

[10] *Ibid.* (pp. 115–116).   [11] *Ibid.* (p. 117, l. 30).

more directly expressed in the *Principles* where he speaks of
"freedom" as the equivalent of "indifference." [12]

In either of these two stages of his view, however, the
freedom of the will maintained by Descartes was a miraculous power given by God to man enabling him to deviate
from the ordinary course of nature. In the earlier stage, though
man's freedom was not powerful enough to resist the divine
grace that disposed him to the true and the good, it was
powerful enough to resist his own natural propensities toward
what is erroneous and sinful. In the later stage, it was powerful enough to resist even divine grace. The power of resist-
ance in either case was a miraculous power with which man
was endowed by God.

But if God has endowed man with the miraculous power to
violate the laws of his own nature, it would be quite reasonable to assume that God would also possess the power to violate the laws of nature in general. And yet Descartes is reluctant to admit that assumption. When a certain miracle
about the body of St. Bernard was reported to him, he re-
fused to believe it, evidently not because he doubted the veracity of the testimony, but rather because he doubted the possibility of a violation of the ordinary course of nature,[13] and
so also, for the same reason, did he refuse to see any miracle
in what was generally believed to be the miracle of trans-
substantiation.[14]

Still more emphatically is the denial of miracles expressed
by him in his *Le Monde*. This work is described by Descartes
himself as a "fable" [15] in which, he says, he is going to tell
the story of the creation of a new world, a story unlike that
of the creation of our present world as told in the Book of
Genesis.[16] But though his fable is indeed unlike the story in

---

[12] *Principia Philosophiae* I, 41.
[13] Lettre CLXVIII (II, 557–558).
[14] Lettre CCCLXVII (IV, 162–172); cf. *Quartae Responsionae* (VII, 248–256).
[15] *Le Monde*, ch. V (XI, 31, l. 18).
[16] *Ibid.*, ch. VI (p. 32, ll. 4–6).

the Book of Genesis, it still contains certain elements to be found in the works of theologians who ever since Philo's *De Opificio Mundi* have tried to rewrite the Book of Genesis in terms of Plato's *Timaeus*. There is in Descartes's fable a pre-existent matter, as there is one in both Plato and Philo. That pre-existent matter is in Descartes's fable created by God,[17] as it is also in the revised story of creation by almost all those who followed Philo, though it is not so in Plato. As in Plato, God divides this matter into various figures,[18] from which He creates the world. Again as in Plato, and also as in Philo, God endows the matter out of which the world is created with various kinds of motion, so that the created world continues these motions "according to the ordinary laws of nature, for God has so marvelously established these laws." [19]

True, however, to the Neophilonic tradition, Descartes declares that the continuity of the divinely established laws of nature are not due to any power of causation which God has imparted to matter or nature. There are no secondary causes in nature. It is God himself who "continues to preserve it in the same way that He has created it," [20] and the regularity of its continuity is due to the fact that "God always acts in the same way and consequently always produces the same effect in substance," [21] the implication being that it is not due to any power of causation possessed by nature itself. If despite the unchangeability of God's will, the world manifests certain deviations from the straight motions which are preserved directly by the will of God, this is due, he says, to matter, and in support of this he quotes a similar explanation in the name of the theologians,[22] though he could have quoted Plato.[23] Like all religious philosophers before him, who found scriptural support for the old Aristotelian laws of motion, he finds support for his own new laws of motion in what he

[17] *Ibid.* (p. 32, ll. 27–28).
[18] *Ibid.* (p. 34, l. 1ff.); cf. *Timaeus* 35 Bff.
[19] *Ibid.* (ll. 18–19).
[20] *Ibid.*, Ch. VII (p. 37, ll. 6–7).
[21] *Ibid.* (ll. 26–28).
[22] *Ibid.* (p. 46, l. 9ff.).
[23] *Timaeus* 48 A; 56 C.

describes as the "truths" which "God himself has taught us," [24] paraphrasing from the apocryphal work Wisdom of Solomon the verse: "But in measure and number and weight Thou hast ordered all things." [25] But then departing from the common traditions of religious philosophy ever since Philo, he declares concerning this new world that "God will never work any miracles there, and that the intelligences, or reasonable minds, which we shall hereafter assume to be there, will never interfere in the ordinary course of nature." [26]

And so Descartes, who on the whole follows the Philonic tradition, departs from the Philonic formula. While lavishing upon man the miraculous power of free will, he begrudges God, in this old world of ours, a few reported miracles; and, in his own imaginary new world, he denies Him outright the power of miracle-working. To Descartes, then, in departure from the Philonic formula, man can break the spell of a moonlit night, but God cannot stay the moonlight.

II

While Descartes endows man with a greater freedom than his conception of miracles would allow him, Leibniz, we shall now try to show, does not endow man with the kind of freedom which he could allow him by his own conception of miracles.

Historically, the monads of Leibniz are in the tradition of the various attempts by philosophers before him to combine Platonic ideas with Epicurean atoms.[27] But true to the Philonic tradition in religious philosophy he did not follow the Epicurean theory of chance as an explanation of the origin and

[24] *Le Monde*, Ch. VII (p. 46, ll. 15–17).
[25] Wisdom of Solomon, 11:20; cf. St. Augustine, *De Genesi ad Litteram Libri* XII, Lib. IV, Ch. III (PL 39, col. 299).
[26] *Le Monde*, Ch. VII (p. 48, ll. 3–6).
[27] An example of such an attempt to combine ideas and atoms in Arabic philosophy is discussed by me in "The Kalam Problem of Nonexistence and Saadia's Second Theory of Creation," *Jewish Quarterly Review*, n.s., 36 (1946): 371–391.

order of the universe. His pre-established harmony, by which he explains not only the harmony between soul and body but also the harmony that prevails throughout the different parts of the universe, attributes the order of nature to God who established it at the time of the creation of the world. But, while true to the Philonic tradition as a whole, he does not follow it either in its original form or in its modified form. With the Neophilonians he rejects the belief in secondary causes; but, unlike the Neophilonians, he does not conceive of God as the immediate cause of events in the world, and in this connection he criticizes especially the occasionalism of Malebranche, which at that time was the latest form of expression given to the old Neophilonic theory. His own view may be regarded as a modification of both the original Philonic theory and the Neophilonic theory, standing midway between them. Like both these theories it assumes that laws of nature were established by God at the creation of the world. But it differs from both these theories in its view as to how these laws operate in the world. According to the Philonic theory they operate by means of secondary causes; according to the Neophilonic theory, they operate by the direct intervention of God; according to the theory of the pre-established harmony they operate spontaneously by the original causation of God.

Still even the doctrine of pre-established harmony may be traced to a tradition in which Philo shared, namely, a rabbinic tradition.[28] But whereas in Philo and the rabbis it was used only as an explanation of miraculous events, Leibniz has extended it to natural events. The literary sources through which Leibniz became acquainted with this tradition are undoubtedly Buxtorf's Latin translations of Judah Halevi's *Cuzari* and Maimonides' *Moreh Nebukim*. In both these works miracles are described as being "natural" (*naturales*),[29] or as "in some respect flowing forth from nature" (*aliquo*

[28] Cf. my discussion of this in *Philo*, I, 351 n. 24.
[29] *Liber Cosri* III, 73 end (Basel, 1660), p. 255.

modo e natura promanare),[30] or as "coming into being by the eternal will of God" (*fiunt voluntate Dei aeterna*),[31] for at the creation of the world God established that certain miracles should happen at certain times in the future. What Leibniz did was to use this principle, which reduces miracles to something "natural," as an explanation of the occurrence of all events which are usually described as natural. As we shall see, Leibniz also makes use of this principle in its original form as an explanation of miracles. His argument that occasionalism introduces into the world perpetual miracles,[32] which reflects Judah Halevi's argument that the Kalam conception of continuous creation removes the distinction between the miraculous and the non-miraculous,[33] may, therefore, be applied to himself, for by his pre-established harmony he explains natural events by a theory used by others in explaining miracles.

But in this harmonious world established by God at the time of its creation, Leibniz, again in the Philonic tradition, believes that God has the power to upset the harmony. His criticism of occasionalism as a theory which introduces into the world perpetual miracles does not imply a denial of the possibility of miracles in his own world governed by a pre-established harmony. Again and again he affirms his belief that the God who established the harmony in the world can also disestablish it by the creation of miracles. Indeed, like many a religious philosopher, he does not want to resort to a miraculous explanation of an event, when a rational explanation was possible,[34] still miracles, to him, are possible and did happen, miracles which he attributes to God who "has

---

[30] *Liber Doctor Perplexorum* II, 20 (Basel, 1629), p. 272.

[31] *Cosri, loc. cit.*

[32] *Théodicée* I, §61; cf. *Système nouveau*, §13. Cf. below at nn. 47, 48.

[33] *Cosri* V, 20, p. 369: "Quod si innovata (*ea quae fiunt*) intentione prima intenderentur a Causa prima, tum singulis horis et momentis nova crearentur (*a Deo*), et possemus dicere de mundo, et iis quae in eo sunt, quod nunc eum creet creator (*per continuas sc. et successivas creationes*), neque in prodigiis et miraculis quicquam foret miraculosi homini."

[34] *Nouveaux essais*, Préface (ed. P. Janet, Paris, 1866, 1900, p. 27; English by G. Langley, London, 1894, p. 55).

the power to change the course of nature." [35] In this statement as well as in similar other statements, he would seem to consider miracles to be due to a direct intervention by God in His own pre-established harmony. But sometimes, in conformity with his own explanation of the order of nature as being due to a pre-established harmony, he explains miracles as being due also to what may be described as pre-established disharmony. "One may say," he declares, "that miracles are as much in the [general] order as the natural operations," [36] maintaining that even miracles follow from God's "general will." [37] This explanation of miracles by a kind of pre-established disharmony of nature is exactly like the explanation we have quoted above from the *Cuzari* and *Moreh Nebukim*. Both these explanations try to show exactly the same thing, namely, that though miracles are a deviation from what is generally called nature, they have been pre-established by God in the same way as natural events. But what is more striking is the statement made by Leibniz, in the course of the explanation of miracles, that "one may say that this nature is nothing but the custom of God." [38] In the same connection, in the Latin translation of the *Cosri* there is the statement: "By nature is understood custom." [39]

With his belief in the possibility of miracles, whether due to a direct intervention of God in His pre-established harmony or to a sort of pre-established disharmony, Leibniz could logically assume that man's will was in a similar miraculous way completely free and undetermined. And yet he does not make that assumption. His discussion of freedom reflects primarily the Greek philosophic conception of it. Freedom, to him, is merely the power of reason to overcome desire.[40] In the metaphysical sense, he maintains, the will

---

[35] *Ibid.* IV, XVI, §13.

[36] *Discours de métaphysique* VII (ed. H. Lestienne, p. 34).

[37] *Théodicée* II, §206.

[38] *Discours* VII (p. 34): "Car on peut dire que cette nature n'est qu'une coustume de Dieu"; cf. below, n. 55.

[39] *Cosri* III, 73 end (p. 255): "Per Naturam intelligitur Consuetudo"; cf. below n. 55.   [40] *Nouveaux essais* II, 21, §47.

is not free from necessity, for, as he says, "the understanding can determine the will," [41] and to be free, he says, is "to be determined by the reason to the best." [42] Freedom of indifference, whether in the choice of good or in the choice of evil, is declared by him to be purely imaginary. [43]

And so Leibniz, too, departs from the Philonic formula. While maintaining with the Philonic tradition that God does sometimes miraculously upset the order of nature, he does not follow that tradition in having God endow man's will with a similar miraculous power.

III

The Philonic conception of divine causality, which on the whole is followed by both Descartes and Leibniz, is directly discussed and rejected by Hume, and he similarly rejects the classical Greek conception of fated causality, though only with a slight allusion to it. In their place, he revives the Epicurean denial of causality.

Hume, like many ordinary people who are not known as profound philosophers, did not believe that the world was created by God. Nor did he, like Aristotle, believe that the world is eternal. In fact, like the ancient Greek skeptics, he declared that all questions concerning the origin of the world lie entirely beyond the reach of human capacity. [44] Still, when for the purpose of explaining the order of the world he needed some theory as to its origin, he ventured to revive the old Epicurean hypothesis of the fortuitous concourse of atoms, giving to it what he calls "a faint appearance of probability" [45] by assuming that the atoms are finite in number instead of assuming, as in the original Epicurean

[41] *Ibid.* II, 21, §8.
[42] *Ibid.* II, 21, §50.
[43] *Ibid.* II, 21, §47; cf. *Théodicée* I, §35.
[44] *An Inquiry Concerning the Human Understanding*, sec. VIII, part II (ed. Selby-Bigge, Oxford, 1896, p. 81).
[45] *Dialogues Concerning Natural Religion* VIII, beginning.

theory, that they are infinite in number but only finite in variety.

Originally the Epicurean denial of causality was aimed against the various conceptions of fated causality which prevailed throughout Greek philosophy. There is an indirect allusion in Hume to this ancient conception of fate, when prefatory to his examination of the origin of the idea of causality he refers to the "universally acknowledged" view that "every object is determined by an absolute fate to a certain degree and direction of its motion." [46] Directly, however, Hume's own denial of causality is aimed against the various conceptions of divine causality held by the theologians and philosophers of his own time. Now of the two main theological conceptions current at his time, the Philonic and the Neophilonic, the latter view, through the influence of Descartes and his followers, especially the occasionalists, was philosophically the more fashionable. It is this view, therefore, that is taken up by him for special criticism. His argument against it is like that used by Leibniz against occasionalism, which reflects, as we have seen, an argument by Judah Halevi. Leibniz argues that occasionalism does nothing but "to have recourse to miracle" [47] or to introduce into the world "perpetual miracles." [48] So also Hume argues that the occasionalists "have recourse, on all occasions, to the same principle, which the vulgar never appeal to but in cases that appear miraculous and supernatural." [49] The original Philonic view is only indirectly alluded to by Hume when, contrasting it with the then current occasionalism, he contends that, from a purely theological point of view, it is more consistent with the traditional conception of God's power and wisdom to have Him "delegate a certain degree of power to inferior creatures" than to have Him "obliged every moment to adjust" the parts of the world. [50] This contention reflects the intestine squabbles

[46] *A Treatise of Human Nature*, bk. II, part III, sec. I (ed. Selby-Bigge, pp. 399–400).

[47] *Système nouveau*, §13.   [49] *Inquiry*, sec. VII, part I (p. 70).

[48] *Théodicée* I, §61.   [50] *Ibid.* (p. 71).

among the theologians themselves, as it is also reflected in Leibniz' contention that God "is skilful enough to make use of this contrivance," that is to say, of the pre-established harmony.[51]

But though in this argument *ad hominem*, Hume maintains that the assumption of secondary causes is theologically preferable to the assumption of occasionalism, he himself rejects both these assumptions, for both of them proceed from the belief in the existence of a creative deity, which Hume does not accept. And since there is no God either to impart the power of causation to His creatures or continuously to act as the immediate cause of His creatures, there is no such thing as causality in nature, for causality in nature always implies either an eternal Fate or an eternal God above nature. What we have in nature is a mere succession of isolated things which are neither connected with each other as causes and effects, nor are they each individually effects of the immediate causality of God's will, nor in fact are they all in their totality the product of God's creation. They are all, according to Hume — whether he would say so explicitly or not — the product of chance, and by chance they follow a certain order, and by chance that order may at any moment disappear. If these things which are in "succession" happen to appear to us to be causally connected, this idea of causation is due to "a customary connexion in the thought or imagination between one object and its usual attendant," [52] and if we seem to have faith that chance succession of the past will continue in the future it is because of our "being determined by custom to transfer the past to the future." [53]

Ever since students of philosophy were told that there was a medieval Hume [54] there has been a search for other me-

---

[51] *Second éclaircissement* (*Opera*, ed. J. E. Erdmann, Berlin, 1840, p. 134).

[52] *Inquiry*, sec. VII, part II (p. 75).

[53] *Ibid.*, sec. VI (p. 58).

[54] Cf. H. Rashdall, "Nicolas de Ultercuria, A Medieval Hume," *Proceedings of the Aristotelian Society*, n. s., 7 (1907): 1–27.

dieval Humes. Now, there was really no medieval Hume, for Hume in his complete denial of causality is an unadulterated Epicurean, whereas all those who may be trotted out as medieval Humes only denied secondary causes, and whatever Epicureanism there was in them was smothered by Philonism. They were all what we chose to call Neophilonists. Still certain phrases or terms in Hume's writings may be traced to medieval Neophilonism. One of these I wish to deal with here, and that is the term "custom." In Muslim Neophilonism, with its denial of causality, in the limited sense of the denial of secondary causes, the order of nature was described by the term custom (in the Latin translations *consuetudo*).[55] Now Averroes in his argument against these Muslim Neophilonists confronts them with the question as to what they mean by the term "custom." If they mean thereby some habit (*habitus*) acquired by God, that, of course, is absurd, for God is unchangeable. And if they mean thereby some habit acquired by the existent things themselves, that also is absurd, for inanimate things do not acquire habits. His conclusion is that they must mean thereby "the *custom* of those who possess *judgment* concerning existing things," i.e., men, but "that there should be in us a *custom* in the *judgment* concerning existent things that *custom* is nothing but an act of the *mind*," [56] and thereupon he tries to show where they are wrong. Now Hume's own summary of his view that, as a result of the recurrence of the same event after the same object, we "feel a new sentiment or impression, to wit, a *customary* connection in the *thought* or *imagination* between one object and its usual attendant," [57] or that "the *mind* is determined by *custom* to infer the one from the appearance of the other" [58] quite obviously reflects the statement quoted from Averroes.

[55] Cf. Averroes, *Destructio Destructionum*, *In Physicis*, Disput. I, *Aristotelis* opera IX (Venice, 1573), fol. 130E; cf. Maimonides, *Doctor Perplexorum* I, 73, Prop. 6 (Basel, 1629), p. 155, and n. 39, above.
[56] Averroes, *Destr.*, fol. 130E–F.
[57] *Inquiry*, sec. VII, part II (p. 78).
[58] *Ibid.*, sec. VIII, part I (p. 82).

Strictly speaking, with his denial of causality and of necessary connection, Hume could not use the terms "cause" and "necessity" and "laws of nature." Similarly, for the same reason, he had all the right to use the term "chance." But philosophic terms, throughout their history, have been loosely handled and have been used in a variety of senses, often in opposite senses. Hume, therefore, wishing to make use of this philosophic license and also wishing to forestall any possible criticism, avails himself of an ancient maxim, which has been used by all sorts of philosophers on similar occasions, and thus says of himself, "I shall not dispute about a word." [59] Now it happens that the term cause, without any implication of necessary connection between two things, is used even by the Epicureans themselves as a description of a thing which always happens to precede another thing; thus they speak of the "cause of existence" [60] or the "cause of disease." [61] Similarly, the term "necessity" without any implication of "fate" is used by them as a description of the periodic recurrence of phenomena,[62] reflecting therein Aristotle's use of the same term in the sense of that which "always comes to pass in the same way." [63] And consequently the term "chance," the opposite of "necessity," has also come to be used simply as a designation of that which does not "always come to pass in the same way." [64] And so also the expression "fixed law of nature" [65] is used by the Epicureans themselves as a designation of the periodic recurrence of phenomena, even though that periodic recurrence is not attributed to a cause, either an inexorable, blind fate or a benevolent deity acting by design.

Evidently taking advantage of the looseness in the use of these terms, Hume uses the term "cause" for that which is

---

[59] *Ibid.*, sec. X, part I (p. 111). See my comment on the history of this maxim in *The Philosophy of Spinoza* (Cambridge, Mass., 1934), I, 190 n. 3.

[60] Lucretius, III, 348: *causa salutis.*

[61] *Ibid.*, 502: *morbi causa.*

[62] Diogenes, X, 77.

[63] *Physica* II, 5, 196b, 10–11, 12–13.

[64] *Ibid.*

[65] Lucretius, V, 924: *foedus naturae certum.*

merely observed always to precede an event,[66] and he quotes with approval, but evidently in a new sense, the philosophic maxim that "nothing exists without a cause for its existence." [67] By the same philosophic license, he applies the term "necessity" to that which to him is a mere constant succession of things; [68] he repeats with approval, evidently again in a new sense, the philosophic maxim that "chance is a mere negative word" [69] or that it has "no existence"; [70] and he uses the expression "laws of nature" [71] as a description of that which only our mind by custom sees in nature as being constantly recurrent.

The constancy in the recurrence of events in the past, which, though only a matter of mere succession, is described by Hume in terms of causality and necessity, is also sufficient, according to him, to assure us of the recurrence of the same events in the future. The judgment that the sun will rise tomorrow, or that all men must die, or that fire will burn human beings and water will suffocate them is indeed based only on past experience. Still it would be ridiculous, says Hume, to express doubt in the recurrence of any of these events in the future.[72] He is therefore opposed to Locke's designation of this type of sure judgment by the term "probability," as distinguished from the term "knowledge," and prefers to designate it by the term "proof," meaning thereby that kind of judgment which is "entirely free from doubt and uncertainty," leaving the term "probability" for that kind of judgment "which is still attended with uncertainty." [73] However, this distinction between "proof" and "probability" is, as Hume himself admits, merely a matter of terminology,

---

[66] *Inquiry*, sec. VIII, part I (pp. 95–96); *Treatise*, bk. II, part III, sec. II (p. 409).

[67] *Inquiry*, sec. VIII, part I (p. 95).

[68] *Ibid.* (p. 82); *Treatise*, bk. II, part III, sec. I (p. 400).

[69] *Inquiry*, sec. VIII, part I (p. 95).

[70] *Ibid.* (p. 96).

[71] *Ibid.*, sec. X, part I (p. 114).

[72] *Treatise*, bk. I, part III, sec. XI (p. 124); *Inquiry*, sec. VI (pp. 56, 57).

[73] *Treatise*, *loc. cit.*; *Inquiry*, *loc. cit.*

which he himself has not always observed. The main point philosophically is that events which in our experience of the past have constantly occurred are to Hume only "probabilities," or a special kind of probability called "proofs," but are not "knowledge."

Now the difference between a judgment which constitutes "knowledge" and a judgment which constitutes only a "probability" of this special kind, according to Hume, is that the former, being based upon the comparison of ideas, not only creates in our mind an assurance free from doubt and uncertainty but is also, by the very nature of the ideas which are compared, necessary and invariable, whereas the latter, being based only on experience and on the conception of cause and effect which does not exist in the nature of things themselves, while it creates in our mind an assurance free from doubt and uncertainty, is by the nature of the things themselves not necessary and invariable. The significance of Hume's view becomes apparent when it is contrasted with that of Aristotle. Hume's distinction between "knowledge," "proof," and "probability," and for that matter Locke's distinction between "knowledge" and "probability," it can be shown, are a development of the terms "knowledge" (ἐπιστήμη), "probability" (τὸ εἰκός), and "proof" (τεκμήριον) as used by Aristotle, Hume's "knowledge" corresponding to the term "knowledge" as used by Aristotle in the sense of judgments which are necessary and cannot be otherwise. But, still, because of his belief in causality, Aristotle, unlike Hume, places constantly recurrent events under "knowledge," and this because he takes the constancy of their recurrence as evidence that the events in question are causally connected and hence by their very nature are necessary and cannot be otherwise. Such judgments as "all men are mortal," which to Hume do not belong to "knowledge," are to Aristotle to be included under "knowledge."

Now since, according to Hume, all those things, which, on the basis of the constancy of their occurrence in the past, are called by him laws of nature, are to be considered only as probable in the future and not as necessary, the reported constancy of their occurrence in the past must likewise make the report of the constancy of their occurrence in the past only a probability and not a necessity. The fact that no exception to certain commonly recurrent events was ever reported in the past is in itself no assurance that such an exception did not or could not take place. Supposing, therefore, that no case were ever reported of fire that did not burn a human being or of a dead man who came to life, the absence of such reported exceptions would not necessarily mean that such exceptions are impossible. Conversely, also, when we do have reports of such exceptions, as, for instance, the scriptural stories about Daniel's friends whom fire did not burn and about Elijah, Elisha, and Jesus who raised the dead, these reported exceptions are not necessarily to be regarded as impossible. On the basis of his own philosophy, therefore, Hume could not declare these events reported in Scripture as impossible; he could only deny that they have been caused by the particular volition of God. It is for this reason evidently that in his attempt to discredit the veracity of religious miracles he does not argue that they are impossible; he only argues that the testimony as to their having occurred is not to be relied upon.[74]

With this conception of the possibility of miracles — miracles in the mere sense of the transgressions of the laws of nature without the assumption of an intervening deity — it should have been logically possible for Hume to assume also the possibility of an absolutely undetermined freedom of the human will. Unencumbered by preconceived notions of fated causality, Hume, unlike Plato, Aristotle, and the Stoics, was under no logical compulsion to force the universally acknowledged capriciousness of human actions into the general framework of universal causality. He could have treated human will and human actions as an area in nature

[74] *Inquiry*, sec. X.

which, by the peculiarities of the fortuitous concourse of its atoms, did not have to conform to those of other areas in nature. Such was the position of the Epicureans.

And yet, in his discussion of freedom, he argues like a follower of Plato, Aristotle, and the Stoics, and not, as he should, as a follower of Epicureanism. His entire discussion in his inquiry on "Liberty and Necessity" is an attempt to uphold the conception, held by classical Greek philosophy, of human freedom against that held by the Philonic, making no reference at all, as he should, to the Epicurean conception of liberty. "All mankind," he says, "have shown a propensity, in all ages, to profess" a belief in the absolutely undetermined freedom of the will.[75] From his subsequent more explicit discussion of the problem,[76] it is evident that by "all mankind . . . in all ages" he meant only those who in the history of Christian theology have stressed the element of human free will against those who stressed the element of divine preordination. And against them he argues, in the manner of Plato, Aristotle, and the Stoics, that freedom of the will means only freedom from external compulsion, which, as he says, belongs to everyone "who is not a prisoner and in chains;" [77] and, if certain human acts seem to us undetermined, it is only because we are ignorant of the causes.[78]

And so in Hume, too, we have a departure from a formula which we should expect him to follow, the Epicurean formula. There is to him no causality in nature, and yet he denies that the human will is absolutely undetermined.

In calling attention to the fact that Descartes, Leibniz, and Hume have departed from certain historical formulas, we did not mean to say that they were inconsistent. In philosophy, there is no inconsistency which cannot be adjusted by clipping off the jutting edges of some concept or by splitting the meaning of some term, and often behind what appears

[75] *Ibid.*, sec. VIII, part I (p. 92).
[76] *Ibid.*, part II (pp. 99ff.).
[77] *Ibid.*, part I (p. 95).
[78] *Ibid.* (pp. 85ff.).

to be an inconsistency is not bad reasoning but only conflicting motives or objectives. The main purpose of our discussion was to show that historically there were two roads to undetermined freedom of the will, the Epicurean road of the denial of causality and the Philonic road of divine causality and miracles, and that Descartes, Leibniz, and Hume — who, as we all know, belong to a new age in the history of philosophy — traveled the same old roads, though for reasons they did not take the trouble to tell us they either made a detour or completely changed their direction. Descartes starts with divine causality and ends with miraculous free will but denies miracles. Leibniz starts with divine causality, continues with miracles, but denies miraculous free will. Hume starts with a denial of causality but denies causeless free will. And what we have found in the case of Descartes, Leibniz, and Hume is also to be found, we venture to say, in the case of all those who after them discussed the problem of free will. If we cut through the jungle of words which so often obscures the discussion of this problem, we shall always find the two old roads, the Philonic and the Epicurean, modernized, perhaps, broadened, lengthened, straightened out, smoothed out, macadamized, and heavily academized — but still the same old roads. Not all who traveled these roads, however, were equipped with good road maps, and so occasionally some of them lost their way and got to the wrong place.

9

THE VERACITY OF SCRIPTURE FROM
PHILO TO SPINOZA *

I. THE PROBLEM AND ITS SOLUTIONS

To religious philosophers, taken collectively, the problem of
the veracity of Scripture presented itself in three parts — one
with regard to the historical narrative before the exodus from
Egypt, another with regard to the historical narrative after
the exodus, and a third with regard to the laws of Moses and
the teachings of the other prophets. These constituted three
distinct problems, each of them presenting a special difficulty
and each of them requiring a special kind of solution.

The part which troubled the mind of religious philosophers
the least, was the historical narrative after the exodus. This
narrative, presented in Scripture as the record of eyewitnesses,
was accepted as authentic history by both Jews and Christians, though not altogether by Muslims. A reflection of this
general attitude on the part of Jews is to be found in Judah
Halevi's *Cuzari*, a work written in the form of a dialogue
between the King of the Khazars and a Rabbi. The Rabbi
first discusses the source of our knowledge of the events before the exodus, but when he comes to the events after the
exodus, he simply says: "And we know what the chronology
is from Moses to the present time," [1] by which he means
that our knowledge of that post-Mosaic chronology is in
need of no proof, inasmuch as it is attested by eyewitnesses.
The argument from the attestation of eyewitnesses is extended by Maimonides even to certain narratives before the
exodus, namely, narratives which contain certain details
which to him bear the intrinsic evidence of their having been

---

* Published in *Alexander Marx Jubilee Volume*, 1950, pp. 603–630, issued
by the Jewish Theological Seminary of America.

[1] *Cuzari* I, 47.

recorded by reliable eyewitnesses.[2] As for the Christian and Muslim views on the historical narratives of the Hebrew Scripture, they will be discussed later in section III of this paper.

More of a problem to all those religious philosophers was the prophetic teachings, both the laws of Moses and the teachings of the other prophets. Presented in Scripture as special revelations from God to men, these laws and teachings seemed to them to be in need of arguments in support of their veracity.

From the very beginning of the attempt to harmonize Scripture and philosophy, four types of arguments were used to establish the divine origin of the laws and teachings of the prophets: (1) the miracles performed by the prophets; (2) the prophetic power to predict future events; (3) the revelation on Mount Sinai; (4) the intrinsic excellency of the laws and teachings of the prophets.

These four types of arguments are all used by Philo. In great detail he describes the miraculous early history of Moses and the numerous miracles performed by him in Egypt and in the desert.[3] He also dwells upon the fulfillment of everything that Moses predicted in the name of God.[4] Then he represents with many explanations the account of the revelation on Mount Sinai when, in a miraculous way, the voice of God — which, of course, was not a physical voice — was heard by the entire people, men and women alike,[5] and which like any direct experience is itself evidence for its veracity. Finally, there is to him the evidence of the intrinsic excellency of the laws of Moses, their comprehensiveness,[6] their permanence,[7] their universal appeal to all mankind,[8] and their establishment of a perfect way of life in accordance with all the requirements of science and philosophy.[9]

Among the Christian theologians, to mention only one of

[2] *Moreh Nebukim* III, 50.
[3] *Mos.* I, 2, 5–59, 327.
[4] *Ibid.* I, 14, 71.
[5] *Decal.* 9, 32–35.
[6] *Mos.* II, 3, 12.
[7] *Ibid.* II, 3, 14.
[8] *Ibid.* II, 4, 17–44.
[9] *Spec. Leg.* I–IV.

the earliest among them, Justin Martyr restates three of Philo's arguments in proof of the veracity of both the Old and the New Testament. Speaking of the Old Testament prophets, he says that while "they did not use demonstrations in their treatises," still (1) "they were entitled to credit on account of the miracles which they performed" and also (2) on account of their true prophetic predictions, for those events which have happened, and those which are happening, compel you to assent to the utterance made by them," and finally (3) on account of the intrinsic excellence of their teachings, for "their writings are still extant, and he who has read them is very much helped in the knowledge of the beginning and end of things, and of those matters which the philosopher ought to know, provided he believed in them." [10] And speaking of Jesus, he says that the divine origin of his teachings is verified (1) "by the works and by the attendant miracles," [11] (2) "by the prophecies announced concerning him," [12] and (3) by the intrinsic excellence of his teachings as is evidenced by the lives of Christians, for "we see and are persuaded that men approach God, leaving their idols and other unrighteousness, through the name of Him who was crucified, Jesus Christ, and abide by their confession, even unto death, and maintain piety." [13]

In Islam, the same three kinds of argument came into play in the discussion of the veracity of the Koran. 'Alī Ṭabarī, among his ten arguments for the veracity of the Koran, includes the following three: the intrinsic merits of its teachings; the miracles wrought by Muhammad; his predictive power. [14] Algazali stresses the importance of miracles, arguing that the allegorical or rational explanation of them by the philosophers is a denial of the claim of Moses as well as of the other prophets

[10] *Dial. cum Tryph.* 7.
[11] *Ibid.* 11; cf. 69.
[12] *Ibid.* 35.
[13] *Ibid.* 11.
[14] 'Alī b. Rabban al-Ṭabarī, *The Book of Religion and Empire*, Arabic text: *Kitāb al-Dīn wa'l-Daulah*, ed. A. Mingana (1923), p. 16, ll. 11–14; pp. 23–44 (English translation by A. Mingana [1922], pp. 14, 23–49).

that their teachings were of divine origin.[15] In opposition to him, however, Averroes, drawing upon Avicenna, argues that the test of the truth of prophecy is to be found in "(1) the communication of things hidden, i.e., prediction, and (2) the establishment of laws which are in agreement with truth and which cause the acquisition of habits of conduct leading to the happiness of all created things."[16]

It is exactly this kind of argument that Judah Halevi uses in his *Cuzari*. He puts into the mouth of his spokesman, the Rabbi, at the beginning of his address to the King of the Khazars in proof of the divine origin of the teachings of Scripture.

He begins, like Justin Martyr, by stating that the truth of the teachings of Scripture, unlike those of the philosophers, are not based upon demonstration.[17] Then he continues to say that the truth of these scriptural teachings may be established by the miracles performed directly by God as well as by those performed by God through Moses,[18] and also by the prophetic power of Moses to know things hidden from everybody and to foretell events that are to take place.[19] Like Philo he dwells upon the revelation on Mount Sinai where the whole assembly of Israel were eyewitnesses to the appearance of God and they themselves heard His voice as He revealed to them the Ten Commandments, which, again like Philo, he tries to explain in conformity with his belief in the incorporeality of God,[20] for before the revelation on Mount Sinai, he says, despite the miracles performed by Moses, "the people did not fully believe that God spoke with man."[21] Finally, he points to the excellency of the teachings of the Law as is evidenced by the lives of those who live according to those teachings[22] and also by their willingness to sacrifice their lives for the sake of those teachings.[23]

This last type of argument is introduced by a question ad-

---

[15] *Tahāfut al-Falāsifah*, Phys. (ed. Bouyges), §§6–12, pp. 271–276.
[16] *Tahāfut al-Tahāfut*, Phys. (ed Bouyges), §9, p. 516.
[17] *Cuzari* I, 13.
[18] *Ibid*. I, 9; I, 11; I, 25.
[19] *Ibid*. I, 9; I, 41.   [20] *Ibid*. I, 89.
[21] *Ibid*. I, 49; cf. I, 87.
[22] *Ibid*. I, 19.
[23] *Ibid*. IV, 16–17.

dressed by the Rabbi to the King: "If thou wert told that the King of India was an excellent man, who deserves that you exalt him and do honor to his name and eulogize his deeds on account of the reports that have reached you of the justice of the inhabitants of his land and the excellency of their characters and the uprightness of their business dealings, would this bind you to revere him?"[24] To this, after some hesitation and after the Rabbi has added the fact that the reports from India were brought by reliable eyewitnesses who had seen the king of India, the king of the Khazars admits that he is convinced that such a king does exist in India and that his power and rule are such as are reported to be.[25] A striking parallel is to be found also in Justin Martyr who, in his attempt to show that a knowledge of God can be attained not by philosophy but only through revelation and tradition, makes the unknown stranger ask the following question: "Now, if one were to tell you that in India there is a living creature unlike all others, of such and such a shape, multiform and of various colors, you would have no positive knowledge of it until you had seen it, nor would you give any description of it, except you had heard from an eyewitness." To which Justin answers: "True."[26]

Maimonides, like his contemporary Averroes, rejects miracles as proof of the authenticity of the divine origin of the teaching of Moses and, like Philo and Halevi, dwells upon the direct evidence of those who witnessed the revelation on Mount Sinai. "Moses was not believed by Israel on account of the miracles which he performed, for he who comes to believe by reason of miracles retains in his heart some suspicion that perhaps those miracles were performed by magic and sorcery. All the miracles which Moses performed in the wilderness were performed by him to meet a certain exigency and not as evidence for the truth of prophecy . . . By what, then, were they ultimately brought about to believe in him?

[24] *Ibid.* I, 19.
[25] *Ibid.* I, 20–24.
[26] *Dial. cum Tryph.* 3.

By the revelation on Mount Sinai," [27] which revelation, like Philo and Halevi, he explains in conformity with his belief in the incorporeality of God.[28] Finally, the truth of the Law is to be established, as he himself tries to prove in his work, by the intrinsic excellency of its teachings. "The general object of the Law," he says, "is twofold: the well-being of the soul, and the well-being of the body." [29]

The most difficult part to defend was the pre-Mosaic part of the Pentateuch. This part, to the mind of religious philosophers, was divided into the history of the universe and the history of mankind. In the history of the universe, the chief teaching of Scripture is that the world was created; in the history of mankind the chief teaching of Scripture is twofold, namely, that mankind had its origin in Adam and that the history of mankind from Adam to Moses was a comparatively short time, approximately 2500 years. An outline of these three problems are given by both Halevi and Maimonides. Halevi, at the outset of his discussion, makes the Rabbi outline the principles of scriptural teachings as containing information as to how the world was created, how all mankind, with all their geographical dispersions and linguistic divisions, trace their descent ultimately to Adam, and how we know the number of years that had elapsed since the time of Adam.[30] Similarly, Maimonides outlines the principles of scriptural teachings as containing the beliefs that "the world was created, that at the beginning there was created only one individual of the human species and that was Adam, and that the time which elapsed from Adam to Moses was not more than about two thousand five hundred years." [31]

The story of creation presented special problems. Here the scriptural narrative seems to come into conflict with certain other views as to the origin of the world with which philoso-

---

[27] *Mishneh Torah, Yesode ha-Torah* I, 8; cf. *Moreh Nebukim* III, 24; *Iggeret Teman, Ḳobes* II, p. 4d, and ed. A. S. Halkin (1952), p. 55 and p. [XI]

[28] *Moreh Nebukim* I, 46; II, 33; III, 9.   [30] *Cuzari* I, 43.

[29] *Ibid.* III, 27.   [31] *Moreh Nebukim* III, 50.

phers, Jewish, Christian or Muslim, became acquainted. The manner in which this problem was dealt by them does not concern us for the present. But two general observations may be made with regard to the story of creation.

First, from Philo throughout Christian, Muslim and Jewish philosophy, there was a general tendency on the part of the philosophers of these religions to disregard the literalness of the story of creation and to harmonize it with what each of them happened to believe with regard to the origin of the world.

Second, irrespective of their individual interpretation of the story of creation in the Book of Genesis, they all considered the act of creation as an act of divine will and hence a miraculous act. Thus Philo,[32] Tertullian,[33] Augustine,[34] Halevi,[35] and Maimonides [36] — all of them invoke the act of creation as proof for the possibility of miracles.

II. THE ORIGIN OF LANGUAGES, THE HEBDOMADAL PERIOD, AND THE DENARY SYSTEM

But whatever their views were with regard to the creation of the world, all religious philosophers took literally the belief in the Adamic descent of mankind. Jews and Christians were bound to this belief by the teaching of the Hebrew Scripture. Muslims considered themselves also bound to this belief by the repetition of the story of the creation of Adam as the first man in the Koran. Halevi speaks for the philosophers of all the three religions when he says that whatever the scriptural teachings with regard to creation may be, it definitely teaches that "the world was created at a certain time and that Adam, through Noah, was the origin of the human species." [37]

[32] *Mos.* I, 38, 212.
[33] *De Resur. Carn.* ch. XI.
[34] *De Civ. Dei* XXI, 7.
[35] *Cuzari* I, 91.
[36] *Moreh Nebukim* II, 25; *Ma'amar Teḥiyyat ha-Metim, Ḳobeṣ* II, p. 10vb; ed. Finkel, c. 42, p. 30.
[37] *Cuzari* I, 67.

Both Halevi and Maimonides, therefore, undertake to prove the Adamic descent of man.

The proofs, logically, are all of the same type. They all try to show that the belief in the Adamic descent of mankind gives the most satisfactory explanation of the origin of certain institutions which exist today. They all seem to start by saying: We have nowadays certain human institutions. These human institutions, they then argue, must have had a beginning. But they could not have had their beginning in a multitudinous society. They, therefore, conclude that all these institutions must have begun with one man, and that man was Adam, the father of the entire human race. Halevi, who leads the discussion on this point, takes as the subject of his argument three human institutions, language, the hebdomadal period, and the denary system.

His discussion of language occurs in three brief passages in different places in his work.[38] These disconnected passages are to be connected and welded into one continuous argument, and to understand the full implication of that argument we must reconstruct the historical background to which certain terms in that argument refer or allude.

In Greek philosophy there was a controversy over the question whether language had a "conventional" or a "natural" origin. Upon examination, however, we find that the terms conventional and natural in this controversy were used in three different senses. To begin with, the term conventional was contrasted with the term natural and meant that names were invented by man and were attached to things arbitrarily without any relation to the nature of the things to which they were attached. It is in this sense that Aristotle contrasts convention and nature when he says that "by a name we mean a sound significant by convention ($\kappa\alpha\tau\grave{\alpha}$ $\sigma\upsilon\nu\theta\acute{\eta}\kappa\eta\nu$),[39] because "nothing is by nature ($\phi\acute{\upsilon}\sigma\epsilon\iota$) a name." [40] Then the term conventional, instead of being contrasted with the term natural,

---

[38] *Ibid.* I, 53–57; II, 72; III, 25.
[39] *De Interpr.* 2, 16a, 19.
[40] *Ibid.* 27–28.

was used as supplementary to it and meant that names were indeed invented by somebody, but their invention as well as their application to things was not arbitrary, for all those invented names expressed the nature of things to which they were applied. It is in this sense that Plato combines the term convention with the term nature when, in his discussion of the origin of names, he says that in addition to "likeness" or "nature" we are compelled to add "convention," [41] so that "he who first gave names, gave such names as agreed with his conception of the nature of things.[42] Finally, the term "natural" was contrasted with the term "conventional" and meant that names were not invented by some name-giver but have rather grown out spontaneously of natural cries like those uttered by animals. It is in this sense that Epicurus contrasts the term natural with the term conventional when he is reported to have said that "the names of things were not originally due to convention or agreement (θέσει), but men's natures (φύσεις) according to their different nationalities, suffering peculiar feelings and receiving peculiar impressions, properly emitted air moulded into shape by each of these feelings and impressions, differing according to the difference of the regions which the nationalities inhabited." [43]

These Greek theories as to the origin of language were brought into play by Philo in his philosophic interpretation of Scripture. Commenting on the verse which reads to the effect that God brought every animal to Adam that he might give them their names,[44] he says that this verse admonishes students of philosophy that "names proceed from agreement (ex positione = θέσει) and not from nature (ex natura = φύσει), for a natural (naturalis) nomenclature is with peculiar fitness assigned to each creature when a man of wisdom and pre-

---

[41] Cratylus 435 C.
[42] Ibid. 436 B.
[43] Diogenes, X, 75. Cf. T. Gomperz, Griechische Denker (4th ed.), I, 327–331; II, 438–440 (English, I, 394–398; III, 164–166); C. Bailey, The Greek Atomists and Epicurus (Oxford, 1928), pp. 267–269, 380–382.
[44] Gen. 2:19.

eminent knowledge appears." [45] The statement in this passage
with regard to the peculiar fitness of the names given by
Adam is elsewhere repeated by him in his statement that the
names given by Adam brought out clearly "the peculiarities
(ἰδιότητας) of the creatures who bore them," [46] or that they
were "their appropriate names." [47] The scriptural proof-text
for his view is the verse which is quoted by him as "What-
soever Adam called anything, that was the name thereof"
(Gen. 2:19).[48] The reason why Adam was given the task of
naming the animals was due to the fact that "he was the first
person who deserved to govern them all as their chief." [49]

From these statements of Philo we may gather the particular senses in which he uses the terms nature and convention. With regard to the term nature, he rejects its use in the
Epicurean sense that names developed out of natural sounds
without any convention, but he uses it in the Platonic and
Aristotelian sense that names express the nature of the objects of which they are names. Then, with regard to the term
convention, he openly rejects its use in the sense that names
are merely arbitrary terms without any relation to the nature
of the things of which they are names, but he accepts, by implication, its use in the sense that names were given to things
by some name-giver and were not merely the spontaneous
outgrowth of natural sounds. His view thus reflects exactly
the view of Plato. He differs, however, from Plato in that the
human name-giver, according to him, was endowed by God
with a special gift for that purpose, for, commenting upon
the verse in which God is said to have given to Adam the
power to have dominion over the animals (Gen. 1:28), he
says that Adam was enabled to give appropriately fitting names
to all things because he "was wise with wisdom self-learned
and self-taught, having been created by the grace of God." [50]

[45] *Qu. in Gen.* I, 20.
[46] *Opif.* 52, 149.
[47] *Mut.* 9, 63.
[48] *Ibid.*; but cf. quotation of this verse in *Qu. in Gen.* I, 22.
[49] *Qu. in Gen.* I, 20; *Opif.* 52, 148.   [50] *Opif.* 52, 148.

From this statement by itself it is not clear whether he means by it that Adam was created by God with a special name-giving faculty or whether he means by it that Adam was directly inspired by God to give those names to all animals. The latter interpretation, however, would seem to be more likely, for elsewhere he uses the expressions "enacted ordinances" (τεθειμένα διατάγματα) and "enacted laws" (τεθέντες νόμοι), by which he means conventional ordinances or laws, in the sense of laws revealed by God [51] and he similarly used the expression "self-learned wisdom" and "self-taught wisdom" in the sense of wisdom which comes by revelation and prophecy, described by him as being caused by God "to spring up within the soul." [52] As for the language used by Adam in giving those names, it may be assumed that Philo believed that it was Hebrew and, as for the subsequent rise of a multiplicity of languages, it may be also assumed that he regarded the story of the confusion of tongues, which was caused directly by God, as an explanation of what he describes as the "origin of the Greek and barbarian languages." [53] How these various languages arose as a result of this confusion — whether the new languages, just as the confusion itself, arose by a direct intervention of God or whether, unlike the confusion itself, they developed naturally — he does not explain. But from his statement that what Moses called "confusion of tongues" means "the division of speech into a multitude of different kinds of language" [54] it may be inferred that God who caused the confusion of tongues also caused the formation of the different languages.

The rabbinic treatment of the names given by Adam to the animals and of the confusion of tongues contain statements which are parallel to those we have quoted from Philo. Like Philo, the rabbis say that Adam "gave to every living being a name suitable to it" [55] or that "everything the Holy One,

[51] *Abr.* 1, 5; cf. my *Philo*, rev. ed. (Cambridge, Mass., 1948), II, 189.
[52] *Sacr.* 22, 78; 23, 79; cf. *Philo*, I, 36.
[53] *Conf.* 38, 190.   [54] *Conf.* 4, 9.
[55] *Midrash ha-Gadol* on Gen. 2:20; cf. *Genesis Rabbah* 17, 4.

blessed be He, created in His world was named by Him according to its disposition." [56] Again, like Philo, they connect the power given to Adam to name the animal with the power given him to govern them. This view is expressed in a comment upon the verse "And the Lord said unto him, who hath made Adam's mouth" (Exod. 4:11), which reads as follows: "God answered Moses, saying unto him: Moses, Moses, who hath made Adam's mouth? It is I who hath made Adam's mouth and tongue, for I have made him overseer of all those who came into the world, to govern with care all the creatures of the world and to call each one of them by its name, that is to say, to give a name to each of them." [57] Like Philo, too, if our interpretation of his statement is correct, they say that Adam "gave names to the living beings by the Holy Spirit." [58] As for the language spoken by Adam, the rabbis evidently held it to be Hebrew, inasmuch as Hebrew is said by them to be the language with which the world was created.[59] According to one rabbinic statement, however, Adam spoke Aramaic.[60] As for the multiplicity of languages, while one rabbi says that seventy languages had already existed prior to the confusion,[61] others say that "the Holy One, blessed be He, together with the seventy angels who surround His throne of glory, came down and mixed up their language so that it became seventy languages, giving to each nation its own script and its own language and appointing an angel over each language." [62]

In Christianity, Origen, like Philo, rejects the view that names are arbitrarily given to things and argues that they ex-

---

[56] Sefer ha-Bahir, 35, ed. Wilna, p. 8d, quoted in M. Kasher, Torah Shelemah on Gen. 2:20.

[57] Midrash Alpha Beta de-Rabbi Akiba, under Pe (Jellinek, Bet ha-Midrash, III, 43), quoted in Kasher, Torah Shelemah on Gen. 2:19.

[58] Midrash Lekah Tob on Gen. 2:19; cf. Ginzberg, Legends of the Jews, V, 82 n. 30.

[59] Bereshit Rabbah 18, 4; cf. Ginzberg, Legends of the Jews, V, 205.

[60] Sanhedrin 38b.

[61] Jer. Megillah I, 11, p. 71b.

[62] Pirke de-Rabbi Eliezer, 24.

press the nature of things.[63] Similarly Tertullian says that the names given by Adam to the animals was "on the ground of the present purpose which each particular nature served" and also that they were called, "as each nature was, by that to which from the beginning it showed a propensity." [64] As for the language spoken by Adam, it is generally assumed by the Church Fathers that it was Hebrew,[65] called the "divine language," [66] and as for the multiplicity of languages, it is explained, as in Scripture, by the story of the confusion of languages at the Tower of Babel.[67]

In Islam, with reference to the names given by Adam, the Koran says, "And God taught Adam names of all things." [68] In the Ikhwān al-Ṣafā, reflecting additional influences going back either to Philo or to rabbinic traditions, it is said: "God breathed into Adam of His Holy Spirit and strengthened Him with His word and taught him the names of all things as well as the properties (*sifāt*) of all things." [69] The language spoken by Adam, however, was not Hebrew but rather Syriac or Nabathean,[70] the latter of which is evidently used as the equivalent of Syriac.[71] This identification of Adam's language as Syriac may be due to the influence of the Talmudic statement quoted above that "Adam spoke Aramaic." [72] But it is also possible that the term Syriac here stands for Hebrew and the statement may therefore ultimately be traced to the influence of Philo who sometimes identifies Hebrew with

[63] *Cont. Cels.* I, 24; V, 45; *Exhortatio ad Martyrium*, 46.
[64] *De Virginibus Velandis*, 5.
[65] Augustine, *De Civ. Dei* XVI, 11.
[66] Origen, *Cont. Cels.* V, 30.
[67] *Cont. Cels.* V, 31; *De Civ. Dei* XVI, 4–5.
[68] Surah 2:19.
[69] *Rasā'il*, ed. Bombay (1305 A. H.) II, 404, ll. 14–15; ed. Beyrouth (1957: 1377) III, 141, ll. 12–14: cf. II, 384, l. 19; III, 112, l. 19: "God taught Adam the names of all things."
[70] Ikhwān al-Ṣafā, II, 385, l. 5; III, 113, ll. 10–11; Mas'ūdī, *Murūj al-Dhahab: Les Prairies d'Or* (ed. C. Barbier de Meynard et Pavet de Courteille, Paris, 1861–77), III, 270; I, 94, 106.
[71] Mas'ūdī, *Murūj*, I, 94; Nöldeke, "Die Namen der aramaischen Nation und Sprache," *ZDMG*, 25 (1871): 122–127.
[72] *Sanhedrin* 38b.

Chaldean,[73] the latter in the sense of Aramaic. In the Koran, however, while there may be a vague reference to the tower of Babel,[74] there is no statement that that was the cause of the confusion of languages. Hence Muslims did not consider themselves bound to accept the scriptural explanation of the origin of the multiplicity of languages. Different explanations are therefore given by Muslim authors. Mas'udi evidently accepts the scriptural story of the tower of Babel, but, going beyond the scriptural story, makes God not only the cause of the confusion of their language but also the cause of the division of languages,[75] that is to say, the formation of the new languages. The Ikhwān al-Ṣafā, however, came out in opposition to the view of those whom they describe as explaining the division of languages by "corruption" (fasād).[76] The reference here is undoubtedly to the scriptural explanation which is usually referred to as the "confusion" of languages, for so also Ibn Janaḥ, in his Hebrew lexicon written in Arabic, takes the Hebrew term balal, which is usually translated "to confuse," to mean (1) "to corrupt" (afsada) and (2) "to change" (ghayyara).[77] The explanation which the Ikhwān al-Ṣafā themselves advance for the rise of the various languages is that it was due to differences in the organs of speech.[78]

Repercussions of all this are to be noticed in Halevi's treatment of the origin of languages as evidence of the Adamic descent of men.

He starts out by prodding the King into committing himself to three propositions with regard to the variety of languages which existed at his own time.

First, he makes the King commit himself to the proposition that languages are not "eternal and without a beginning" but

[73] Mos. II, 5, 26; cf. C. Siegfried, Philo von Alexandria (Jena, 1875), p. 144.
[74] Surah 16:28.
[75] Murūj, I, 78–79; III, 270.
[76] Ikhwān al-Ṣafā, II, 388, ll. 20–21; III, 118, ll. 6–7.
[77] Ibn Janaḥ, Sefer ha-Shorashim, s. v.
[78] Ikhwān al-Ṣafā, II, 388, ll. 19–20; III, 118, ll. 5–6.

that they "undoubtedly had come into existence as a result of convention." [79] By denying that languages are "eternal and without beginning" he means here to deny the Epicurean contention that language sprang up originally without an agent but by that process of chance which they describe as nature, that is to say, out of the natural cries uttered by men. The term "eternal" here is loosely used in the sense of "without a beginning," that is, without a cause. As proof of this he points to the fact that languages "are made up of nouns, verbs, and particles, all of which consist of sounds (al-aṣwāt, Hebrew: otiyyot = letters) derived from the organs (makhārij: moṣo'im) of speech." [80] This, we take it, is an argument against the Epicurean theory of the natural origin of language. Languages, he seems to say, could not have developed out of natural sounds like those of animals, for there is a fundamental difference between them. The sounds of cries of animals, while they may be significant, are irrational, whereas language is speech which is not only significant but also rational, consisting as it does of certain parts of speech arranged in a certain order. The passage thus interpreted reflects the following statements with regard to language. Sounds (al-aṣwāt) are divided into significant (mafhūmah) and insignificant, the former being those of animals and the later those of inanimate objects. Significant sounds, again, are divided into rational (manṭiqiyyah) and irrational, the former being those of men and the latter those of other animals. The rational sounds of men are called speech (manṭiq), for "speech consists only of sounds which proceed from the organs of voice (makhārij) and can be decomposed into letters." [81]

[79] Cuzari I, 53-54. The Arabic term muṣṭalaḥ, Hebrew: muskam, in this passage (istilāḥiyy: heskemi, in Cuzari II, 64, and in Moreh Nebukim II, 30) is the Greek συνθήκη, κατὰ συνθήκην, "by convention" (see above, n. 39). The term maudū': munnaḥ, or waḍ'iyy: hannaḥi (Moreh Nebukim II, 40) is the Greek θέσει, κατὰ θέσιν, "by agreement" (see above, nn. 43, 45). Both of these terms are in opposition to ṭabī'iyy: ṭibe'ī, φύσει, κατὰ φύσιν, "by nature" (see above, nn. 40, 45). [80] Ibid. I, 54.
[81] Ikhwān al-Ṣafā, II, 377, ll. 1-6; III, 101, ll. 10-15. Cf. the following

Second, while admitting that languages have come into existence as a result of convention, the King is forced to answer in the negative to the question put to him by the rabbi "Did you ever see any one who contrived a language, or didst thou hear of him?" [82] The implication of this negative answer is that while in theory language could not spring up naturally but must have its origin in the act of a rational agent, practically he could not conceive of the possibility of such an origin for language. Why he could not conceive of such an origin of language he does not tell us here in this connection. But elsewhere in connection with the problem of chronology he tells us why it is impossible to conceive of the Mosaic chronology to have originated by convention. How did that convention come about? he asks there. If it were the result of a collusion on the part of many people, then, the argues, even if it involved only ten people, it would be impossible for them to carry out their plan "without their having a falling-out and betraying the secret of their collusion." [83] And if it were the concoction of an individual, then, he argues again, it would be impossible that "they should not reject the words of him who would try to impose upon them the belief in such a chronology." [84] The same kind of argument was undoubtedly in the mind of Halevi here when he makes the king say that he never saw or heard of a language coming into existence by contrivance or convention. In fact, Epicurus, in his argument against the theory of the conventional origin of language, assuming that one man invented language and then tried to impose it upon others, argues in exactly the same way. "One man," he says, "could not avail to constrain many, and vanquish them to his will, that they should be willing to learn all his names for things." [85]

---

outline based upon Diogenes, VII, 55 and 57; De Anima II, 8, 420b, 29–33; Voice (φωνή) is either (a) a mere noise (ἦχος) or by (b) the inarticulate sound (ψόφος) of an animal, the latter of which may be significant (σημαντικός). Speech (λέξις) is articulate and rational (ἀπὸ διανοίας).

[82] *Cuzari* I, 55–56.
[83] *Ibid*. I, 48; cf. below, n. 124.
[84] *Ibid*.; cf. below n. 125.
[85] *Lucretius*, V, 1050–1051.

And so the King is forced to deny that the multiplicity of languages of his time had either a natural beginning, that is, uncaused by any agent, or a conventional beginning, that is, caused by a human agent. But still he is forced to admit that "undoubtedly languages appeared at some time." [86] How, then, did these languages appear? The answer, he wants us to conclude, is to be found in the scriptural story of the Tower of Babel. It came as a result of the confusion of languages. But how this division of languages did result from the confusion of languages, whether, as in Philo and Mas'udi, God himself not only caused the confusion of languages but also caused the division of languages, or whether God only caused the confusion of languages but their division afterwards came about in some other way, Halevi does not say. His contemporary Abraham Ibn Ezra advances three interpretations of the confusion and division of languages. "Some say that they began to hate one another and each one invented a new language. Others say that He who teaches man knowledge caused them to forget the knowledge of their language. What appears to me as the correct interpretation is that they were scattered abroad [by God] from thence . . . and after many years, when the first generation died, the original language was forgotten." [87] From all this it would appear that whatever God's share in the confusion or the forgetfulness of the original language, the invention of the new languages was due to natural causes. This is evidently contrary to the view of Philo and Mas'udi. Whether Halevi's view was in agreement with that of Ibn Ezra cannot be ascertained.

But then the King continues to say that undoubtedly also "before this division of languages there were no different languages which had been adopted by different peoples as a result of different conventions." [88] What he means to say is this: Inasmuch as we are bound to accept the scriptural story of the confusion and division of languages as the best possible

---

[86] *Cuzari*, I, 56.
[87] Abraham Ibn Ezra on Gen. 11:7.   [88] *Cuzari* I, 56.

explanation of the origin of the languages which exist today, we must also accept the scriptural story that before that division of languages there was only one language and that one language did not originate in a multitude of people, either naturally or conventionally. That one language originated with one man who existed alone and who formed the beginning of the human race. With that one man language originated by a divine act. It was a "divine" language, "created and instituted" by God who "taught it to Adam and placed it on his tongue and in his heart." [89] Again that language which Adam was taught by God was "the most perfect of languages and the most fitted to describe the objects named by it," [90] for every living creature given a name by Adam "deserved that name which fitted it and explained its nature." [91] This, as we have seen, is exactly the view of Philo. Like Philo, therefore, we may say, while Halevi would not describe the origin of language as conventional in the sense of man-made and natural in the sense of being without an agent, he would describe it as conventional in the sense of God-made and as natural in the sense of expressing the nature of things.

Thus the origin of language is used by Halevi to explain the Adamic descent of man, for by that theory alone, he argues, we can extricate ourselves from the difficulties as to the origin of language.

A suggestion of the argument for the Adamic descent of mankind from the origin of languages is to be found also in Maimonides' statement that it was in order to lend credence to the belief that "at the beginning there was created only one individual of the human species and that is Adam" that the Pentateuch describes the cause of "the formation of their different languages after they had . . . spoken one language, as would be natural for the descendants of one person." [92]

[89] *Ibid.* IV, 25 (ed. Hirschfeld, p. 269, ll. 25–26). Cf. II, 72 (p. 129, l. 2): "Our created and produced language."
[90] *Ibid.* IV, 25 (p. 269, l. 27).
[91] *Ibid.* IV, 25 (p. 271, l. 1).   [92] *Moreh Nebukim* III, 50.

Put in the form of argument, this statement tries to show how Scripture gives a satisfactory explanation for the rise of languages by the story of the Tower of Babel and the story of Adam. As to how language originated with Adam, Maimonides tells us in another passage. Commenting on the verse, "And Adam gave names" (Gen. 2:20), he says: "This teaches us that languages are conventional, and that they are not natural, as has been assumed by some." [93] This statement has been taken to mean that names of things, according to Maimonides, are only arbitrary terms without telling us anything of the nature of the things of which they are names,[94] thus siding with Aristotle's view against the view which is generally identified with Plato and the Stoics. According to some commentators, this statement also means that the language spoken by Adam was man-made and not created by God, so that Hebrew, the language spoken by Adam, is called sacred, according to Maimonides, not because it was instituted by God but only because it is a chaste and refined language,[95] and consequently also Maimonides is taken to be in opposition to Halevi.[96] None of these inferences, however, necessarily follow from Maimonides' statement. The term "conventional," as we have seen, may mean not only "arbitrary" but also "man-made" or "God-made" and the term "natural" may mean not only to be expressive of the nature of things but also to be grown up spontaneously without a founder. Accordingly what Maimonides may mean by his statement here is merely the assertion that languages are "conventional" in the sense that they are founded by somebody, that is, Adam, who was taught by God; and are "not natural" in the sense that they have not grown up spontaneously without a founder. The "some" in the expression "as has been assumed by some" would thus refer to the Epi-

---

[93] *Ibid.* II, 30.

[94] See Narboni, Shem-Ṭob, and Munk (II, 254 n. 2), *ad loc.*

[95] See Shem-Ṭob, *ad loc.* For Maimonides' explanation of "sacred language" see *Moreh Nebukim* III, 8.

[96] Cf. Munk (*loc. cit.*) and Friedländer (II, 157 n. 3), *ad loc.*

cureans. In another passage, Maimonides speaks of language as a "boon with which God favored man" and quotes scriptural verses to show that it is God who "gave a mouth" (Ex. 4:11) or "a learned tongue" (Is. 50:4) to man.[97] This, too, may not mean merely that God endowed men with a capacity to institute language by convention; it may mean exactly the same as Halevi's statement that the language spoken by Adam was "created and instituted" by God who "taught it to Adam and placed it on his tongue and in his heart."[98]

Halevi's other two arguments for the Adamic descent of mankind, those of the hebdomadal period[99] and the denary system,[100] are based upon two assumptions. First, both the hebdomadal period and the denary system are universally accepted by all mankind. Second, both of them have no foundation either in nature or in reason. On the basis of these assumptions, how then, Halevi seems to ask, did these originate? To say that they originated by convention must be rejected on the same ground that the theory of convention had been rejected by him in the case of the origin of language. Hence it must be assumed that they originated in some "divinely mysterious way"[101] with one man, and that is Adam,[102] from whom all his descendants inherited it as a tradition.

Maimonides uses neither of these arguments as proof for the Adamic descent of mankind. Whether he omitted these arguments because he did not happen to discuss this problem directly or whether he omitted them because he was informed that the hebdomadal period was unknown among the ancient Persians, Greeks and Romans and that the denary system had its rival in the quinary and vigesimal systems cannot be ascer-

---

[97] *Moreh Nebukim* III, 8.   [98] Cf. above, n. 89.

[99] *Cuzari* I, 57–58; II, 20 (p. 85, ll. 2–4).

[100] *Ibid.* I, 59; IV, 27 (p. 285, ll. 8–10). Cf. Pseudo-Plutarch, *De Placitis Philosophorum* I, 3, 8 (Diels, *Doxographi Graeci*, p. 281, ll. 13–16; Arabic translation, ed. Badawi, p. 100, ll. 7–8): "All people, whether Grecians or Barbarians, reckon from one to ten, and thence return to one again."

[101] *Ibid.* IV, 27 (p. 285, l. 10), in connection with the denary system; so undoubtedly also in the case of the hebdomadal period.

[102] *Ibid.* II, 20 (p. 85, ll. 2–4), in connection with the denary period.

tained. On one point, however, it is certain that he differed from Halevi. He held that the hebdomadal period had both a natural and a rational explanation, for "the period of seven days is the unit of time intermediate between the natural day and the lunar month and it is also known how great is the importance of this period in nature." [103] Similarly Philo makes no use of either of these arguments as proof of the Adamic descent of mankind, believing in a natural or rational origin for both the denary system and the hebdomadal period. Number ten to him is the perfect number which he found in nature.[104] As for the hebdomadal period, while in one place he says that without the guidance of the divine spirit Moses could not have announced the Sabbath,[105] in another place he says that "nature taught men the only, or to speak more cautiously, the chief festivals, namely, the recurring periods of seven days and seven years." [106]

III. THE SCRIPTURAL CHRONOLOGY

While the Jewish belief in the creation of the world and the creation of Adam was shared by both Christianity and Islam, the belief in the scriptural chronology was shared only by Christianity but not by Islam. This last belief, unlike the first two beliefs, did not have to defend itself against any theory of an eternal chronology. Among Greek philosophers, even Aristotle, who believed in the eternity of the world and hence the eternity of the human race, admitted the recency of the arts and, hence, of our present social history and civilization in general, though this recency is explained by him as being due to the devastation of former civilizations in these parts of the world inhabited by us.[107] Philo, starting with this commonly admitted belief in the recency of our civilization, argues in favor of the scriptural teaching of the recent origin of the human race,[108] concerning which he ac-

---

[103] *Moreh Nebukim* III, 43.
[104] *Decal.* 7, 24–28, 31.
[105] *Mos.* II, 48, 265.

[106] *Praem.* 48, 265.
[107] *Meteorologica* I, 14, 351b, 8ff.
[108] *Aet.* 24, 130.

cepts the scriptural story that it began with the creation of
Adam.[109] Though he does not dwell directly on the veracity
of the scriptural chronology, the fact that he places the
historical part of Scripture by the side of the story of creation and the legislative part [110] shows that he considered it of
equal veracity. Undoubtedly Philo was acquainted with the
legend reported by Plato concerning an Egyptian priest who
had told Solon of the founding of Athens nine thousand years
before his time,[111] but, if challenged with it, he would have
undoubtedly dismissed it, as he does all myths in general,
as an "imposture" in contrast to the "truth" of Scripture.[112]
In fact, later in Christianity, when Celsus tried to refute the
scriptural chronology by "Plato" and "the most learned of
the Egyptians," evidently referring to the legend we have
quoted from the *Timaeus*, Origen declared that "the dialogues of Plato" and the "fables" of the "boastful Egyptians"
are not by any means to be regarded as more trustworthy than
the Mosaic account in the Pentateuch.[113] Augustine equally
dismisses as untrustworthy "those mendacious documents
[of the Egyptians] which profess to give the history of many
thousands of years, though, reckoning by the sacred writings,
we find that not 6,000 years have yet passed." [114]

In Islam, however, a distinction was made between scriptural beliefs which happen to be restated in the Koran and those
which do not happen to be restated in it. Accordingly, the
belief in the creation of the world and in the creation of
Adam which are restated in the Koran is accepted, whereas
the scriptural chronology which is not restated in the Koran
is not accepted. Mas'udi thus declares that religious philosophers among the Muslims say that "demonstrations may establish the creation of the world" as well as the belief that "the
beginning of men is from Adam" but that "it is impossible for
us to determine and count up the years," [115] adding that "God

---

[109] *Opif.* 23, 69ff.
[110] *Mos.* II, 8, 46; *Praem.* 1, 1–2.
[111] *Timaeus* 23 D–E.
[112] *Praem.* 2, 8; cf. *Philo*, I, 32.
[113] *Cont. Cels.* I, 19–20.
[114] *De Civ. Dei* XII, 10; cf. XVIII, 40.
[115] Mas'ūdī, *Murūj*, IV, 110.

has informed us in His Book that He created Adam . . . but He has not furnished us any information with regard to the extent of time that has elapsed since then." [116] Muslims, therefore, gave no more credence to the scriptural chronology than to the other chronologies known to them. Of such other chronologies known to Muslims were not only those of the Greeks but also those of the Indians [117] and Sabians.[118]

It is against this disregard of the scriptural chronology by the Muslims and the equal regard given by them to the Indian and Sabian chronologies that Halevi undertakes to defend the scriptural chronology. It will be noticed that the Muslim in his speech is made by Halevi to say that he believes in "creation of the world and the genealogical descent of all men from Adam through Noah." [119] But he does not express his belief in the scriptural chronology. This was advisedly omitted by Halevi from the speech of the Muslim. When the Rabbi, however, comes to speak, Halevi makes him say that he believes not only in the creation of the world and in the Adamic descent of mankind but also in "the chronology from Adam up to this day." [120] But no sooner does the Rabbi say that than the King is made by Halevi to take him up on the last point, asking him: "It is strange that you should possess authentic chronology to the creation of the world." [121]

In his answer, Halevi tries first to establish by positive arguments the authenticity of the scriptural chronology.

To begin with, he advances in its support the principle of consensus. "There is no difference," he says, "between the Jews of Khazar and Ethiopia in this respect." [122] The force of this argument can be realized only when we recall that it is addressed to Muslim readers, for among Muslims, the principle of consensus (ijmā') plays an important part in their own religion.

Then he tries to show that such a consensus among the Jews

[116] *Ibid.*, p. 111.
[117] *Ibid.*, p. 105.
[118] *Ibid.*, p. 106.
[119] *Cuzari* I, 5.

[120] *Ibid.* I, 43.
[121] *Ibid.* I, 44.
[122] *Ibid.* I, 45.

make it humanly impossible for that chronology to have come about by "convention" or rather collusion. The argument used here by Halevi is, as we have pointed out above, analogous to one of the arguments reported by Lucretius in the name of Epicurus to show that language could not have come about by convention.[123] It is an argument of *reductio ad absurdum*. Suppose, says Halevi, the chronology is not true, then it must have been invented by somebody. But how was it invented? It could have been invented either by the collusion of many people or by the private invention of one individual. But in the former case, "it would have been impossible even for ten people to have concocted this chronology by a collusion without their having a falling-out and betraying the secret of their collusion." [124] And in the latter case, again, even if only ten people were involved, it would have been impossible that "they should not reject the words of him who would try to impose upon them the belief in such a chronology." [125] Clinching his argument, Halevi concludes: "How much more was this impossible when so many multitudes of people were involved and when also the period involved was not long enough to admit untruth and fiction." [126]

Having thus established by positive arguments the authenticity of scriptural chronology, he tries to refute the rival chronologies. Of these rival chronologies he mentions two. First, the various Indian chronologies, with their millions of years, and the claim of the Indians of having antiquities and buildings to prove these chronologies.[127] Second, the chronology based upon a book written in Arabic in the 10th century entitled "On the Nabatean Agriculture" and purported to be a translation from the Aramaic of an ancient author, in which reference was made to "ten thousands of years" and to three men, Dewan, Saghrith and Yanboushad, who are supposed to have lived before Adam.[128] Halevi's refutation of these chronologies is like Origen's and Augustine's refuta-

---

[123] Cf. above, n. 85.   [125] *Ibid.*   [127] *Ibid.* I, 60.
[124] *Cuzari* I, 48.   [126] *Ibid.*   [128] *Ibid.* I, 61.

tion of the Egyptian chronology.[129] He simply dismisses them as untrustworthy and unreliable.[130]

Maimonides does not discuss the Indian and the Nabatean chronologies in connection with the scriptural chronology. But he has a detailed discussion of the religious beliefs and forms of worship as described in the book "On the Nabatean Agriculture." [131] The views expressed in that work represent, according to him, the views of the Sabians of whom he says that the Indians are remnants [132] and who, he adds, believed that Adam came to Babylon from a place near India.[133] He refers also to a story contained in that book about a tree which stood in Nineveh twelve thousand years.[134] These Sabians are dismissed by him, as the Indians are by Halevi and the Egyptians by Origen and Augustine, as unreliable, having "manufactured ridiculous stories, which prove that their authors were very deficient in knowledge and very far removed from philosophy; they certainly were of extreme ignorance." [135]

IV. SPINOZA

It is this conception of Scripture common to all religious philosophers, whether Jewish, Christian or Muslim, ever since Philo, that became an object of attack by those who before Spinoza began to nibble at traditional philosophy and by Spinoza himself in his grand assault on it. He attacks this conception of Scripture on every point.

To begin with, he denies that the information contained in the pre-Mosaic account of history, whether the story of creation or the story of mankind, was known to Moses either by revelation or by an inherited continuous tradition. That part of the Pentateuch, according to him, was made up of various

---

[129] Cf. above, nn. 113, 114.
[130] *Cuzari* I, 61.
[131] *Moreh Nebukim* III, 29–30.
[132] *Ibid.* III, 29.

[133] *Ibid.*
[134] *Ibid.*
[135] *Ibid.*

contradictory narratives collected at a much later time.[136] Nor is the historical account in the Pentateuch and in the other books of Scripture from Moses on to be considered as contemporary records of eyewitnesses. These too, were made up of various conflicting accounts collected at a much later period.[137] And so even those parts of Scripture which were originally meant to be history should not be accepted as authentic history in every detail. Only the main outline of that history is probably true, and this not because it was written down by eyewitnesses but because they were evidently transmitted in good faith.[138]

Then, he denies that the Law was divinely revealed. He was aware of the various kinds of evidence for the veracity of the Law that were advanced throughout the history of religious philosophy ever since Philo and, drawing directly upon Maimonides' restatement of these kinds of evidence, he proceeds to discuss them. Like Maimonides, he argues that miracles, even according to Scripture, are no evidence of the truth of revelation and, again, like Maimonides, he points to the fact that the Israelites themselves were not fully convinced by the miracles performed by Moses as to the truth of what he had taught them about God.[139] Unlike Maimonides, however, he does not consider the revelation on Mount Sinai as more convincing evidence, for the story about that revelation, like many other scriptural stories, though "narrated in Scripture as real and were believed to be real, . . . were in fact only symbolical and imaginary." [140] Indeed he is willing to call Scripture "sacred and divine" [141] and "the word of God," [142] but this only in the sense that any book that teaches morality may be so described,[143] and to prove that it is

---

[136] *Tractatus Theologico-Politicus*, ch. 9 (*Opera*, ed. Gebhardt, Heidelberg, 1925, III, 130.1–131.11).

[137] *Ibid.*, chs. 8–10.   [138] *Ibid.*, ch. 12 (III, 166.12–21).

[139] *Ibid.*, ch. 6 (III, 87.9–35); ch. 7 (III, 99.18–20).

[140] *Ibid.*, ch. 6 (III, 92.35–93.8); cf. ch. 1 (III, 19.3ff.).

[141] *Ibid.*, ch. 12 (III, 160.11).

[142] *Ibid.* (III, 162.31).

[143] *Ibid.* (III, 160.11; 162.31); cf. *Epistolae* 43 (IV, 222.10ff.).

"sacred and divine" and "the word of God" in this sense, he is willing to accept the argument which alone according to Maimonides proves the divine origin of Scripture, namely, the intrinsic excellency of its teachings.[144] "Wherefore," he says, "the divine origin of Scripture must consist only in its teaching true virtue" [145] and "the certainty of divine revelation can be based only on the wisdom of the doctrine, and not on miracles, that is, on ignorance." [146]

With subtle irony, we shall now try to show, he turns the tables on Maimonides and declares that the miraculous stories of Scripture, including the story of creation, are no more credible than the fables of the Sabians ridiculed by Maimonides himself. Speaking of the traditional belief in the creation of the world, he says: "I fully expect that those who judge things confusedly . . . erroneously ascribe to substances a beginning like that which they see belongs to natural things; for those who are ignorant of the true causes of things confound, everything and without any mental repugnance represent [1] trees speaking like men, or imagine that [2] men are made out of stones as well as begotten from seed, and that [3] all forms can be changed the one into the other." [147]

In this passage, it will be noticed, Spinoza makes three statements as illustrations of human credulity. Let us see what these three statements refer to.

The first statement, that with regard to trees speaking like men, undoubtedly refers to a passage in Maimonides, where, trying to expose the credulity of the Sabians, he mentions their belief in the existence of a "tree which in its roots resembles a human being and lets out a loud sound and utters certain words." [148]

The second statement, that with regard to men being made

[144] Cf. above, n. 29.
[145] *Tractatus Theologico-Politicus*, ch. 7 (III, 99.20–21).
[146] *Epistolae* 73 (IV, 307.15–17).
[147] *Ethics* I, Prop. 8, Sch. 2.
[148] *Moreh Nebukim* III, 29. Cf. above nn. 131–135.

out of stones as well as begotten from seed, has a twofold reference. First, it refers to the following preaching of John the Baptist: "I say unto you, that God is able of these stones to raise up children unto Abraham." [149] Second, it refers to the Greek legend of Deucalion and Pyrrha, according to which stones thrown by Deucalion became men and those thrown by Pyrrha became women. [150]

The third statement, that with regard to substances and forms being changed into one another, has also a twofold reference. First, it refers to the common Jewish and Christian conception of miracles as the change of substances into one another, illustrated in Maimonides, by the story of Moses changing water into blood [151] and in St. Thomas, by the story of Jesus changing water into wine. [152] Second, it refers to the Greek legends about the metamorphosis of men and gods, which is ridiculed by Tatian in his address to the Greeks: "There are legends," he says, "of the metamorphosis of men: with you the gods also are metamorphosed. Rhea becomes a tree; Zeus a dragon, on account of Persephone; the sisters of Phaëthon are changed into poplars, and Leto into a bird of little value." [153] Tatian himself, it is to be remarked, believed in a still greater metamorphosis, namely, the creation of the world out of a formless pre-existent matter, which was itself created out of nothing. [154]

This passage, then, is Spinoza's challenge to all religious philosophers who ever since Philo defended their belief in the creation of the world on the ground of the power of God to work miracles. Maimonides' belief in a miraculous creation of the world out of nothing, he seems to argue, rests on no more solid foundation than the belief of the Sabians in a tree speaking like a man, which is ridiculed by Maimonides himself. Similarly Tatian's belief in the miraculous creation of the world out of a pre-existent created formless matter, as

[149] Matt. 3:9.
[150] Ovid, *Metamorphoses* I, 411–413.
[151] *Moreh Nebukim* II, 29.
[152] Thomas Aquinas, *In 2 Sent.* 18, 1, 3c.
[153] *Orat. ad Graec.* 10.
[154] *Ibid.* 5.

well as John the Baptist's preaching that men will be raised from stones, and, in general, all the Jewish and Christian stories about the miraculous change of substances into one another, he again seems to argue, are no more credible than the Greek legends about Deucalion and Pyrrha and about the metamorphoses of men and gods, the latter of which are ridiculed by Tatian himself.

10

SPINOZA AND THE RELIGION OF
THE PAST*

A COMPREHENSIVE study of Spinoza's attitude toward religion would of necessity fall into three parts. For Spinoza, who is known to us primarily as a philosopher, was also a historian of religion and a political thinker. As a historian of religion, which in his time meant a student of the Bible, he had certain definite views on the development of religious ideas and institutions in both the Old and the New Testament. These views are to be found in his *Tractatus Theologico-Politicus*. As a political thinker Spinoza, like many of his contemporaries, was especially preoccupied with the problem of the relation between Church and State, concerning which he had certain definite views. These views are to be found, again, in his *Tractatus Theologico-Politicus* and also in his unfinished *Tractatus Politicus*. Finally, as a philosopher he dealt with all the abstruse and abstract problems of traditional religious philosophy. The discussion of these problems is to be found in the *Ethics*. It is with the *Ethics* that I am going to deal tonight.

The *Ethics* — as I have tried to show in *The Philosophy of Spinoza* — is primarily a criticism of fundamental principles of religious philosophy, which at the beginning of the Christian era were laid down by Philo and were still in vogue at the time of Spinoza in the seventeenth century. This criticism is constructed according to an old forensic device which may be described as "yes" and "but." The "yes" part is an expression of Spinoza's assent to the external formulation of some of the principles of traditional religious philosophy. The "but" part is a statement of the special sense in which he himself is willing to use that formulation. Between these two

* Delivered as the Horace M. Kallen Lecture at the New School for Social Research in 1949; published by the New School in 1950, and reprinted in *The Menorah Journal* (1950), 146–167.

parts is a whole chain of complicated arguments. To the
general reader this structure of Spinoza's thought is not obvious, for it is obscured by the artificial form in which the
Ethics is written — the geometrical form. It is for this reason
that the *Ethics* is one of the most difficult books in philosophic
literature. It is for this reason also that the *Ethics*, in my
opinion, has so often been misunderstood and so often mis-
interpreted.

Spinoza begins from the very beginning. He asks himself,
What is the most fundamental assumption underlying the
religious philosophies of Judaism, Christianity, and Islam?
And after examining various possibilities he settles on one.
It is the belief that over and above and beyond the aggregate of things which make up this our physical universe
there is something unlike the universe.

Had Spinoza written his *Ethics* after the manner of the
rabbis and the scholastics he would have quoted here verses
from Scripture in which men are challenged to produce
something which is like unto God. As to what that unlikeness
between God and the universe consisted in, Spinoza must
have found a variety of opinions among religious philosophers.
Most of them, and Philo at their head, following the tradition
of Plato and Aristotle, interpreted that unlikeness between
God and the world as meaning that, unlike the world which
is material, God is immaterial. Others, of whom Tertullian is
the chief example, either consciously or unconsciously following the Stoics, argued that the unlikeness between God
and the world meant that, unlike the world which consists
of one kind of matter, God consists of another kind of matter.

But there is one sense of unlikeness between God and the
world upon which, Spinoza must have found, all religious
philosophers were in agreement. They all believed that, unlike the world which is dependent upon God, God is independent of the world. This independence of God may be
expressed by the term separateness — separateness in the sense

that the existence of God does not necessarily imply the existence of the world. For believing, as all of them did, that the world came into existence after it had not been in existence, they also believed that prior to the existence of the world there was a God without a world. And believing, as some of them did, that some day the world will come to an end, they also believed that after the ultimate destruction of the world there will be God, again, without a world. And since God was and will be without a world, even now when the world exists, God's existence is independent of the world, separate from it, and apart from it.

To this principle Spinoza begins by saying "yes." Yes, he is willing to admit that there is something over and above and beyond the aggregate of things which constitutes this physical universe of ours. He is not an antiquated Epicurean to whom the world was a mere conglomeration of aimlessly flying indivisible particles of bodies. He is even willing to call that something by the name of God, for, as he so often says, he does not care to argue about words. But — and here his first "but" comes in — he is unwilling to admit that the something unlike the constituent parts of the universe is separate from the universe. Within the universe itself and inseparable from it, he maintains, there is something unlike its parts. And as he proceeds in his argument he explains that by that something he means the wholeness of the universe, which he contends is not the mere aggregate of its parts. In support of this contention, he alludes to two old propositions which by his time were already philosophic commonplaces. The first proposition is that the universe is an organic living being, a view which ever since Plato had been expressed by various philosophers in various ways. The second proposition is that in an organic living being the whole is something different from the mere sum of its parts.

This is a clear and simple thought which Spinoza could have expressed in clear and simple language. But being a philosopher, he felt that he owed it to his profession to express himself in technical language, even at the risk of making clear things obscure and simple things complicated. And so, rummaging through the stockpile of philosophic terminology, he came upon the term *substance*. This he pasted as a label upon that wholeness of the universe of which we have been speaking: a label used by Spinoza as the equivalent for the traditional term God.

The choice, it must be said, was not a happy one. For already by the time of Spinoza the term *substance* had a variety of conflicting meanings, and the one exclusive meaning which he now gave to it only tended to add to the confusion of those who later began to study his *Ethics*.

Then from the same stockpile Spinoza pulled out the term *mode*, which he used as a label for the particular things in the universe. And inasmuch as the particular things are many and can be classified in a variety of ways, Spinoza has a variety of *modes* variously classified.

The choice of the term *mode* as a designation for particular things was also unfortunate. For the term *mode*, historically, had already acquired the meaning of something unreal, something which is only apparent. And so its use by Spinoza led many of those who later began the study of his *Ethics* to read a false meaning into what he meant by particular things.

Finally, out of several reminiscent terms and expressions, Spinoza coined a new phrase of his own, "the face of the whole universe," which he uses as a description of the aggregate of particular things of the universe, or of the particular *modes*, which to him is to be distinguished from the wholeness of the universe.

All this is the first point in Spinoza's criticism of traditional philosophy. He then takes up another point.

To traditional philosophy, God, though independent of the universe, is still not unrelated to it. His relation to the universe, which is that of creator and preserver, is expressed by traditional philosophers in their description of God as the efficient and formal and final cause of the world. They could not exactly agree on the manner in which God created the world — whether it was after the manner of a potter who molds a vessel out of clay, or after the manner of a magician who pulls rabbits out of the emptiness of his hat. But whether God created the world out of a pre-existent matter or whether He created it out of nothing, they all insisted that He created it by will and design. For, if He willed it, He need have created no world at all. And, again, if He willed it, He could have created a different kind of world.

And so, not only is the world we live in the creation of God, but also the order we observe in the world was designed by God. For at the time of the creation of the world God implanted in it certain laws, laws of nature and laws of causality, by which it is to be governed. Philo, who first formulated this principle for all religious philosophers who were to follow him, calls it in Greek "the divine Logos"; and later medieval philosophers continue to call it their own Latin *"ratio divina."*

This is a sort of constitution which God Himself has drawn up for His own governance of the world. On the whole, God is conceived by most of the religious philosophers as a constitutional monarch who rules in accordance with the laws He designed for the world. But still they all agree that God, obedient to His own law though He is, has not abandoned His power nor His freedom. Should the good of His subjects demand it, He will upset the laws of nature which He has implanted in the world and produce what is called miracles.

Here again, Spinoza starts with a willingness to adopt the religious vocabulary and describe the relation of his God to the universe — the wholeness of it in relation to its parts from which it is inseparable and with which it is eternally coexistent — as a relation of cause and effect. For *cause*, in philosophic language, is one of those weasel words which may be used by different men in different senses. In ordinary

speech, a *cause* is what brings about the existence of something. But in the philosophic language of Spinoza's time any
kind of relation between two things, or even within one thing,
any kind of relation between two distinguishable aspects of
the thing, could be described as a causal relation. Especially
was the term *cause* used as a description of the relation of the
whole to the part.

But — and here the second "but" comes in — Spinoza is
unwilling to admit that there is a God who is the *cause* of the
world in the sense that He created it by will and design, so
that if He willed it, there need have been no world, or there
might have been a different kind of world; nor is Spinoza
willing to admit that, once God created the world after a
certain order, He can miraculously upset that order. The
world as it now exists, as well as the order which we observe
in it, is fixed, immutable, and inexorable; and it has so existed,
without any change, from eternity.

For Spinoza, we must bear in mind, was an old-fashioned
philosopher, who knew nothing of what we now call "evolution." He was in this respect more old-fashioned than the
religious philosophers to whom he was opposed. In the case
of religious philosophers, homiletical historians of religion
may find in their vague descriptions of the process of creation
certain adumbrations of evolution. But no homiletical historian of philosophy — even those who have discovered in
Spinoza adumbrations of Marxian dialectics, Freudian psychology, and Einsteinian relativity — will be able to find in
his conception of the eternally complete and fixed universe
any traces of a theory of cosmic evolution.

Spinoza's description, then, of the wholeness of the universe in relation to its parts as *cause* was simply a concession
to his opponents. It was justified only by the license exercised by philosophers in the use of the term *cause*, and also
by his own disinclination to quarrel about words. But, having once expressed his willingness to describe his own God
by the traditional term *cause*, Spinoza goes even further to

express his willingness to describe Him as a cause in the various senses in which traditional philosophers described their
God as *cause*. His wholeness of the universe is thus to Spinoza
not only a mere *cause* but also a *first cause*, a *principal cause*,
a *universal cause*, an *efficient cause*, an *essential cause*, an *immanent cause*, a *free cause*. However, in every one of these
instances, he shows in what special sense he uses these terms.
In some instances, he also shows how his use of these terms
is even more justifiable than that of his opponents.

Spinoza's criticism of the traditional conceptions of the
separability and causality of God — conceptions which, as
fundamental principles of scriptural religious philosophy,
were first formulated by Philo — led him to an examination
of a philosophy which is quite the opposite of the philosophy
of Philo — that is, the emanationist theory of Plotinus.

The philosophy of Plotinus may, indeed, be considered as
the counterpart of the philosophy of Philo. Just as Philonism
is a rationalization of Hebrew Scripture, so the Neoplatonism
of Plotinus is a rationalization of pagan mythology; and, if the
truth were known, it originated as a pagan reaction to Philonism. In opposition to Philonism, emanationism denies that
God, either after the manner of a potter created the world
from a pre-existent matter, or after the manner of a stage-
magician created it out of nothing. Emanationism maintains
instead that, after the manner of a spider which spins its web
out of itself, God caused the world to emanate out of His own
essence. Again in opposition to Philo, it maintains that this
process of emanation is an eternal process and a necessary
process. But then, while rejecting the Philonic belief in the
separateness of God in the sense that He could exist without
the world, it maintains His separateness in the sense of His
being immaterial.

Here, again, Spinoza is willing to adopt the emanationist
vocabulary and describe the relation between the wholeness
of the universe and its parts as a process in accordance with

which the parts flow from, or follow from, the whole. Logically, he sees no difference between the emanationist God, who coexists with the world from eternity and acts upon it as a necessary cause, from his own conception of God *as the wholeness of the universe*. He is even willing to describe his own God as the emanative cause of the universe. In fact, when he decided to build up his few religious heresies into an imposing system of philosophy, it was the system of emanation that he took as his model.

But — and here his third "but" comes in — Spinoza does not admit that his God is separated from the world in the sense that He is immaterial. He shows how, by the assumption of an immaterial God, there is no adequate explanation under the theory of emanation for the rise of matter. Of course, he was aware of the answer provided by the emanationists — in their theory of an intermediary mind as the immediate emanation from God and the immediate emanative source of matter. But he shows how the interposition of such an intermediary between God and matter fails to solve the difficulty, how furthermore it gives rise to new difficulties, and how in fact the emanationist theory is really nothing but a disguised form of the belief in creation out of nothing. He concludes, therefore, that if the relation between the wholeness of the universe and its parts is to be described in terms of emanation, then the wholeness cannot be described as immaterial.

Proceeding now to recast his own few simple views into a philosophic system modelled after that of emanationism, Spinoza tries to express the difference between these two systems — his own and emanationism — in technical terms. The technical terms which Spinoza uses for this purpose are *attribute*, *thought*, and *extension*.

Attribute is a term he borrows from the vocabulary of religious philosophy, where it was used as a description of the way we conceive of God and speak of Him in terms derived from His manifestation in the world. *Extension* and *thought* are terms used in the more fashionable vocabulary of Spinoza's own time for the old-fashioned terms "matter" and "form." And so he contrasts the emanationist view with his own by saying that to the emanationists God has only *the attribute of thought*, whereas to him God has both the *attribute of thought* and *the attribute of extension*.

Again, to the emanationists, whose God has only the *attribute of thought*, the immediate thing that follows from God is an intellect; to Spinoza, whose God has both the *attribute of thought* and the *attribute of extension*, the immediate thing that follows from God is twofold, an intellect and motion. These he describes, respectively, as the *infinite immediate mode of thought* and the *infinite immediate mode of extension*.

As in emanationism, all the particular things in the world are described by Spinoza as following from these two immediate infinite modes, and hence in their totality are described by him as mediate infinite modes or as "the face of the whole universe," which phrase, as we have said, he himself has coined out of reminiscent terms and expressions. Finally, from somewhere in that stockpile of philosophic terminology he dragged out the expressions "naturating nature" (*natura naturans*) and "naturated nature" (*natura naturata*), and used them as designations, respectively, of *substance* and *modes*.

Behind the imposing façade of Spinoza's philosophic system, with all its intricacies of design and vocabulary, there is thus a simple philosophic faith. Directly, this philosophic faith is presented in opposition to the traditional religious faith. But indirectly, as may be judged from certain expressions in Spinoza's correspondence, it is also aimed at the old Epicurean faith, which in his time was still the bugbear of both theologians and philosophers. In opposition both to the religious faith, which professed a belief in the creation of the world by the will of an eternal God, and to the Epicurean

faith, which professed a belief in the emergence of the world
out of the accidental collision of aimlessly drifting eternal
atoms, Spinoza's philosophic faith protested that the world in
its present form existed from eternity.

Again, in opposition to the religious faith, which saw in the
order of the universe certain laws of causality which were
implanted in it by the will of God, and which God by His
will can miraculously upset — and in opposition also to the
faith of the Epicureans, who saw in the order of the universe
only an accidental equilibrium of stray forces, liable at any
moment to be upset — this simple philosophic faith of Spinoza sees in the order of the universe certain eternally fixed
laws of causality, with which all the apparently wayward behavior of particular things is indissolubly connected by an
imperceptible chain of causes.

But then a question arose in the mind of Spinoza. How do
we know that the Epicurean faith is mistaken? Perhaps, after
all, the world is only a conglomeration of atoms which had
come together by chance. Perhaps what appears to us as
causal order is only the result of a chance equilibrium of
atoms. Moreover, what guarantee have we that the order
which has existed till now will continue to exist in the future?

When this question occurred to religious philosophers,
they answered it by what is known as the proofs of the existence of God. The proofs used by them, with one exception,
contain nothing new; they inherited them from pagan philosophers. On the whole, these proofs of the pagan philosophers fall into two classes.

Those philosophers who believed that all our knowledge
is derived ultimately from sense perception maintained that
the existence of God could be proved only indirectly from
our various sensible perceptions of the world. This gave rise
to those proofs for the existence of God which are known
nowadays as the cosmological proofs, of which the best
known is that syllogistic jingle, which begins with the prem-

ise, "All things that are in motion must be moved by some-thing." On the other hand, those who believed that some of our knowledge, indeed the most valid portion of it, is born within our own mind, maintained that the existence of God is a direct kind of knowledge within our own mind.

These two modes of proving the existence of God, invented by pagan philosophers, were adopted by later religious phi-losophers, though some of them rejected the second type of proof. But these later religious philosophers added a new kind of direct knowledge of the existence of God, namely, the historical revelation of God as recorded in Scripture, and the divine illumination which may be experienced by certain favored individuals. Moreover, in imitation of those proofs known to us as cosmological, the various assertions of the immediacy of our knowledge of the existence of God have in later days been resolved into syllogistic jingles which came to be known as the ontological proofs.

Here, again, Spinoza begins by admitting that the exist-ence of what he has already agreed to call God is a direct kind of knowledge within us, for Spinoza believed our mind is capable of generating knowledge of itself. But he refuses to admit that we can have a direct knowledge of God either by revelation or by divine illumination. Following in the footsteps of those who asserted a direct knowledge of the existence of God, he is not content with merely stating his profession of faith; he presents his profession of faith in the form of various syllogistic demonstrations, describing these demonstrations by the term *a priori*.

Altogether he advances three such *a priori* demonstrations. In one instance, he performs before our eyes the verbal trans-formation of an indirect proof of the existence of God, or what he calls an *a posteriori* demonstration, into a direct proof, or an *a priori* demonstration.

From a consideration of God, Spinoza passes on to a con-sideration of Man.

To religious philosophers, man as the crown of creation occupies a unique place in the universe. In this view, man's uniqueness does not consist in the mere fact that he possesses a soul; for, not only from the works of philosophers but also from their own Scripture, they gathered that other living beings also have a soul.

The singularity of man consisted in the fact that he had a special soul of special origin. Spinoza himself, in his book called *Cogitata Metaphysica*, which is really not a book but a scrapbook, alludes to the three theories of the origin of the human soul held by various religious philosophers. In technical language they are known as the theories of creation, pre-existence, and traducianism. In plain English they may be described, respectively, as the theory of custom-made souls, the theory of ready-made souls, and the theory of second-hand souls.

According to the custom-made theory, at the birth of each child God creates a soul especially for that child. According to the ready-made theory, at the time of the creation of the world God in His foresight created individual souls which in number and variety were sufficient to supply the need of all the future generations of men. These souls are kept in a place the exact name of which is variously given by various authorities who are expert in the knowledge of these matters. At each child's birth a soul suitable to his body is placed within him — though, judging by the great number of misfit souls in the world, one may infer that mistakes frequently occur. According to the second-hand theory of the soul, God, at the time of the creation of the world, created only one soul, and that is the soul of Adam. All our souls are only slices of the soul of our first ancestor, so remade as to fit our own peculiar bodies.

The common element in these three theories of the origin of the human soul — which is of philosophic interest to Spinoza — is that the human soul is of divine origin, and has been especially created by God apart from the body, so that even after it is placed in the body it continues to exist there as something apart from it.

As usual, Spinoza has no objection to adopting the vocabulary of his opponents and describing the human soul as being of divine origin. The technical vocabulary in which he has clothed his thought allows him to say that "the human mind is part of the infinite intellect of God." [1] In fact, this statement is so phrased as to allude to a medieval discussion of the nature of the divine origin of the soul. But — and here another "but" comes in — he does not admit that the soul is separable from the body.

Everything in the world, Spinoza argues, has a double aspect. In one respect, everything in the world may be looked upon as something simple and isolated. Looked upon in this way, everything in the world has only one simple mode of behavior. It is always in flux, constantly in a process of change: it is always ceasing to be what it is and becoming something else. Earlier philosophers called it matter, and matter was defined as extension. Spinoza, in his own technical vocabulary, calls it *extended thing*, or a *part of the infinite immediate mode of motion*, or a *finite mode of the attribute of extension*.

In another respect, everything in the world, however simple, is composed of parts and, however isolated, is part of something else. Looked upon in this way, everything in the world, in relation to itself, has a structure and, in relation to other things, has a function. Earlier philosophers called it form. But form is not one single thing. There is a hierarchy of forms. Some philosophers enumerated the several stages in the hierarchy of form by such general terms as cohesion, nature, soul, mind. Other philosophers, however, used a different kind of vocabulary and, instead of speaking of a hierarchy of forms and of everything as having a form, spoke of a hierarchy of souls and of everything as having a soul. Spinoza adopts this vocabulary and hence says, "all things have a soul

[1] *Ethics* II, 11, Corol.

(*omnia animata*)," adding immediately the qualifying phrase "in different degrees." [2]

And so, Spinoza argues, the human soul is only one of the degrees of soul which all things possess; and just as the cohesiveness, which is the soul of a clod of earth, or growth, which is the soul of a plant, is inseparable from the body of the stone or the plant, so is mind, which is the soul of man, inseparable from the body of man. In his own vocabulary, mind and body are respectively *finite modes* of God's attributes of *thought* and *extension*; and, just as in God these two attributes are united together, so are mind and body in man. Referring therefore to this argument of his, Spinoza concludes: "Hence we see not only that the human mind is united to the body, but also what is to be understood by the union of the mind and body." [3]

As a corollary of the conception of the soul as being of divine origin, and separate from the body, is the conception of its freedom.

On the whole, to religious philosophers man, though occupying a special position in the world, is still a part of nature, and his actions, like all natural actions in the world, are determined by certain laws of causality which are of divine design and implantation. There are no free actions in man, as there are no free motions in the world. Still there are certain exceptions. In the world, God may change the order of nature and create miracles; in man, the mind is endowed with a similar power to change the order of human nature and produce actions which are miraculously free. Philo, who was the first to formulate the philosophic basis of this kind of undetermined human freedom, says that God endowed the human mind with a proportion "of that free will which is His most peculiar possession and most worthy of His majesty," and that by this gift of free will the human mind "has been made to resemble God." [4] And both the miracles worked by God

[2] *Ethics* II, 13, Schol.   [3] *Ethics* II, 13, Schol.   [4] *Immut.* 10, 47–48.

in nature and the miraculous power of the freedom of the human mind are two forms of the selfsame providence by which God governs the world. What is the purpose of miracles? To protect man against the evils of the external forces of nature. What is the purpose of freedom? To protect man against the evil forces of his own nature.

Spinoza is willing to describe man as free. But he denies that his freedom is undetermined. To him, as there are no miracles in nature, so there is no miraculous freedom in human nature. Freedom is power, the power of reason by which man may control and guide the forces of his own nature, just as by the same power of reason he can control and guide the forces of external nature. Every conflict in man is looked upon by Spinoza as a conflict between two physical forces, which he calls by their old philosophic names, reason and emotion; and as in every conflict between two opposite physical forces, the stronger force will subdue the weaker. Man is called free only in the sense that by an increased knowledge of his own nature reason will grow in strength to overcome all the adverse forces of his emotions.

There is nothing miraculous about this kind of freedom. Referring to those who, like Philo, saw in human freedom an endowment of the human mind with a miraculous power by which it is made to resemble God, Spinoza observes that by the same token "they say that the mind can by its own strength create sensations or ideas which do not belong to things, so that in a measure they make it out to be a God." [5] It is doubtful whether Spinoza had a direct knowledge of Philo; but the Philonic view is also restated by Descartes when he says that free will "in a certain sense renders us like God in making us masters of ourselves." [6] By aiming directly at Descartes, Spinoza indirectly hit Philo.

Religion, to religious philosophers, was not only a truth,

[5] *Tractatus de Intellectus Emendatione* 60.
[6] *Les Passions de l'Ame* III, 152.

a way of knowing, but also a good, a way of living. To them God in His governance of the world, by His individual providence, has in His infinite wisdom not only endowed men with freedom but has also revealed to them laws of conduct by which, through the exercise of their freedom, they are guided to their destined good. These divinely revealed laws — it was insisted upon by the religious philosophers — were not the prescripts of an arbitrary ruler; they were based upon reason. In fact, they were the virtues which philosophers, in their fumbling way, were trying to discover by their own faulty reason as rules of conduct whereby men were to attain their highest good.

Here, again, Spinoza begins by saying "yes." Yes, he admits that the practical teachings of Scripture, unlike its intellectual teachings, contain some merit. But — and here another "but" comes in — he denies that they are divinely revealed, or that they are of the same nature as the virtues dealt with by the philosophers. They are the practical wisdom of simple-minded men, based upon their limited experience in a simple form of life.

And so in direct opposition to traditional philosophy, which presented its ethics in the form of a systematization of the teachings of the various philosophers interspersed with quotations of scriptural proof-texts, Spinoza reproduces the same systematization without the benefit of any supporting scriptural quotations. Following in the footsteps of Aristotle, the Stoics, and their successors, he defines the nature of the highest good, of happiness, and of virtue; and out of the writings of these philosophers he draws up a list of virtues and vices to take the place of the positive and negative commandments of religious legislation.

In addition to its being a truth, a way of knowing, and a good, a way of living, religion is also a promise, a way of attaining happiness.

The promise of happiness held out by religion, as Spinoza

sees it, is twofold: happiness in the present life and happiness in what is called the hereafter. Spinoza describes the happiness religion promises in this world by the phrase *"mentis acquiescentia."* An English translation of this phrase, partly literal and partly free, would be "peace of mind"; though, judging by the current lists of best-sellers, it would be more fashionable to translate it by "peace of soul." The God of traditional religion is not only the powerful architect of the universe and the wise lawgiver for mankind. He is also the great provider, the great comforter, the rock of salvation, the refuge in the day of evil. To man, burdened with trouble, old-time religion offers one sovereign remedy. "Cast thy burden upon the Lord, and He will sustain thee" (Ps. 55: 23/22); "Take my yoke upon you . . . and ye shall find rest unto your souls" (Matt. 11:29).

Again, in a way, Spinoza says "yes." He does not deny that religion offers consolation to the true believers. But — and here still another "but" comes in — there is a consolation of philosophy as there is a consolation of religion. Reason, he claims, can restore peace of mind, or peace of soul, without benefit of the soothing words of the Psalms or the Gospels. And he thus undertakes to prescribe philosophic remedies for the various ailments of the soul.

In a series of twenty propositions, Spinoza tells us how we can be happy though miserable. He tells us how we may overcome anxiety, fear, worry, desire, ambition, envy, disappointment, frustration, hatred, self-pity, and all the other innumerable ills that stem from the emotions. In the past generations, readers of Spinoza saw in these propositions a distillation of the cumulative wisdom of the ages, wisdom writ large in the form of proverbs in the pages of copy-books. Readers of today see in them adumbrations of the newly discovered science of the mind, its traumas and its therapies. Spinoza himself presents them in profound technical language as a philosophic cathartic for the emotions, as a metaphysic for bilious souls.

The promise held out by religion for happiness in the hereafter is the promise of immortality. Here, too, we may gather from Spinoza's discussion that, on the one hand, while he is willing to admit that the soul is immortal — or eternal, as he prefers to call it, following one of Cicero's usages — on the other hand, his own conception of its immortality is of a somewhat special kind. But what he means exactly by that special kind of immortality is not quite clear. Let us try to find out.

At the time of Spinoza there were three distinct views of immortality. Each of these views has a long and complicated history, and a variety of subtly distinguishable aspects. But for our present purpose we shall describe them briefly in their main outlines.

The first view may be described as that of individual immortality by the grace of God. According to this view, the soul is a creation of God and begins its existence as an individual entity. As a creation of God, the soul by its own nature cannot be eternal, for only God is eternal. By His infinite grace and power, however, God confers immortality upon the souls of certain individuals as a reward for their conduct during their lifetime. Accordingly, it is only the souls of those who are stamped as righteous that are immortal; the souls of those who are stamped as wicked are annihilated.

This, on the whole, is a conception of immortality to which, theoretically, all religious philosophers would subscribe; though, historically, many of them preferred to see the wicked eternally punished rather than utterly annihilated. But the difference between utter annihilation and eternal punishment is only a matter of taste, not a matter of theory. The belief in eternal punishment does not exclude the possibility of utter annihilation. In fact, certain theologians, learned in these matters, speak of both eternal punishment and utter annihilation and interpret either one in terms of the other.

The second view may be described as that of universal immortality by nature. According to this view, the soul does not begin its existence as an individual entity, but as part of a universal soul of which each man gets a portion. Since the universal soul is homogeneous, all portions of it distributed among individual men are alike in nature. It is only through their contact with different bodies that the souls of different individuals appear to act differently. But this contact of souls with bodies leaves no permanent effect upon them. As soon as the bodies die, the accidental individual differences between their respective souls disappear. The souls of all men, in their original undifferentiated nature, return to the universal soul and, reabsorbed within it, retain no trace of their erstwhile temporarily acquired accidental individuality.

The third view is a modification of the one just described. It may be called individual immortality by nature. This view, too, assumes that there is a universal soul, of which the soul of every individual human being is an undifferentiated portion, and that whatever individuality it displays during its existence in the body is owing to its contact with that body. Yet such contact, especially as it results in the knowledge of the external world, and of what lies beyond that world, leaves upon the soul a permanent mark. It essentially transforms the nature of the soul; it changes it into something distinct and individual. This distinctness and individuality, by the eternal order of nature, is retained by the soul even after it departs from the body. It is as an individualized soul that it returns to its native source, the universal soul. It is not reabsorbed by it; it only finds shelter in it. The universal soul is a sort of heaven, to which the disembodied souls of philosophers, if not of saints, return in their naked spirituality to enjoy bliss for evermore in the presence of God.

These are the three views with which Spinoza, we assume, started his speculation concerning immortality. He must have examined each one of them, trying to find out which one he could accept without involving himself in contradictions.

The first view he must have found himself compelled to

reject at once, for it was contradictory to his entire conception of God and of the human soul.

The second view he must have thought, at first, he could accept. For in the philosophic system he had built up after the model of the emanationist philosophy there is a universal soul which he calls the infinite intellect of God; and of that soul the human soul is, as he has said, a part; and that part of the infinite intellect of God is certainly not annihilated with the death of man: it is reabsorbed in the source whence it came. For with his denial of creation out of nothing, Spinoza also denied the destruction of anything into nothing. Quite consistently, therefore, he could express himself as willing to accept the immortality of the soul in the sense of the universal immortality of the soul.

But after some reflection Spinoza decided, we presume, to reject this kind of immortality. He would only stultify himself, he reasoned, if he were to speak of a universal immortality of the soul, when, on the basis of his own philosophy, he could also speak of a universal immortality of the body. For in his own philosophy there is a universal body as there is a universal soul, and both are inseparably united, and of that universal body the individual human body is a part, and, upon the death of man, just as his soul is reabsorbed in the universal soul, so is his body reabsorbed in the universal body. What sense is there in speaking of the immortality of the soul unless the soul, unlike the body, in its reabsorption in the universal soul retains a certain kind of individuality which is not found in the body in its reabsorption in the universal body?

And so Spinoza must have come to examine the third view of immortality. With regard to this view he must have found that there is nothing in his philosophy to preclude the assumption that, by the eternal order of nature, that portion of the infinite intellect of God which constitutes the human mind acquires, through its experience in life, a certain distinctness and individuality which remains with it even after death when it is reunited with that infinite intellect of God whence it originally came. If he were asked how that happened, he would answer that it was so determined by the eternal order of nature. For it must be borne in mind that the eternal order, to Spinoza, was a sovereign explanation for everything inexplicable, just as the will of God was to the Philonic religious philosophers. Nothing is impossible in an eternally ordered world, such as is conceived by Spinoza, just as nothing is impossible in a world governed by the will of God, such as is conceived by Philonic philosophers. It is only in a world where everything new must arise in a process of evolution that certain things may be conceived as impossible.

Having found this third view of immortality not inconsistent with his philosophy, Spinoza accepted it. The terms he uses in his restatement of it reflect exactly the terms commonly used in the descriptions of this view. It is not in all its faculties, Spinoza maintains, that soul is immortal, for the faculties of imagination and memory are destroyed with the body.[7] This is quite in accordance with the third view of immortality. Still, he continues, "the human mind cannot be absolutely destroyed with the body, but something of it remains which is eternal";[8] and that something of it which remains eternal, he explains, is conditioned upon the acquisition of knowledge of a certain kind. This, again, is in accordance with the third view of immortality. He then concludes, "The essence of the mind consists of knowledge . . . therefore the more things the mind knows . . . the greater is that part of it which remains."[9] This, once more, is in accordance with the explanation given by the exponents of the third view of immortality for the individual differences between immortal souls.

And so here again Spinoza begins by admitting that there is individual immortality of the soul. But — and here the last

[7] *Ethics* V, 21.
[8] *Ibid.*, 23.
[9] *Ibid.* V, 38, Demonst.

"but" comes in — this individual immortality belongs to man not by grace but by nature.

Yet, while Spinoza's assertion of individual immortality is not inconsistent with his philosophy, it does not necessarily follow from it. It is a gratuitous principle; it is an expression of faith rather than of reason. On the rational basis of his philosophy he could have said — just as he has said in his discussion of God, of the human soul, and of the revealed law — yes, I am willing to use the word immortality and use it even in the sense of individual immortality, but I do not mean by it the immortality of man's soul; I mean by it the immortality of man's achievements. In fact, this is exactly what most students of Spinoza take to be the meaning of his statements about the eternity of the soul. But while Spinoza might have spoken in this vein, he does not in fact so speak; and there is no indication that he meant his writings to be treated as divinely inspired sacred texts which pious readers were constantly to modernize by constantly giving them allegorical interpretations.

And so, while Spinoza's conception of immortality betrays no logical inconsistency of thought, it betrays an inconsistency of mood. Departing from the method followed by him in his speculations about God, about the soul, or the revealed law, he is here willing to accept more than the mere use of a term; he is willing to accept a certain belief.

This change of mood is to be noticed also in his attempt to cite scriptural proof-texts for his belief in immortality. Such citation marks a departure from his general practice in the *Ethics*. Nowhere in the *Ethics* does he quote scriptural verses in support of his view. And yet here, after developing his views on the individual immortality of the soul, he tries, almost like Maimonides or Thomas Aquinas, to tell us how his conception of immortality is in agreement with that of Scripture. He describes the state of immortality by such New Testament terms as salvation, liberty, regeneration, and blessedness, all of which consists in the love of God, or union with Him, and then concludes, "This love or blessedness is called Glory in the sacred writings." [10] In fact, this last statement of Spinoza's is a paraphrase of the following statement in St. Thomas: "Hence this blessedness is many times described as glory in the sacred writings: thus it is said (Ps. 149:5), 'The Saints exult in glory.'" [11] Similarly, Abraham Ibn Ezra, who is quoted by Spinoza in his *Tractatus Theologico-Politicus*, commenting upon the verse of the Psalm quoted by St. Thomas, says: "Let the saints exult in that glory which awaits them, namely, in the eternal existence that they shall enjoy, referring thereby to the eternal existence of their souls, or to what is called the hereafter."

Still further evidence for this change of mood is to be found in the new kind of opponent whom Spinoza visualizes in his discussion of immortality. As I have said, the *Ethics* is a critique of the philosophy of certain unnamed opponents. The opponents visualized throughout the *Ethics* are the religious philosophers. Now the opponent visualized in his discussion of immortality, as may be judged from the context, is a religious heretic, Uriel Acosta, who died when Spinoza was a boy of about fifteen. Eight years before Spinoza's birth Acosta became known as a heretic through the publication of a work in which he denied the immortality of the soul, showing that there was no such belief in Scripture. This book evoked a great deal of opposition, which continued for many years after its publication. In Spinoza's discussion of immortality there are several passages directed against Uriel Acosta.

What brought about this change of mood in Spinoza cannot be exactly determined. If we were writing historical fiction, we might invent all kinds of situations to explain this change. As historians, trying to reconstruct the true doctrine of Spinoza, all we can say is that Spinoza, despite all his philosophizing, felt, even as you and I, the need of the consolation of this belief.

[10] *Ethics* V, 36, Schol. [11] *Cont. Gent.* III, 63.

The picture which I have drawn of Spinoza in his relation to religion is not the picture with which we are familiar. Spinoza is daring, but he introduces no novelty. His daring consists in overthrowing the old Philonic principles which by his time had dominated the thought of European religious philosophy for some sixteen centuries. But in overthrowing these principles, all he did was to reinstate, with some modification, the old principles of classical Greek philosophy. That is what he did in dealing with the concepts of God, the soul, freedom, ethics, and immortality, though, in the case of immortality, he follows a medieval variation of the Platonic conception of immortality.

Perhaps this is all one could expect of Spinoza or of any other philosopher. For on all these religious issues there are only two alternatives. One was stated in the Hebrew Scripture, and the other in the various writings of Greek philosophers. Thereafter, the great question in the history of religious philosophy was whether to follow the one or the other, or to combine the two. And in the history of religious philosophy, so conceived, two figures are outstanding, Philo and Spinoza. Philo was the first to combine the two; Spinoza was the first to break up that combination.

11

SERMONETTE
THE PROFESSED ATHEIST AND THE
VERBAL THEIST*

The fool hath said in his heart,
There is no God. (Ps. 14: 1)

THE fool, who in the Scripture lesson this morning is quoted as saying to himself, There is no God, was not a fool in the ordinary sense of the term. He was not a fool in the sense of lacking in intelligence or of lacking in knowledge. He was a fool in the sense of being perverse and contrary. He denied what others affirmed. But he was also a downright honest and plain-spoken fellow. People, he knew, believed in God; and by God, he knew, they meant a Being over and above and beyond the world, the creator and governor of the world, a God who revealed himself to men and told them what to do and what not to do and promised them reward for obedience and threatened them with punishment for disobedience. This, he knew, is what people believed in and this is what he did not believe in. And so, honestly and bluntly he said to himself and said to others, There is no God. He was quite willing to be known as an atheist. He did not start to quibble about the meaning of God. He did not offer a substitute God.

But, unlike him whom Scripture called fool, those who called themselves lovers of wisdom, philosophers, made quibbling about the meaning of God one of their chief occupations. Ever since Xenophanes rejected the gods of popular religion and put something else in their place to which he gave the name God, it became the practice of the Greek lovers of wisdom not to deny God but to change the meaning of God. Plato carried around a label, with the name God in-

---

* Delivered in Appleton Chapel, March 17, 1955, and published in the *Harvard Divinity School Bulletin*, 20 (1954–55): 69–70.

scribed on it, even though he did not know where exactly in his philosophy to paste that label. Aristotle's God sat motionless on the top of the world, without, however, being able to detach himself from it. The God of the Stoics was imprisoned within the entrails of the world, from which he could not extricate himself. Even the Epicureans had their gods, ageless human beings, squatting on empty spaces between the worlds and, without a worry in their heads and without a care in their hearts, beholding with sublime indifference the happenings in the infinite worlds around them.

We are told that at the beginning of the Christian era Scripture-bred religious thinkers, on becoming acquainted with the array of deities of the Greek lovers of wisdom, were at a loss to know how to take them. They studied them, they examined them, they scrutinized them, and finally arrived at the conclusion that, while some of them were the paltry result of the blind groping of human reason for a truth which can be known only by faith and revelation, most of them were only polite but empty phrases for the honest atheism of the fool in Scripture.

Nowadays, lovers of wisdom are still busily engaged in the gentle art of devising deities. Some of them offer as God a thing called man's idealized consciousness, others offer a thing called man's aspiration for ideal values or a thing called the unity of the ideal ends which inspire man to action, still others offer a thing called the cosmic consciousness or a thing called the universal nisus or a thing called the élan vital or a thing called the principle of concretion or a thing called the ground of being. I wonder, however, how many of the things offered as God by lovers of wisdom of today are not again only polite but empty phrases for the downright denial of God by him who is called fool in the Scripture lesson this morning!

INDEX OF
NAMES, SUBJECTS, AND TERMS

Abū al-Hudhayl, 56

Abū Hāshim, 183

Acquisition, theory of, in the Kalam, 189–191

Adam — fall of, 160; language spoken by, 229

Aëtius. See ps.-Plutarch

Aëtius the Arian, 127–128

Albertus Magnus, 57

Albinus, 29

Alexander of Alexandria, 127

Alexander of Aphrodisias, 19

Alfarabi, 186

Algazali. See Ghazālī

Altmann, A., 21

Ambrosiaster, The, 97–98

Ammonius Hermiae, 48–49

Ammonius Saccas, 45–46, 139

Annihilation and eternal punishment, problem of, 76–77

Apollinaris and Apollinarianism, 126, 147–149, 151–157

Apologists, The — and Philo, 39–42, 105

Arabic terms:
  'adah, 179, 180
  al-fi'l fī ta'aqqul, 187
  al-'aql al-fa''āl, 187
  al-'aql al-tajribiyy, 187
  al-'aql al-tamyīziyy, 187
  al-'aql bil-fi'l, 187
  bi-lā kayfa, 194
  fikr, 187, 188
  ḥāl, 52
  ikhtiyār, 186
  iktisāb, 189
  iqtirān, 180
  irādah, 186
  iṣṭilāḥiyy, 231
  kasb, 189
  musabbib al-asbāb, 179
  muṣṭalaḥ, 231
  qaṣd, 186
  mauḍū', 231
  ma'na, 51
  ṣifah, 51, 56, 57, 229
  ṣifāt al-ma'āniyy, 181
  ṣifāt ma'nawiyyah, 181

taṣawwur, 186

waḍ'iyy, 231

Archer-Hind, R. D., 33

Aristotle — and Arianism, 126–131; definition, 12; faith, 106–107; fate, 158; free will, 159, 196, 215; God, 146, 178; psychology of human action, 185–186; immortality, 102–103; knowledge, probability, proof, 213; necessity, 172–173, 211; origin of language, 224–225, 235; primary premises, 13; providence, 104; recency of civilization, 237; relation, 15; syllogism and division, 129. See also 6, 30, 34, 35, 37, 42, 79, 83, 108, 138, 154, 166, 172, 173, 178, 187, 232

ps.-Aristotle, Liber de Causis, 179

Arnim, H. v., 100, 105, 107, 108, 158

Arius and Arianism, 47, 126–147, 149–153, 155–157, 173

Arnobius, 71, 77

Ash'arī and Ash'arites, 21, 56, 182, 183, 189, 195

Assent and faith, 107–108

Athanasius — Arianism, 133, 134, 140, 142, 157; homoousios, 118, 119, 121, 122; Logos, 127, 141, 143; Sabellianism, 47

Athenagoras, 104

Attribute, Arabic and Greek terms for, 51; Hebrew terms for, 56; Latin terms for, 56–57; in Islam, 49–52, 53, 54, 56, 181–182; in the Church Fathers, 52–53; in the Schoolmen, 60–64; in Descartes, 65–66; in Spinoza, 66–67, 68, 253–254

Augustine — concupiscence, free will, grace, love, necessity, original sin, predestination, 161–176; eternal punishment, 77; God, 42, 59, 95; immortality, 73–74, 101; miracles, 223; palingenesis, 75; philosophy, 113; providence, 104, 203; resurrection, 81–82, 88, 89, 93, 94, 105; salvation, 97; scriptural chronology, 238; transmigration, 76

Averroes, 23, 180, 189, 210, 220
Avicenna, 220

Badawi, 'A, 187, 236
Baghdādī, 52, 189
Bailey, C., 92, 225
Bāqillānī, 182
Barbier de Meynard, C., 229
Bardenhewer, O., 179
Bardy, G., 46, 119
Basil — Arianism, 126; homoousios, 118, 119, 122, 123, 124
Baumgarten-Crusius, L. F. O., 132
Baur, F. Ch., 131
Beatific vision, 95
Bethune-Baker, J. F., 120
Bouyges, M., 18, 180, 220
Bréhier, É., 45
Busse, A., 48
Buxtorf, J., Fil., 204

Capitaine, W., 72
Cause and causality, 179–180, 207–213, 249–252
Celsus, 105
Chadwick, H., 21
Chroust, A. H., 98
Chrysippus, 99
Cicero, 8, 166
Clement of Alexandria — faith and reason, 108–111, 113, 114, 115; Logos, 40, 46, 143; palingenesis, 75; providence, 104; salvation, 197; the three mansions, 94–95
Common notions, 13
Concupiscence, 164–167
Continuous creation, 202–203
Cornford, F. M., 33
Creation and eternity, 8–9, 204, 207, 222–223, 249–253, 266
Cureton, Wm., 183
Custom and causality, 179–180, 209–210
Cyril of Alexandria, 147
Cyril of Jerusalem, 104–125

Deane, W. J., 167
Demos, R., 28
Definition, 28
Denary system, 236–237
Descartes — attributes, 64–66; continuous creation, free will, grace,

miracles, soul, 198–203, 260; innate ideas, 13
Deucalion and Pyrrha, 244, 245
Diels, H., 236
Dieterici, Fr., 186
Diogenes Laërtius, 166, 211, 225, 232
Division and syllogism, 129
Dodds, E. R., 1
Dorner, I. A., 136
Duns Scotus, 62, 63–64

Elder, E. E., 182
Emanation, 252–254
Empedocles, 76
Epicurus and Epicureanism — and Spinoza, 254–255; causality, 207–208, 211; free will, 196, 197–198; immortality, 84, 87, 91; origin of language, 225, 232; static pleasure, 92, 93
Epiphanius, 47, 119, 126, 127
Erigena, John Scotus, 54–55, 58–59
Eusebius of Caesarea, 46, 118, 129, 147
Eusebius of Nicomedia, 141
Evil, problem of, 8, 16–17

Faḍālī, 181
Faith and reason, 106–117
Fate, 100, 158, 169–170, 196
Finkel, J., 223
Free will, 158–161, 170–176, 188–189, 196–216, 259–260

Galen, 83
Gebhardt, C., 242
Ghazālī, 18, 57, 179, 180, 193, 195, 219–220
Gibson, A. B., 200
Gilberts of la Porrée, 55–56, 58–59
Gilson, É., 54, 62, 200
Ginzberg, L., 228
God, as artisan and as begetter, 41–42, 145–146; existence of, 14–15, 177–179, 255–256; goodness of, 7–8, 16–17; incorporeality of, 85; infinity of, 5–11; power of, 8–11, 17–25; Spinoza on, 248; unity of, 37, 144–145, 180–181; unknowability of, 6–7, 12–16; unlikeness of, 85, 247
Goichon, A.-M., 186

Gomperz, Th., 225
Grace, divine, 71, 168–169, 200–201
Grant, R. M., 19
Greek chemistry, 154–155
Greek terms:
 ἀγέννητος γέννησις, 127
 αἰώνιος, 77
 ἀκατάληπτος, 6
 ἀκατονόμαστος, 6
 ἀκριβὴς πίστις, 109
 ἀνυπόστατος, 119
 ἄρρητος, 6
 βαστάζειν, 135
 γένος κοινὸν ὑπερκείμενον, 122
 ἐγκρατής, 167
 εἶδος, 80
 εἶναι, 40–41, 139
 ἐνυπόστατος, 121
 ἐπιστημονικὴ πίστις, 109
 κρᾶσις, 154
 κόσμος νοητός, 32
 λόγος σπέρματος, 81
 μετασχεῖν, 135
 μίξις, 154
 ὅμοιος, 117, 120
 ὁμοιπρόσωπος, 121
 ὁμοούσιος, 117–125
 ὁμοϋπόστατος, 121
 οὐσία προϋποκειμένη, 121
 πρᾶγμα, 51
 πρῶται οὐσίαι, 48
 πίστις, 106–107
 πνοή, 84
 σύγκατάθεσις, 107–108
 σύγχυσις, 154
 σύνθεσις, 154
 ὑλικὸν ὑποκείμενον προϋπάρχον, 122
Gregory of Nazianzus, 155
Gregory of Nyssa — Apollinaris,
 148, 155; Arianism, 126, 127, 129,
 130; dialectic reasoning, 130; immortality, 100–101; resurrection,
 81, 82, 83; secular knowledge, 115;
 transmigration, 76
Guillaume, A., 182

Halkin, A. S., 222
Harvey, W. W., 95
Hebdomadal week, 236–237
Hebrew language, 229–230
Hebrew terms:
 balal, 230

dabar, 36
hannaḥi, 231
middah, 56
munaḥ, 231
neshamah, 84
'olam, 77
otiyyot, 231
to'ar, 56
Hefele, K. J. v., 119, 136
Henry, P., 45
Hermann, K. Fr., 28
Hippolytus, 29, 140, 147
Holy Spirit, 41, 42, 150–151
Homer, 105
Homoousios, 117–125
Huber, J., 55
Hume — causality, creation, custom, free will, knowledge and
 proof and probability, laws of
 nature, miracles, necessity, occasionalism, 207–216; infinite goodness of God, 16–17; omnipotence
 of God, 22–23; revelation, 11; unknowability of God, 13–16

Ibn Ezra, Abraham, 233, 268
Ibn Gabirol, 57
Ibn Ḥazm, 18, 182
Ibn Janaḥ, 230
Ibn Khaldūn, 177–195
Ideas, 27–68
Ikhwān al-Ṣafā, 229–230
Immortality, 69–103, 263–268
Impossibilities, 17–21, 99
Individuation, principle of, 80–81
Innate ideas, 13
Intelligible world, 32–33, 39, 40–41,
 44
Irenaeus, 70, 71, 76, 81, 85, 87, 88, 89,
 94–95
Isaac Israeli, 21

Jabarites, 189
Janet, P., 205
Jansen, B., 62
Jansenism, 200
Jellinek, A., 228
Jesus — immortality and resurrec-
 tion, 69–70; unity of God, 144
Johanan ben Zakkai, 69
John of Damascus, 53
Jones, M., 29

Judah Halevi — denary system, 236; hebdomadal week, 236; miracles, 204, 205, 223; origin of language, 230–234; scriptural chronology, 239–241. *See also* 217, 220, 221, 222, 223, 224

al-Junayd, 195

Justin Martyr, 13, 70, 71, 96–97, 99, 219, 221

ps.-Justin Martyr, *Cohortatio ad Graecos*, 29, 74

Kalam and Mutakallimūn, 50, 52, 177, 179, 181, 182, 194, 196–197

Kasher, M., 228

Lactantius, 71, 75, 76, 77, 88, 89, 99–100, 104

Landauer, S., 18

Langley, G., 205

Language, origin of, 224–236

Latin terms:
   assignatio, 57
   attributio, 56, 57
   attributum, 56, 57, 59
   concupiscentia, 164–166, 171
   consuetudo, 210
   continens, 167
   cupiditas, 166, 171
   dispositio, 56
   distinctio conceptus, 63
   distinctio formalis, 62
   distinctio rationis, 65
   ex positione, 225
   fatum, 170
   habitus, 210
   immortalis natura, 72
   libido, 166, 171
   meritum fidei, 111
   nominatio, 56
   ratio, 80, 81
   spiraculum, 84

Lawlor, H. J., 46

Laws of nature, 158, 211–212

Leibniz — free will, miracles, monads, pre-established harmony, 203–207, 215–216; occasionalism, 208

Lestienne, H., 206

Locke, 213

Logos, in Philo, 33–37, 137, 150; in St. John, 38–39, 137; in the Apol-ogists, 39–42, 137–140; in Origen, 44–47; in Arianism, 47; in Sabellianism, 47

Louis, P., 29

Lucretius, 84, 87, 91, 211, 232

McCarthy, R. J., 182

Macdonald, D. B., 181

Maimonides — attributes, 56; equivalence of cause and effect, 22; hebdomadal week, 237; impossibilities, 17–18; Latin translations of his work, 56–60, 204–205, 206, 210; miracles, 204–205, 223; origin of language, 234–236; scriptural chronology, 241; Sabians, 243; veracity of Scripture, 217–218, 221–222. *See also* 21, 24, 25, 223, 231

Masʿūdī, 229, 230, 238–239

Maximinus the Arian, 138

Mill, John Stuart — infinite goodness of God, 17; omnipotence of God, 23–25; revelation, 11

Milman, H. H., 131

Mingana, A., 219

Miracles, 99, 196, 201–202, 203, 204–206, 213–214, 243–245, 250, 251

Mode — in Kalam, 52, 56; in Spinoza, 249

Molière, 105, 125

Monads, 203

Montefortino, H. de, 63

Morin, G., 98

Muckle, J. T., 57

Müller, M. J., 181

Munk, S., 235

Muʿtazilites, 21, 182

Narboni, Moses, 235

Neander, A., 148

Necessity, 172–174, 211–212

Nemesius, 75

Neophilonism, 196–197, 199, 202, 208, 210

Neoplatonism — and Philo, 46–47, 252; and Spinoza, 252–253; its theism, 146; its trinity, 139–140

Newman, J. H., 118, 131

Nöldeke, Th., 229

Occam, 59, 62–63, 64

Occasionalism, 204, 205, 208, 209

Oral Law, 5
Origen — eternal generation, 44–47, 139; faith and reason, 110–111, 112–113, 115–116; fifth element, 79; immortality, 73; impossibilities, 18, 19, 21, 99; incorporeality, 85; intelligible world, 40; origin of language, 228–229; palingenesis, 75; principle of individuation, 80–81; providence, 104; resurrection, 78–81, 87–88, 99, 105; scriptural chronology, 238; transmigration, 76; Trinity, 44–46, 122, 123; universal restoration, 77
Oulton, J. E. L., 46
Ovid, 244

Palingenesis, 74–75, 99–100
Parmentier, L., 141
St. Paul — pre-existent Christ, 38; unity of God, 144
Paul of Samosata, 118–119
Pavet de Courteille, A. J. B., 229
Pelagius, 161–163, 169, 176
Peter Lombard, 57, 59
Philaster, 147
Philo — and the Apologists, 39–42, 105; and Arianism, 136, 140–146, 150–151; and Pelagianism, 162–163; and Plotinus, 46–47, 252; cessation of prophecy, 32; free will, 159–160, 162–163, 196, 197–198, 259–260; God, 2–11, 37, 41, 85, 247; hebdomadal week, 237; Holy Spirit, 32, 150; ideas, intelligible world, Logos, 28–38, 137, 150, 250; immortality, 71, 94–95; incorporeality, 85; intermediaries, 135–136; miracles, 99, 159, 193, 204, 223; origin of language, 225–227; powers, 143; recency of civilization, 237–238; revealed religion, 3–11; salvation of non-Jews, 96; soul, 84, 86, 90; the strange woman, 115; veracity of Scripture, 218; world soul, 32
Plato — and Arianism, 131–134; division, 129; faith, 106; fated laws, 7, 158; free will, 196, 215; God, 6, 7, 133, 146, 178; ideas, 27–68; immortality, 71, 100, 102; origin of language, 225, 235; prov-

idence, 7; recollection, 13; soul, 89–90; transmigration, 76. See also 34, 74, 79, 83, 95, 166, 202, 238
Plotinus — and Philo, 46–47, 252; God, 30; ideas, 30; resurrection, 105; his three hypostases, 44–47; vision of the One, 95. See also 19, 22, 90
Plutarch, 8
ps.-Plutarch, De Placitis Philosophorum, 29, 30, 236
Pre-established harmony, 204–206, 209
Pythagoras, 76

Rashdall, H., 209
Relation, 15
Resurrection, 69–103, 105
Revelation, 3–12, 242–243
Ritter, H., 132, 183
Rosenthal, F., 177, 187

Saadia, 18
Sabellianism, 47, 49, 51, 52, 119
Salvation, 96–98
Schwyzer, H. R., 45
Scripture references: Old Testament, 70, 84, 90, 92, 94, 99, 108, 114, 115, 140, 143, 145, 148, 151, 163, 165, 170, 203, 225, 262, 268, 270; New Testament, 19, 69, 70, 74, 77, 78, 93, 94, 95, 97, 99, 105, 106, 112, 113, 120, 121, 137, 143, 144, 148, 149, 160, 164, 244, 262; Koran, 50, 229, 230
Scythianus, 104
Selby-Bigge, L. A., 207, 208
Shahrastāni, 21, 52, 56, 182, 183, 189
Shem-Ṭob, Joseph ben, 235
Siegfried, C., 230
Socrates, 35, 69
Socrates Scholasticus, 126, 127, 128
Sophocles, 105
Soul, 84, 86–87, 90, 151–153, 156, 198, 257–259
Sozomen, 119
Spinoza — and the religion of the past, 246–269; and the veracity of Scripture, 241–245; infinite goodness of God, 16; omnipotence of God, 17–21; revelation, 11; unknowability of God, 12–13

Stählin, O., 75, 104
Stern, S. M., 21
Stöckel, A., 72
Stoics — assent, 107, 108, 109; common notions, 13; fate, 100, 158, 169–170; free will, 159, 196, 215; God, 146; incorporeality, 84; nothing impossible, 99–100; origin of language, 235; palingenesis, 74–75, 87, 99, 104, 158–159
Syllogism and division, 129

Ṭabarī, ʿAlī, 219
Taftāzānī, 182
Tatian, 71, 75, 81, 104
Talmudic references, 69, 97, 227, 228, 229
Terms. See Arabic terms, Greek terms, Hebrew terms, Latin terms
Tertullian — Adam's naming of animals, 229; eternal punishment, 77; faith and reason, 110, 111, 112, 113; free will, 163, 167; God, 247; immortality, 72–73; Logos, 40, 142; miracles, 223; resurrection, 81, 82, 83, 92, 93, 99; soul, 84–86; transmigration, 76; Trinity, 122, 123
Theism, Greek philosophical, 26, 146, 270–271

Theophilus, 71, 142–143, 146
Thomas Aquinas — and Maimonides, 59–60; attributes, 60–61, 63; equivalence of cause and effect, 22; God, 13, 14, 42; ideas, 58; immortality, 268; impossibilities, 17–18; miracles, 244
Tischendorf, C., 165
Traducianism, 86, 257
Transmigration and resurrection, 75–76
Trinity, 38–49, 50–52, 53–55, 117–125, 126–146

Universals, 55
Unwritten Law, 5

Vignaux, P., 59, 62
Vision of God, 59
Voigt, H., 136

Watt, W. M., 189
Weinberg, J. R., 24
Wendland, P., 29
Whitehead, A. N., 27
Wisdom and Logos, 38, 41
Wisdom of Solomon, 6:20, 165; 8:21, 167; 11:20, 203
World soul, 32

Zeller, E., 28
Zeno of Verona, 142